AF540104

Horticultural Pests:
Detection and Control

GEORGE FOX WILSON (1896–1951)

Horticultural Pests: Detection and Control

George Fox Wilson

2025

Biotech Books

ISBN 978-81-7622-059-0

Published by : **BIOTECH BOOKS**
4762-63/23, Ansari Road, Darya Ganj,
New Delhi - 110002
Phones : 011 4300 3222
Email : biotechbooks@yahoo.co.in

PRINTED IN INDIA

Foreword

THE first edition of this work entitled 'The Detection and Control of Garden Pests' is a lasting memorial to my colleague the late G. Fox Wilson.

The book provides a vast fund of information, and enables persons of all walks of life to have a ready means of recognizing the many symptoms of pest damage, and the methods of controlling the pest concerned. This approach is simpler for the layman than getting bogged down with the intricacies of the habits and life-cycle of the creatures concerned. The fact that a second edition was published two years later, underlines the merit of the work, which in time will be regarded as a classic in its own subject.

It is perhaps a little unfortunate that the earlier editions were published at the same period as a number of new synthetic chemicals were introduced, including the now familiar DDT and BHC, because in the succeeding years these chemicals have provided new and simpler methods of controlling horticultural pests, and in consequence some of the control measures advocated in the earlier editions are outdated. It is therefore very appropriate that a third edition should be published, and it is still more fitting that this formidable task should be undertaken by Dr. P. Becker, Entomologist to the Royal Horticultural Society at Wisley, where G. Fox Wilson carried out his studies for over thirty years.

Dr. Becker's task has not been a simple one because he regarded it imperative to maintain the same high standard set by his predecessor, and whilst desiring to keep to the same format as closely as possible, it was also necessary to present a résumé of up-to-date knowledge of this very wide field of pest control and hygiene. Dr. Becker has achieved all these objectives and he is to be congratulated for the high standard and competent manner in which he has achieved his goal. It is particularly appropriate that this third edition should originate from Surrey, and from Wisley, where G. Fox Wilson did most of this work.

The addition of coloured plates and the large number of half-tone photographs add very materially to the value of this practical manual which is assured of continued success.

A. M. MASSEE.

Author's Preface to the First Edition

THE experience of the author as an advisory officer, a teacher and an examiner in entomology, has been of value in indicating the angle from which a knowledge of plant pests is viewed by those whose knowledge of plant pathology is limited.

This book is designed to meet the needs of the horticultural student, of Advisory Horticultural Officers and Inspectors, and of commercial and amateur growers who require guidance both as to the animal organisms that are primarily responsible for injury to crops and as to the direct and indirect methods for avoiding and controlling pest outbreaks.

Technical terms have been reduced to a minimum, and lengthy descriptions of individual pests in the several stages of their life-cycle have been omitted, as such information is readily available elsewhere.

The untrained worker finds considerable difficulty in identifying species of insects from the descriptions given in scientific works, and he must of necessity rely chiefly upon the type of injury produced on plants by such organisms. It is highly desirable for all who are concerned with the growing of plants to possess a general knowledge of pests, their life-cycles and their feeding habits, and to have some understanding of the factors that promote healthy growth by carrying out the principles of good cultivation. Special stress is, therefore, laid upon the diagnostic characters of pest injury, and the excellent series of photographs by the author's colleague, Mr. F. C. Brown, should aid the reader to recognize without difficulty the more important pests of horticultural plants from the nature of the damage they do.

This book is a revised and considerably expanded version of a series of articles on the 'Symptoms of Pest Attack on Plants' that appeared in 'The Gardeners' Chronicle' during the years 1932–6, and the author expresses his appreciative thanks to the Editors for their permission to reproduce in part the subject matter previously published by them.

The term 'Advisory Entomologist' is a partial misnomer, by reason of the wide range of animal organisms that command his attention—in the rôle of an Applied Zoologist, he becomes a General Practitioner with a definite bias towards diagnostic characters in plant injuries. A vast amount of diseased plant material is submitted to him in the course of the year, and some is passed to his colleagues for their specialized knowledge in virus, bacterial and fungal diseases and in nutritional and functional disorders.

The outstanding work of the late Prof. H. Marshall Ward, entitled 'Disease in Plants', exerted a great influence on the author's outlook early in his career, and was a source of inspiration in studying cause and effect in problems relating to plant pathology. The relationship that exists between host and parasite requires the close attention of the plant pathologist to enable him to make a correct and speedy diagnosis of diseased material submitted for examination. The correspondent in seeking advice can ease the burden of the Advisory Officer by submitting adequate and typical material of diseased plants. Too often, unfortunately, meagre samples that are carelessly packed so that they are completely desiccated upon arrival will try the patience of the recipient and cause disappointment to the victim of the outbreak when he is notified that the material submitted is totally inadequate for purposes of identification.

The measures outlined for the control of the various pests are partially or completely effective as far as our present state of knowledge allows. Continual progress is being made in the field of pest control, and it is inevitable that certain measures herein outlined will become outdated in a short time. The Entomologist requires the co-operative aid of the Chemist as well as that of the Mycologist, Plant Pathologist, Physicist and Physiologist before many of the problems that confront the grower are solved. One criticism often levelled against the plant pathologist is that he is concerned only with direct methods of control, chiefly chemical in the application of insecticidal and fungicidal washes and dusts, but the indirect methods of pest and disease avoidance by good, clean and thorough cultivation are the concern of all whose interest lies in the production of healthy crops and plants.

A further criticism is the vexed question of scientific names, which change from time to time owing to the fact that the Systematist must perforce follow the laws of priority as laid down by the International Rules of Nomenclature. This somewhat difficult matter cannot be overcome until a final standardization of names has been settled.

This book is dedicated with the author's compliments and grateful thanks to his Entomological Colleagues, without whose direct and indirect aid through personal discussion of their problems and a close study of their published work this book would not have been attempted. The value that may be in this book is due to them; the errors are those of the author.

The author desires to express his sincere thanks to the Council of the Royal Horticultural Society for permission to publish this book, and to his colleague, Mr. F. C. Brown, whose continued interest in preparing the illustrations has been a source of inspiration, and who has kindly helped in proof-reading. He also expresses his warmest thanks to his wife for executing the drawings, preparing the Indexes, proof-reading, and for her valued help and encouragement during the preparation of the typescript.

G. FOX WILSON.

List of Colour Plates

BETWEEN PAGES 124 AND 125

Contents

Preface to the Third (Revised) Edition

THE untimely death of G. Fox Wilson in 1951 robbed us of a pioneer in entomology. He was the first to give his undivided attention to the study of the wide range of pests of horticultural plants, particularly ornamental plants, and in more than thirty years' service with the Royal Horticultural Society he amassed an unrivalled wealth of knowledge of their biology and control. During his lifetime he wrote many papers and articles in which he described the symptoms of attack of these pests and in 1947 this valuable information was gathered together, augmented and published as a book under the title 'The Detection and Control of Garden Pests'.

The revision of this book has been made necessary primarily because of the considerable advances in the field of chemical control which have been made during the last twenty years and the opportunity has also been taken to bring the nomenclature up-to-date and to include a few new pests and also some which have since become more important. However, although chemical control measures have undergone great changes since the last edition was published care has been taken to preserve the author's remarks on the maintenance of cleanliness and hygiene in the garden and on the use of cultural methods of the prevention and control of infestations. In view of the increasing number of cases of resistance to pesticides these practices are as important today as they ever were.

It should be emphasized that the book is concerned solely with the practical means of recognizing the many symptoms of pest damage and with methods of controlling the pest responsible. In a book of this size it is impossible to give many details of the pests themselves, although this has been requested by a number of people. With this limitation in mind, the general lay-out of the earlier editions has been retained as most suitable for the purpose and for ease of reference. Minor changes in the arrangement include the bringing together of the different types of leaf discoloration, leaf distortion, etc., under single headings. Also, to make recognition somewhat easier the illustrations have been placed as near as possible to the relevant text. The indices have been compiled to assist diagnosis of damage, the symptoms of attack being listed under each item in the plant index, and the main host plants under each name in the pest index. Lastly. a short new chapter on damage to lawns has been added along with a number of appendices giving information which could not easily be incorporated in the main body of the book.

Considerable changes have been made in the illustrations, their number having been substantially increased. The best of the original photographs, by the late Mr. F. C. Brown, and the drawings on Figures 1 and 3, by Mrs. Fox Wilson, have been retained. For the new photographs, duly acknowledged, I am indebted to Mr. K. J. Coghill, the Controller of H.M. Stationery Office, East Malling Research Station, Dr. A. M. Massee, O.B.E., Rothamsted Experimental Station, Mr. R. P. Scase, the Shell Photographic Unit and the Sports Turf Research Institute. The drawings on Figures 2, 4 and 5 were executed by Miss J. Maynard.

My special gratitude is due to the Shell Chemical Company for the provision of a substantial grant which made the inclusion of the colour plates possible.

I wish to express my thanks to the Council of the Royal Horticultural Society for permission to revise this book. The work was greatly helped by the suggestions and advice of many entomologists in the National Agricultural Advisory Service and I am particularly grateful to Dr. A. M. Massee, Mr. J. J. M. Flegg and Mr. V. W. Fowler who kindly read and criticized the manuscript. To Dr. Massee I am also indebted for writing the Foreword to this new edition.

Finally, I should like to thank my wife, Miss J. Maynard and Mrs. V. Kelleher, who all assisted in various ways with the preparation of the typescript and the proof-reading of the revised edition.

P. BECKER.

How to use this book

THIS book is divided into chapters corresponding to the main parts of plants, i.e., Bulbs, Corms and Tubers; Roots; Stems and Shoots, etc., all of which are liable to be attacked by insects and other pests. The signs of attack which may be found on that particular part of the plant are described under various sections which are arranged alphabetically and listed at the head of each chapter. Where the damage may fall under several categories the reader is referred to the section and page where a full description and control measures are given.

The indices have also been arranged to assist in the diagnosis of damage. In the plant index, under each name, are listed the signs of attack which may be found on the plant. Under each name in the pest index are listed the host plants mentioned in the book.

The months given after the names of most pests (with the exception of Scale Insects) are an indication of when the particular damage described may be expected. In the case of Scale Insects they indicate the best time to use sprays, i.e., when the young 'crawlers' are most plentiful. In all cases the timings are approximate and will vary somewhat in different parts of the country and according to climatic conditions.

CHAPTER ONE

Introduction

VAST damage is caused annually to horticultural plants and crops of all kinds by insect and other pests, and it behoves the grower and all who are concerned with maintaining plant health to become familiar with the signs of attack and the cause as contributory to the effect, so that appropriate measures may be taken before irreparable damage is done.

Those who cultivate plants show a definite desire for guidance as to the organism responsible for a particular type of injury. While it is essential to gain knowledge of the various organisms that attack plants, and to have some idea of their life histories, it is beyond the scope of the average horticulturist to comprehend technical details concerning the distinctive characters of every group of animals that may prey upon his crops.

It is in the rôle of the diagnostician that the average agriculturist and horticulturist can hope to achieve success in overcoming crop losses, which may be due, however, to causes other than pests, namely, to unfavourable conditions of soil and site, to nutritional deficiencies, and to disease organisms. The term 'diagnostician' is used here in the pathological sense, and implies one who possesses or cultivates the art of recognizing disease from its symptoms, signs or distinctive marks.

The presence of some phytophagous (plant-eating) species of insect or related animal (e.g. Woodlice, Millipedes) only too often becomes apparent from the unhealthy condition of the host plant. A tardy recognition of the responsible agent may be due to several reasons. For instance, the culprit may be nocturnally active, and hidden during the daytime among rubbish and other shelter (e.g. Woodlice and Vine Weevils); it may be a true soil-inhabiting organism (e.g. Keeled Slugs and Wireworms); or, again, owing to its microscopic size (e.g. Eelworms) its presence is made apparent from the effect it produces on the plant.

A knowledge of the signs of attack produced by the numerous enemies of plants is of inestimable value in pest control work. Attention was first directed to the value of symptomatic detection of plant pests and diseases by Marshall Ward, and was emulated by other authors, including Chittenden, Green, Miles, Kenneth Smith and others.

While there are doubtless some who may consider themselves competent to identify the *species* of insect from an examination of the type of injury produced, the identification of the causal organism solely by means of the signs of attack is scientifically inaccurate. It is true to state, however, that certain types of injury can be correlated with certain types of pest and disease organisms. To rely entirely upon causal effects in determining the species of the organism concerned with any particular diseased condition may be unwise if the effects of other factors are overlooked.

The plant may, for example, be affected by a non-parasitic disorder (physiological or nutritional), or by a virus, bacterium or fungus, and its reaction to any one of them may in certain instances resemble closely the characteristics of insect damage. This is likely to cause confusion in the minds of those who are untrained in plant pathology, and doubtful instances of diseased condition in plants should be submitted to a competent authority.

THE PLANT AS A FACTOR

The plant in health constitutes an individual living organism in which all parts maintain due and appropriate order with regard to one another, and serious injury to one portion, more especially to the root, the stem or the leaf, affects the entire plant. On the other hand, injury to such organs as the flower, fruit and seed is localized and may not unduly affect the whole organism. The plant should, therefore, be studied as a unit, for it is the disease organism that must receive primary consideration by the grower.

It is necessary to appreciate the fact that *every* part of *a* plant—though not of *every* plant—is apt to be attacked by one or more species of insect or related pest. Not only the aerial portions—the stem, branch, shoot, bud, leaf, flower, fruit and seed—may be attacked, but also the underground portions—the root, stem, tuber, bulb, corm and rhizome. The early recognition of the signs of attack on the several portions of a plant is frequently the means of avoiding a serious infestation by a particular pest, so that early measures can be taken to prevent serious damage.

The injury caused by primary pests may often result in secondary invasions by other organisms, both animal and vegetable, many of which are capable of extending the initial injury, while some may mask the effect of the organism primarily concerned with the damage.

TYPES OF PESTS

Before considering the various signs of injury that arise from pest attack, it is necessary to consider briefly the various groups of animals concerned, so that early recognition of the culprit is possible, the general outline of its life history known and the method by which

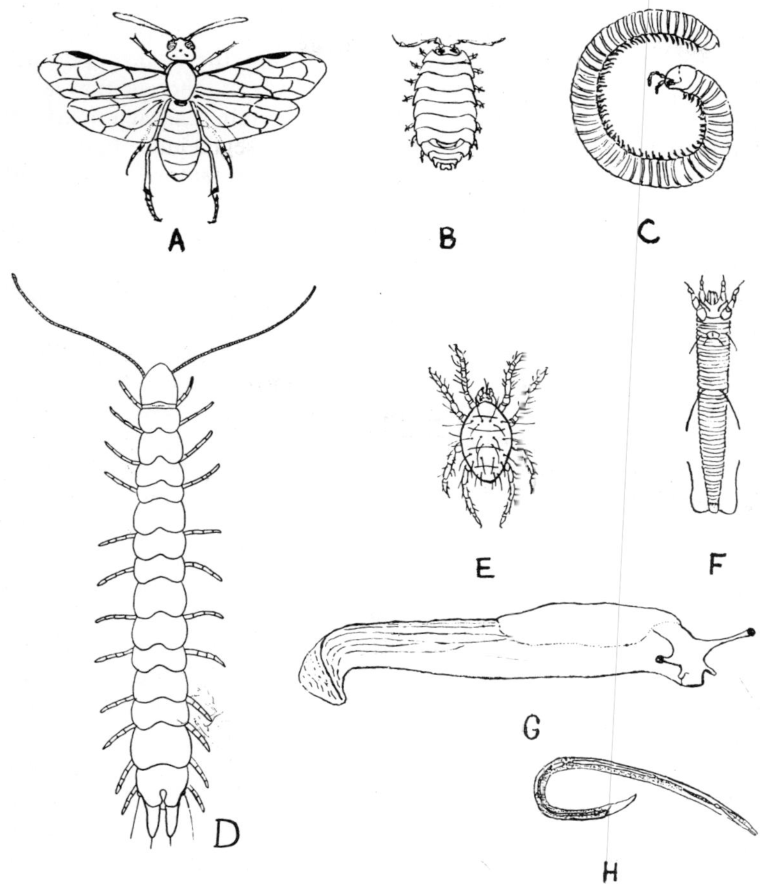

FIG. 1. TYPES OF PLANT PESTS

A. Insect—Sawfly (× 2); B. Crustacean—Woodlouse (× 2); C. Diplopod—Millipede (× 2); D. Symphylid (× 10); E. Acarine—Red Spider Mite (× 10); F. Eriophyid—Gall Mite (× 115); G. Mollusc—Slug (natural size); H. Nematode—Eelworm (× 45).

it feeds is clear, and thus an intelligent approach can be made to the methods by which an outbreak can be avoided or controlled.

The Animal Kingdom is grouped into a number of divisions or *Phyla* (Gr., a tribe), of which three, namely, the *Arthropoda* (Gr., jointed feet), the *Mollusca* (L., soft), and the *Nematoda* (Gr., thread-like), are of special importance to the plant pathologist, for within these three *Phyla* are found all the major pests of agricultural and horticultural crops. The term 'insect' is often loosely applied to any small animal that attacks plants, but among the Arthropods are forms that are closely related to insects and yet, though they arise from a common ancestry and possess certain characteristics in common (namely, an external skeleton, a segmented body and jointed feet), are sufficiently distinct in certain features to warrant their arrangement into definite classes.

The *Arthropoda* are divided into a number of classes, six of which are of special interest to the applied entomologist.

(1) *Crustacea* (L., a shell) are predominantly aquatic animals, and include crabs, lobsters, shrimps, prawns, water-fleas (*Daphnia*), fish- and sea-lice. The Order *Isopoda* (Gr., equal-footed) includes the Wood-lice (Fig. 1, B), which are characterized by possessing two pairs of antennae (feelers), three body divisions—head, thorax, and abdomen—and seven pairs of legs attached to the thoracic segments.

(2) *Chilopoda* (Gr., lip-footed) or Centipedes (Fig. 5, G) have long, flattened, segmented bodies with one pair of legs attached to each segment, the first pair being modified into jaw-like poison claws. The head is prominent, and bears a pair of long antennae with numerous segments. They are active, predaceous creatures and feed on various soil-inhabiting animals, and are entirely beneficial.

(3) *Diplopoda* (Gr., double-footed) or Millipedes (Fig. 1, C) are elongated, worm-like animals with a distinct head bearing short antennae, and a horny, smooth, cylindrical (e.g. Spotted Millipede, *Blaniulus guttulatus*), or a broad, flattened body (e.g. *Polydesmus*), with two pairs of short legs attached to most of the body segments. They are sluggish creatures, feeding on vegetable material in the soil, often curling up when disturbed. They attack plants and usually act as secondary pests, following attacks of other soil pests and extending the initial injury.

(4) *Symphyla* are small elongate soil-dwelling animals. They are active and fast-moving creatures with twelve pairs of walking legs and a distinct head with long many-jointed antennae. In general they feed on decaying vegetable matter, but one species, the Glasshouse Symphylid, *Scutigerella immaculata* (Fig. 1, D), attacks a wide variety of plants grown under glass. This species is white in colour and grows to $\frac{1}{4}$ in. in length.

(5) *Arachnida* (Gr., a spider) include the scorpions, spiders, Mites, ticks, and Gall Mites. The body is separated into two divisions, the cephalothorax (fused head and thorax) and abdomen. They possess

four pairs of legs, and no antennae. There are a number of Orders, including the *Araneae* or true spiders, which are beneficial animals, and the *Acarina* (Gr., not cut) which include the so-called 'Red Spiders' (Fig. 1, E) and other Mites, which are distinguishable by their small size, an inconspicuously divided body, and whose larvae have only three pairs of legs when newly hatched; and the Gall Mites (*Eriophyidae*), which are microscopic in size with a peg-shaped segmented body bearing two pairs of legs attached immediately behind the head (Fig. 1, F).

(6) *Insecta* (L., cut into) or *Hexapoda* (Gr., six-footed) or Insects (Fig. 1, A) have the body divided into three main sections—the head thorax and abdomen. The head bears a pair of antennae, the thorax bears three pairs of legs and usually two pairs of wings (though many are wingless and members of the Order *Diptera* possess only one pair), and a segmented abdomen upon which are borne such appendages as cerci, cornicles, forceps and, in the female, the ovipositor.

The *Mollusca* are divided into a number of classes and sub-classes, and include oysters, cockles, winkles, limpets, squids, cuttlefish and octopods. The Order *Pulmonata* includes Snails and Slugs, which possess two pairs of tentacles—the eyes being borne on the tips of the hinder pair—walk on their stomachs, and possess either a rudimentary shell (Slugs) (Fig. 1, G) or live within a prominent shell (Snails).

The *Nematoda* are rounded, worm- or eel-shaped animals with unsegmented bodies, and include both free-living and plant-parasitic eelworms (Fig. 1, H). Most species are microscopic in size, and many are important parasites of the roots, stems, buds and leaves.

LIFE HISTORIES OF PESTS

Insects undergo a series of changes or metamorphoses, which are termed complete or incomplete. *Complete* metamorphosis occurs in Butterflies and Moths, Beetles and Weevils, Flies, Sawflies, Gall-wasps, Wasps, Bees and Ants. It comprises four stages, namely, the egg, the larva (otherwise known as the caterpillar, grub or maggot), the pupa or chrysalis, and the adult (Fig. 2). There is little or no resemblance between the animal in its larval and adult stages, and the insect undergoes a complete change from the one to the other during its period of quiescence as a pupa.

Insects with an *incomplete* metamorphosis, such as Earwigs, Leaf-hoppers, Cockroaches, Crickets, Thrips, Capsid bugs, Aphids (plant lice), Psyllids (suckers), Aleyrodids (whiteflies) and Coccids (scale insects and mealy bugs) undergo only a slight pupal stage, and the

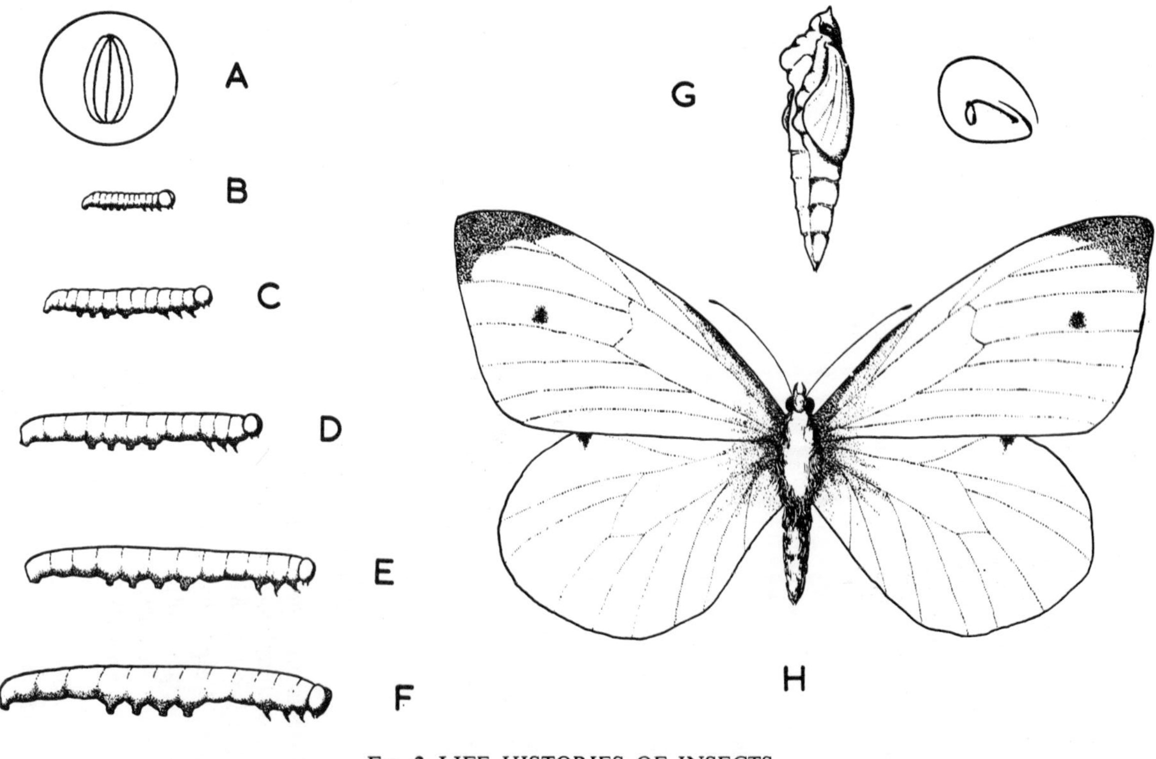

FIG. 2. LIFE HISTORIES OF INSECTS

Butterfly (Complete metamorphosis). A. Egg; B.–F. Immature stages (larvae); G. Pupa; H. Adult Insect.

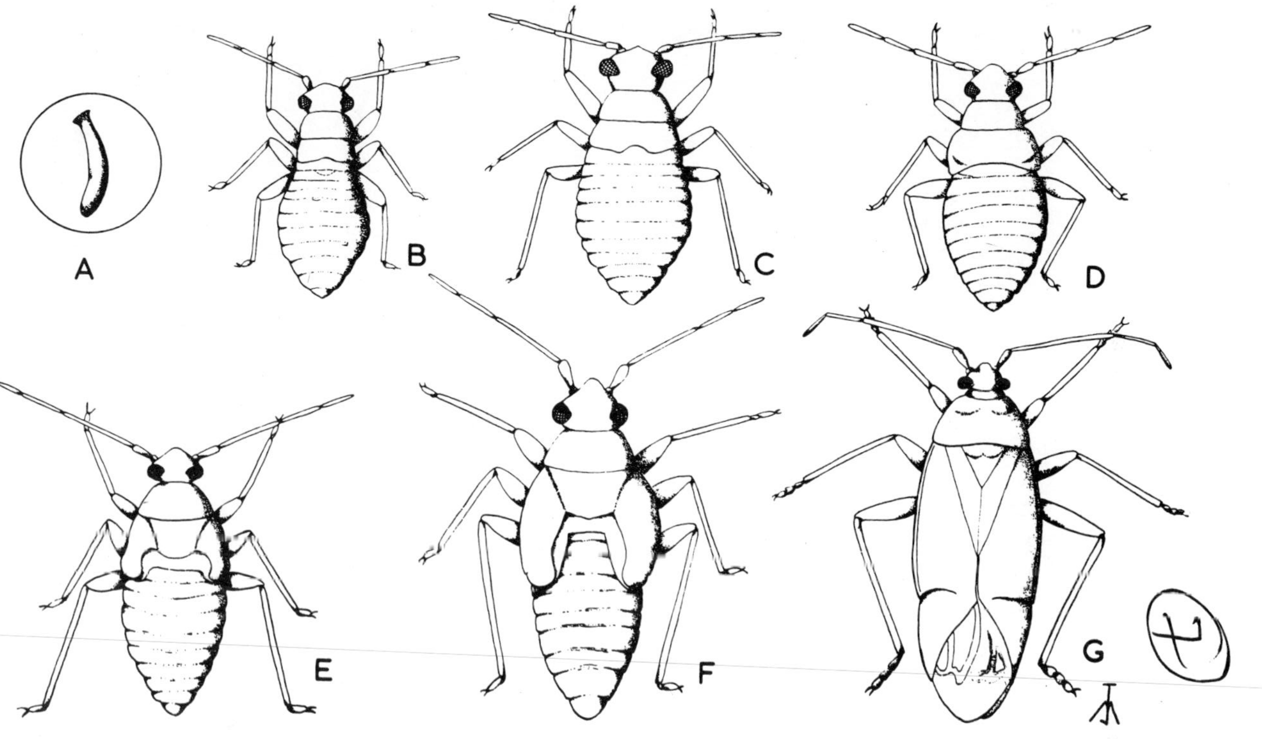

FIG. 2 (*contd.*). Capsid (Incomplete metamorphosis). A. Egg; B.–F. Immature stages (nymphs); G. Adult Insect. (*Drawings not to scale, from various sources.*)

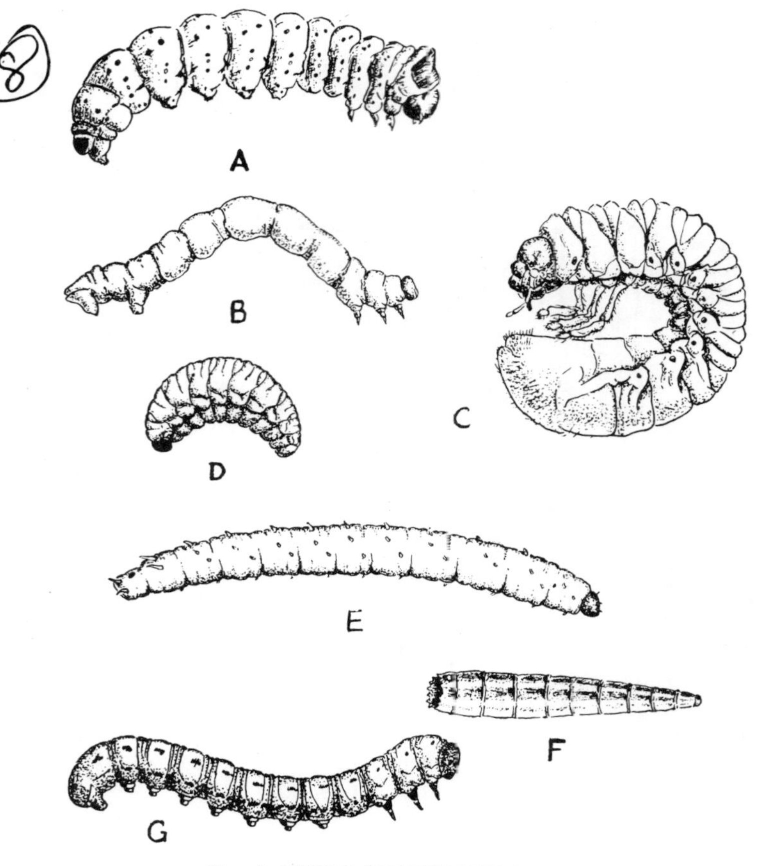

FIG. 3. TYPES OF INSECT LARVAE

Order *Lepidoptera* (Butterflies and Moths)

A. Caterpillar of a Moth (Wood Leopard), with prominent head, 3 pairs of thoracic legs and 5 pairs of abdominal feet (pro-legs); B. Looper Caterpillar of a Geometrid Moth, with prominent head, 3 pairs of thoracic legs and 2 pairs only of pro-legs.

Order *Coleoptera* (Beetles and Weevils)

C. Larva of a Beetle (Cockchafer), with prominent head, 3 pairs of thoracic legs and no abdominal feet; D. Larva of a Vine Weevil with prominent head and a curved legless body.

Order *Diptera* (Two-winged Flies)

E. Larva of a Bibionid (St. Mark's Fly), with a defined head and a legless body; F. Larva of a Muscid (Bluebottle), with no defined head region and a legless body.

Order *Hymenoptera* (Sawflies)

G. Caterpillar of a Sawfly, with a prominent head, 3 pairs of thoracic legs and 6, 7 or 8 pairs of abdominal feet.

resemblance in most instances between the immature insect (nymph) and the adult is so marked that there is little or no confusion in identifying the creature. The nymphs are, however, without functional wings and are sexually immature (Fig. 2).

A small group of wingless insects which includes the *Collembola* (Springtails) do not undergo any metamorphosis. The young hatch from the eggs as miniature replicas of the adults. Among the pests which are not members of the Class *Insecta* such as Woodlice, Slugs and Eelworms, the young are also similar in form to the adults, but the young of Millipedes, Symphylids and Mites hatch from their eggs with fewer legs than the adults. Additional legs are grown during the period of development.

Among the members of the *Arthropoda* growth takes place mainly during the immature stages and, in many cases, e.g. *Insecta*, stops after the adult stage is reached. Since their bodies are covered with a tough, horny cuticle (exoskeleton), which is incapable of much expansion, they must replace this periodically to allow for further growth. This is done by a series of moults which mark each stage of the life-cycle.

The stage during which damage is done to plants by insects varies considerably with the species concerned. Some are injurious *only* in the larval stage (e.g. the larvae of Butterflies, Moths and Sawflies); some as adults only (leaf-eating *Phyllobius* Weevils, and Wasps); while others are injurious both in the larval *and* adult stages (Capsid Bugs, Raspberry Beetle, Cockchafer, Vine Weevil, Bark Beetles and so on).

FEEDING HABITS

The majority of insects and other plant pests bite or chew their food by means of jaws or mandibles, e.g. Woodlice, Millipedes, Springtails, Cockroaches, Earwigs, the caterpillars of Butterflies and Moths, Beetles and Weevils together with their grubs, certain Fly maggots, and the larvae of Sawflies (Fig. 4, B and C). In a few insects, the larvae of some Flies particularly, the jaws are modified for rasping at the plant tissues to obtain their food in a finely-divided or semi-liquid form (Fig. 4, D). Snails and Slugs have no jaws but possess a tongue or radula covered with thousands of tiny hooked teeth which are used to rasp away portions of the plant.

Other pests, namely those belonging to the Orders *Hemiptera* (Capsid Bugs, Leafhoppers, Aphids, Psyllids, Whiteflies, Scale Insects and Mealy Bugs) and *Diptera* (Two-winged Flies), have the mouthparts greatly modified to form organs either for piercing the tissues and extracting the sap (Fig. 4, A) or merely for sucking (the non-blood-sucking Flies). Among the *Thysanoptera* (Thrips), the imperfectly suctorial mouthparts are adapted for rasping plant tissue, while further modifications in piercing and sucking organs are found in the *Acarina* (Mites). Eelworms possess a hollow mouth-spear which is used to pierce the plant cells and suck out the sap.

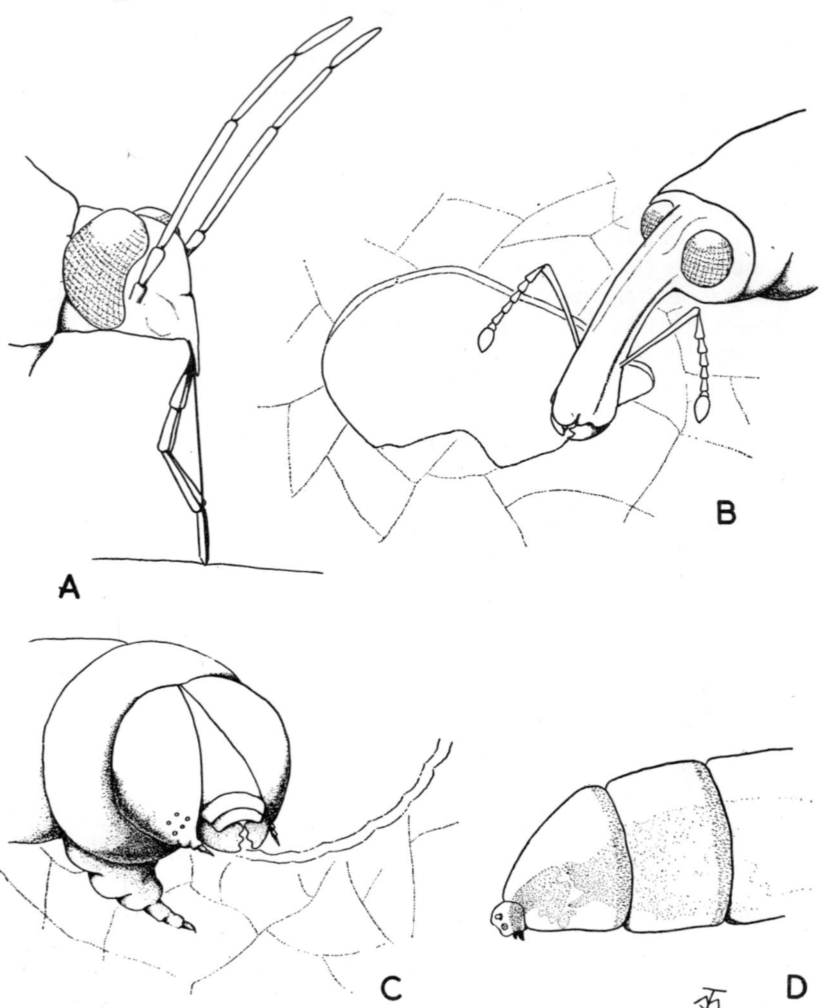

FIG. 4. TYPES OF INSECT MOUTHPARTS
A. Sucking Type (Capsid); B. Biting Type (Weevil); C. Biting Type (Caterpillar); D. Rasping Type (Fly larva).

THE EFFECTS OF PESTS ON PLANTS

Insects and other pests injure plants both directly and indirectly and the chief effects of their feeding are outlined below.

I—Biting Insects

(A) *Direct Damage* consists of (i) a reduction of assimilative tissue, thereby hindering food formation and growth (leaf-eating insects); (ii) a lowered vitality due to the strain imposed upon plants in producing new growth; (iii) the destruction of the floral (corolla and calyx) and reproductive organs (anthers and pistil) thereby lessening the chances of pollination and fertilization (Pollen Beetles, Earwigs, Apple Blossom Weevil); (iv) a reduction in the amount of conductive tissue (stem-tunnelling caterpillars and wood-boring beetles); (v) a reduction in the amount of stored food—water and elaborated food materials—in bulbs, corms, tubers and other storage organs; (vi) a hindrance to the passage of elaborated food materials and a reduction in assimilative tissue (leaf-mining insects); (vii) the destruction of roots thereby reducing water- and nutrient-absorbing tissue (Cockchafer grubs, Vine Weevil larvae); (viii) the destruction of buds, thereby checking growth and producing distortion, proliferation and 'blindness' (Tarnished Plant Bug, Swede Midge, Bud Moth); (ix) the accumulation of food materials due to localized stimuli (Gall Wasps); and (x) the destruction of seeds, thereby affecting fertility (Seed Weevils), and a reduction in reserve food, thereby lessening the powers of germination (Bruchid beetles).

(B) *Indirect Damage* is concerned chiefly with the wounding of tissues, through which may enter bacterial and fungal organisms, including weakly parasitic forms, setting up diseased conditions, and rain causing rapid decay of internal tissues.

II—Sucking Insects

(A) *Direct Damage* consists of (i) the extraction of cell sap and chlorophyll, thereby lowering vitality and producing wilting, discoloration (false chlorosis) and distortion of foliage and flowers, gall formation, and proliferation and 'blindness' in buds (Capsid Bugs, Aphids); (ii) the extraction of cell contents from roots and underground storage organs, thereby reducing water- and nutrient-absorbing and conducting tissues (root Aphids and Mealy Bugs); (iii) the hindering of the free passage and exchange of elaborated food materials by the tapping of conductive tissue and by the severance of veins (Capsid Bugs, Leafhoppers, Aphids); (iv) the laceration of epidermal and sub-epidermal tissues (Capsid Bugs); and (v) the injection into the tissues of salivary juices which have a toxic effect and produce proliferation, distortion and tumours (Capsid Bugs, Aphids, Woolly Aphid).

(B) *Indirect Damage* includes the (i) wounding of tissues, thereby resulting in lesions through which bacteria and fungi enter (e.g. Woolly Aphid and Canker spores); (ii) the transmission of virus diseases by Aphids, Leafhoppers and Thrips; and (iii) the deposition of 'honeydew' by Aphids, Whiteflies, Scale Insects and Mealy Bugs on the foliage, thereby hindering the normal functions (assimilation and respiration) and, in addition, providing a medium favourable to the growth of non-parasitic fungi (Sooty Moulds).

CONTROL MEASURES

A criticism frequently levelled against the plant pathologist is that he appears to stress direct or remedial measures against pests and diseases rather than the indirect or cultural and preventive methods of control. The axiom that prevention is better than cure deserves the attention of all who cultivate plants, and the adoption of a defensive spirit is desirable and is accomplished only by applying hygienic principles to plant growth and by recognizing that good cultivation is the essence of prevention.

The factors governing the increase of an insect species are climatic and biological. Unfavourable weather conditions exercise a marked influence on insect populations, and many examples could be given of threatened outbreaks being naturally controlled by low temperatures, prolonged drought, high winds and gales and rainstorms, all of which may influence the pest at some stage in its development. Biological factors include the availability and attractiveness of its food plants, and the presence of natural enemies, including insectivorous birds and other animals, predacious insects and other Arthropods, parasites whose larvae live within the body of the insect host, and protozoal, bacterial, fungal and other diseases that may cause high mortality among insects.

The control of pests will be considered under five headings, namely, (I) Cultural, (II) Mechanical, (III) Physical, (IV) Biological and (V) Chemical.

I—Cultural Control

The operations that are practised to avoid outbreaks are considered under the following sub-headings:

(i) *Cultivation.* Good and thorough cultivation affects insects directly by rendering conditions unfavourable to them, by exposing them to the attacks of insectivorous birds and to adverse weather conditions. Such operations as regular hoeing destroy many soil pests by the mechanical action of the hoe-blade, while frequent rolling of lawns crushes many pests and consolidates ground loosened by their workings beneath the turf. Clean cultivation destroys weeds, many of which serve as host plants for pests and as 'bridging hosts' for eelworms. The effect of trenching and double-digging is that the pupae are buried to a depth sufficient to cause suffocation or from which ascent to the surface by the emerging adult is rendered impossible.

(ii) *Drainage*. The provision of an effective drainage scheme is desirable, expecially in heavier soils that are inclined to remain waterlogged for long periods, for overmoist soils prove attractive to Slugs and Snails, Millipedes, Springtails and Leatherjackets.

(iii) *Rotation*. Apart from the manurial benefits accruing from crop rotation, the system should be practised in the smallest garden to compel migration of pests thereby tending to reduce the incidence of attack. The re-arrangement of crops annually under horticultural conditions is less effective than under agricultural ones, for there is invariably danger arising from re-infestations from neighbouring gardens where adequate control measures are not practised. The distance that can be arranged between the site of the previous and the current years' crops is negligible in such small areas as gardens and allotment-sites, and high local populations of pests may be rapidly built up. Eelworm attack may be largely avoided by rotation practices, so that a crop subject to infection by a particular biologic race of nematode is withheld from infected ground for a period of 3–5 years. For instance, land infected with the Narcissus strain of the Stem and Bulb Eelworm (*Ditylenchus dipsaci*), should not be planted with onions, and so on. So-called 'Potato sick' ground should remain free of potatoes for a few years to starve out the Potato Root Eelworm (*Heterodera rostochiensis*).

(iv) *Date of Sowing*. Damage by some pests may be avoided by timing the growth of a crop so that the period when it is vulnerable to attack does not coincide with the peak periods of activity of the harmful insect. Plants that become established before the appearance of a pest are enabled to withstand an attack more successfully. For instance, Cruciferous crops that have reached their 'rough leaf' stage before the appearance of Flea Beetles are less affected than those in the cotyledon (seed-leaf) stage. Late-sown (July) carrots and early-sown peas are less subject to damage by Carrot Fly, and by Pea Moth and Pea Thrips respectively.

(v) *Date of Harvesting*. Similarly, the time chosen for harvesting will frequently affect the degree to which a crop is attacked. For instance, early (October) lifting of a carrot crop infested with Carrot Fly will avoid a substantial increase of damage by the maggots, and possibly by frost. Again, a potato crop lifted early (mid- to late August) from ground heavily infested with Wireworms will be far less damaged than when the tubers are allowed to remain until October or later, for the peak feeding period of the grubs will then be avoided.

(vi) *Manuring.* The judicious application of organic (farmyard and stable manure, spent hops, composted material) and of inorganic (chemical fertilizers) manures will ensure a balanced food supply, thereby promoting health, rapid growth and tolerance of certain pests.

Excessive amounts of nitrogenous manures tend to the production of lush, sappy growth that is conducive to Aphid attack, while luxuriant growth may mask the effect of eelworm attack, e.g. Leaf and Bud Eelworm on chrysanthemums and Stem and Bulb Eelworm on phlox. Quick-acting fertilizers (e.g. nitrate of soda and sulphate of ammonia) tend to stimulate growth during a critical period of lowered vitality arising from pest attack (e.g. Flea Beetles and Beet and Mangold Leaf Miner).

Heavy annual applications of dead and decaying organic matter may raise the population of such pests as Slugs and Millipedes, and it may be necessary to change the system of manuring for a year or so by substituting chemical fertilizers.

(vii) *Rubbish Disposal.* Many insects overwinter at the bases of hedges, in stacks of old pea sticks, cut grass, dry leaves, pulled weeds and dead herbaceous stems, and find harbourage among heaps of broken bricks, flower-pots, clinker, rubble and similar material. Measures should accordingly be taken to dispose of such hibernacula by making a compost heap of vegetable material and by using broken bricks, etc., as a foundation for paths or similar purpose.

Other insects (Flea Beetles, Pea and Bean Weevil) hibernate among fallen leaves in hedge bottoms, and may be destroyed by raking out and burning the accumulated rubbish during the winter. Crop remnants in the form of eelworm-infested stems of chrysanthemums and phloxes should be burned and not placed on the compost heap. All prunings and dead and dying branches should be burned and not stacked, so as to discourage the breeding of Bark Beetles and similar pests. Brassica 'stumps' galled by the Turnip Gall Weevil should be pulled before April and loosely stacked to facilitate the speedy drying-out of the stems and roots.

(viii) *Pest Introduction.* A careful examination should be made of all plant material received from outside sources, whether from gardens or nurseries, to avoid the establishment of additional pests. Such pests as Gall Mite ('Big Bud') on black currants, Aphid eggs on the shoots of fruit and ornamental trees and bushes, Woolly Aphid colonies on apple stocks and cotoneaster bushes, Rhododendron Bug eggs within the leaf tissues of rhododendrons, Mealy Bug on tender ornamental plants, Bruchid beetles in seed of pulse, Sawfly pupae among the roots of roses, and Eelworms in narcissus bulbs, chrysanthemum cuttings and phlox stools, together with many others, are unwittingly introduced on plants and on plant material.

II—Mechanical Methods

(i) *Handpicking*. This primitive and somewhat laborious method may still be regarded as a means of checking outbreaks in small areas. It is employed against Slugs and Snails; colonies of Cabbage White Butterfly caterpillars on brassicas, nasturtium (*Tropaeolum*) and stocks; Cutworms among China asters, chrysanthemums, marigolds, zinnias and vegetable crops; egg-masses and 'bracelets' of the Vapourer, Lackey and March Moths; Leaf Miners on celery, chrysanthemum and cineraria; Gooseberry Sawfly larvae; and so on.

(ii) *Trapping*. Many kinds of traps are employed against pests, including: (*a*) Grease bands on the stems of top fruits in autumn to capture the wingless females of Winter and allied Moths and, later, to prevent the wingless, immature Apple Capsid Bugs from regaining the shoots after dropping to the ground during spraying operations; on standard roses against the ascent of Ants; and on standard rhododendrons against wingless weevils (Vine and Clay-coloured). (*b*) Sack and corrugated-paper bands on fruit trees to capture the Apple Blossom Weevil, and to provide shelter and pupating quarters for Codling Moth caterpillars. (*c*) Rolled pieces of sacking placed among plants damaged by Earwigs, and nocturnally-active Weevils. (*d*) Pared portions of potato, carrot and mangold attached to skewers and buried in the ground to attract Millipedes and Wireworms. (*e*) Scooped-out potato tubers for capturing Woodlice in plant-houses. (*f*) Jam-jars suitably baited and sunk to their rims in the ground against the strawberry-devouring Carabid or Ground Beetles, Cockroaches and Crickets, or hung among branches to capture Wasps and the Tomato Moth. (*g*) Inverted straw-filled plant pots, the hollow stems of broad bean, delphinium and similar herbaceous plants, and split bamboo-canes to serve as traps for Earwigs. (*h*) Toboggan traps for Flea Beetles.

(iii) *Jarring*. Shaking the branches of fruit and ornamental trees and bushes over a beating-tray, an open inverted umbrella, or on to sheets of white paper, canvas or linen spread on the ground may be employed against diurnally-active leaf-eating *Phyllobius* weevils, Garden Chafer on apple and rose blooms, Nut Weevil on nut hedges, and Raspberry Beetle on raspberry and loganberry canes, and the nocturnally-active Vine and Clay-coloured Weevils.

III—Physical Methods

The chief physical means for the destruction of plant pests include the application of high or low temperatures, and electricity. Measures employing heat are: (i) steam sterilization of glasshouse soils and of infected plant pots against soil organisms, especially Eelworms; (ii) hot-water baths for the immersion of narcissus bulbs and of chrysanthemum and phlox stools for the control of Eelworms, and of strawberry runners infested with Tarsonemid Mites; (iii) flame-throwers against Locust hopper-swarms, flame-guns against Fungus Gnats on mushroom beds, and blow-lamps for destroying Woolly Aphid colonies and caterpillar 'tents' of Lackey and Ermine Moths, and of the Social Pear Sawfly on fruit trees. Hot air is employed against certain pests of stored products.

Low temperatures such as exist in cold-storage plants render conditions unfavourable to the breeding of Clothes Moths in fur and woollen garments.

Electricity as an agent in pest control is governed by power charges and, in countries where the costs are low, electricity is used for supplying light for light-traps in orchards and vineyards against Moths, and for electrifying gauze fitted to windows, doors and ventilators of stables, cowsheds, dairies and mushroom houses for the electrocution of House and Stable Flies and of Fungus Gnats. A limited use is made of electrical power for soil-sterilizing apparatus.

IV—Biological Control

While this book is devoted to the damage caused to plants by insects and other pests it must be remembered that the number of injurious species is relatively small and that the great majority of insects, mites, eelworms, etc., are quite harmless. Many indeed are actively beneficial and help to reduce the number of pests by killing and eating them or by parasitizing them. The effect of these creatures on pest populations is variable and in most cases has not been adequately investigated, but it has been shown that many of them play an appreciable part in pest control. For this reason it is in the interest of everyone concerned with the growing of plants to become acquainted with these beneficial creatures and to make every endeavour to preserve them.

The increasing use of modern contact insecticides which leave persistent deposits on plant foliage and in the ground constitutes a great hazard to beneficial insects. In general their breeding potential is lower than that of the pest on which they feed with the result that if both pest and predators are reduced in numbers by insecticides, the population of the latter takes far longer to recover, and before this happens the pests have increased to such an extent that further chemical control is necessary. The net result is that, where insecticides are used extensively, the numbers of predators and parasites are kept at a constant minimum.

It is, therefore, important that, if full use is to be made of beneficial insects, insecticides be used only when really necessary. Such advice can be followed more easily by the private gardener than the commercial grower who has to face stiff competition in marketing his produce. Parasites and predators seldom give full control of pests, but in the garden much expense and time can be saved by allowing for a certain degree of damage before using insecticides, thereby enabling the beneficial insects to play their part.

Among the more important beneficial insects and related creatures are:

(*a*) *Predacious Bugs*, the best known being the Black-kneed Capsid (*Blepharidopterus angulatus* Fall.) which is common in orchards and feeds on Red Spider Mites and also on Thrips and Aphids. Other predacious Capsids have a similar diet and there are also many predacious species in the Anthocoridae and Pentatomidae.

(*b*) *Lacewings*. The adults and larvae of the Green Lacewings (*Chrysopidae*) feed mainly on Aphids, including Woolly Aphid, and Adelgids. They are slow-flying, bright green insects with metallic golden eyes. The larvae are variable in colour with long sickle-shaped jaws and bear bristles to which some species attach the empty skins of their prey. The Brown Lacewings (*Hemerobiidae*) which feed on Aphids and Red Spider Mites, and the Powdery Lacewings (*Coniopterygidae*) which feed on Red Spider Mites, also belong to this group (Fig. 5, D).

(*c*) *Ladybirds*. Both adult and larval Ladybirds (*Coccinellidae*) feed on large numbers of small pests such as Thrips, Aphids, Scale Insects, Mealy Bugs and Red Spider Mites. The small, round, red-and-black or yellow-and-black beetles are familiar to all, but the bluish-black, yellow spotted larvae are not so well known (Fig. 5, C).

(*d*) *Ground Beetles*. Though a few species are pests of strawberries most Ground Beetles (*Carabidae*) are predacious, both as larvae and adults. There are hundreds of species in this country and they vary greatly in size. Those which are most often noticed in gardens are

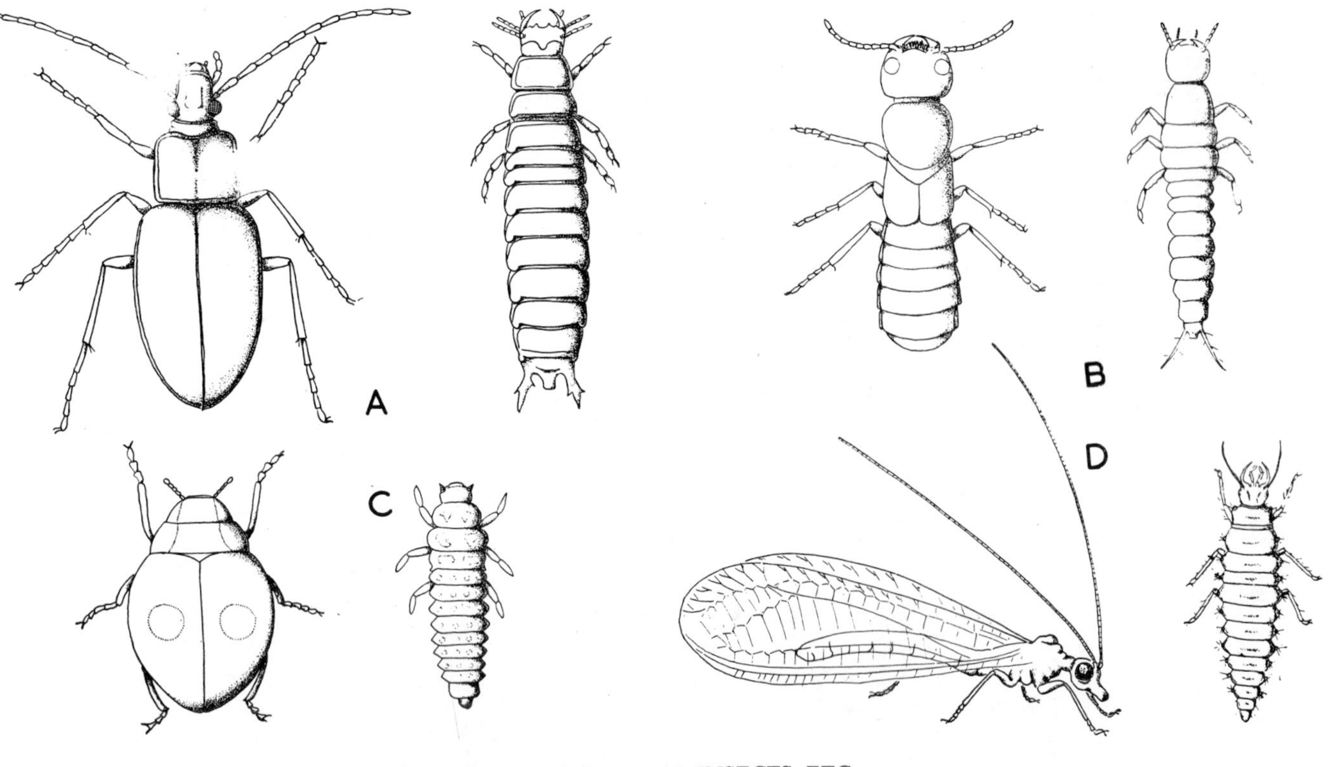

FIG. 5. BENEFICIAL INSECTS, ETC.

A. *Carabidae*—Violet Ground Beetle (*Carabus violaceous* L.), adult and larva (× 2); B. *Staphylinidae*—Devil's Coach-horse (*Staphylinus olens* Müll.), adult and larva (× 2); C. *Coccinellidae*—Two-spot Ladybird (*Adalia bipunctata* L.), adult and larva (× 6); D. *Chrysopidae*—Green Lacewing (*Chrysopa carnea* Steph.), adult and larva (× 2).

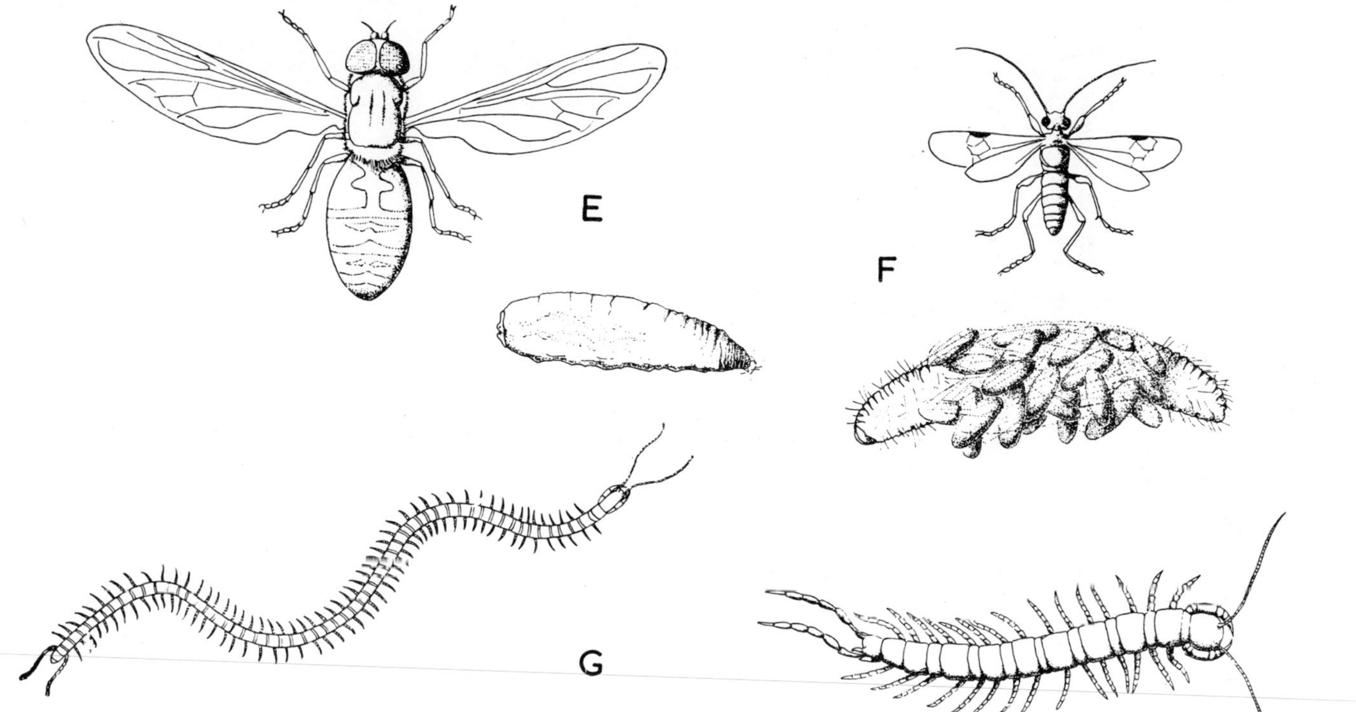

FIG. 5 (*contd.*). E. *Syrphidae*—Hoverfly (*Syrphus balteatus* Deg.), adult and larva (× 6); F. *Braconidae*—Parasitic Wasp (*Apanteles glomeratus* L.), adult and cocoons on parasitized caterpillar (× 4); G. *Chilopoda*—Centipedes, *Geophilus* species (*left*) and *Lithobius* species (*right*) (× 2). (*Drawings from various sources.*)

comparatively large and black in colour. The larvae are quick-moving, well-armoured creatures with strong curved jaws. Both adults and larvae feed mainly at night on a wide variety of prey (Fig. 5, A).

(*e*) *Rove Beetles* (*Staphylinidae*). Narrow, fast-moving beetles with very short wing-covers which leave much of the abdomen exposed. The larvae are very similar to those of ground beetles. Both adults and larvae are carnivorous, feeding on many types of pests (Fig. 5, B).

(*f*) *Hoverflies*. The larvae of many species of Hoverflies (*Syrphidae*) are voracious predators on Aphids. The adult lays its eggs near a colony of the pests and, on hatching out, the pale, soft-bodied maggots start feeding on them. Red Spider Mites are also eaten by some species (Fig. 5, E).

(*g*) *Parasitic Flies*. The most important parasitic flies belong to the *Tachinidae*. The adults are similar to houseflies in general appearance and the maggot-like larvae feed as internal parasites of Earthworms, Snails, Caterpillars and many other types of the larger insects.

(*h*) *Parasitic Wasps*. These mostly belong to three groups, the Ichneumon Flies (*Ichneumonidae*), Braconids (*Braconidae*) and Chalcids (*Chalcidoidae*). The larvae of these wasps are internal parasites of the larvae, pupae and eggs of other insects, including those of Moths and Butterflies, Sawflies and beetles (Fig. 5, F). Also parasitized are Aphids and Scale Insects. The wasps vary in size from the $1\frac{1}{4}$ inch-long Ichneumon *Rhyssa*, which parasitizes a wood-boring sawfly larva, to the tiny Chalcid *Trichogramma*, twenty of whose larvae can develop in a single Moth egg.

(*i*) *Centipedes*. Elongate, with many long legs, Centipedes (*Chilopoda*) are active and fast-moving, in contrast to the harmful, short-legged Millipedes which move more slowly. They feed on a wide variety of soil life which they catch and kill by means of their poison fangs (Fig. 5, G).

(*j*) *Mites*. Little is known about beneficial mites but from the work that has been done there is no doubt that there are large numbers of them. The most well known is the large, brightly-coloured Red Velvet Mite (*Allothrombidium fuliginosum* Herm.) which is often seen running rapidly over the ground or on vegetation. It is often confused with the much smaller Red Spider Mite but, in fact, feeds on small insects including Woolly Aphids. The family *Laelaptidae* also contains many beneficial species, in particular *Typhlodromus tiliae* Oud. which feeds on the Fruit Tree Red Spider Mite.

For many years considerable attention has been paid to the problem of controlling pests by the deliberate introduction of large numbers of parasites or predators to the affected area. Such methods have met with spectacular success in a certain number of instances in various parts of the world, particularly where the pest has been introduced from other countries. In Britain, however, there have been only two cases where control by introduced insect parasites has met with any degree of success. A good control of Woolly Aphid can be obtained by the introduction of the Chalcid parasite *Aphelinus mali* Hald. to infested orchards. Another Chalcid, *Encarsia formosa* Gah., has been used with great success for the control of the Glasshouse Whitefly. Other methods of biological control which can be used to advantage in this country are the introduction of fish (Golden Carp and Orfe) into ornamental ponds to destroy Mosquito eggs, larvae and pupae, the introduction of toads into greenhouses to catch Woodlice and insects and the use of poultry and pigs in orchards to feed on fallen infested fruit and pupating fruit pests.

V—Chemical Methods

The intensive research which has been carried out since the war on chemical methods of pest control has resulted in a flood of new synthetic insecticides and acaricides. In general these are more efficient and easier to use than the older insecticides, and these factors, as well as the skilful advertising of the manufacturers, have encouraged gardeners and growers to employ chemical control measures on a larger scale than ever before. This trend has all too often taken place at the expense of the other methods of control. Cultural control and the principles of general garden hygiene, being more laborious or expensive to operate, tend to be neglected. The unwise or reckless use of these powerful new weapons has resulted in the evolution of resistant races of pests and the slaughter of pollinating insects. Also, the destruction of beneficial parasites and predators has given rise to the increase in numbers of some pests which were previously of little importance.

It is therefore imperative that insecticides should be used with the utmost caution. The principles of cultural control and garden hygiene should be constantly borne in mind and put into practice. Then, making intelligent use of his knowledge of the important pests prevalent in his district, the gardener or grower should only apply insecticides when the pests are likely to reach dangerously high proportions.

Whereas most insecticide manufacturers maintain high standards of their produce and are fairly conservative in the claims made for their products, these principles are unfortunately not universally applied throughout the industry as a whole. To protect growers from sub-standard products and extravagant claims of performance, the Ministry of Agriculture operates the Crop Protection Products

Approval Scheme which gives official approval to products voluntarily submitted to them. These must comply with certain standards of composition and fulfil the claims made on the labels. A list of the approved products is issued each year and the labels of these products bear the official sign of approval (Fig. 6). While it is not suggested that products which are not approved are necessarily substandard the grower would do well to use them with caution or only on a trustworthy recommendation. It should also be remembered that, owing to the time needed to test them, it may be some time before new products are given official approval.

There are a number of different ways by which an insecticide may kill a pest. (*a*) Contact insecticides, as the term implies, kill when they come in contact with the cuticle either during spraying or when the pest walks over the deposit which remains. (*b*) Stomach poisons kill when they are eaten together with the treated tissues of the plant. (*c*) Systemic insecticides are stomach poisons which are absorbed through the leaves and by the roots and carried in the sap to all parts of the plant. (*d*) Fumigants are materials producing a gas or vapour which is breathed in through the spiracles or breathing pores. Most modern insecticides come under two or more of these categories and for this reason the list below is given in alphabetical order with no attempt at grouping.

FIG. 6. The sign appearing on the labels of officially approved control chemicals.

In the following list some materials (marked with an asterisk (*)) are highly poisonous and are subject to the provisions of the Agriculture (Poisonous Substances) Act, 1952, and its subsequent Regulations, which lays down strict rules for the handling of these chemicals, including the use of protective clothing. These chemicals are normally available only to commercial growers.

Aldrin. A persistent contact and stomach poison of the chlorinated hydrocarbon group. Used mainly as a soil insecticide because of its volatility this material has not the disadvantage of causing tainting of root vegetables grown on treated ground. It is obtainable as a dust or a spray, and should not be used on edible crops within 3 weeks of harvesting.

Pests controlled include Cutworms, Swift Moth Caterpillars, Wireworms, Chafer and Vine Weevil Grubs, Leatherjackets, Strawberry Seed Beetle, Cabbage Root Fly, Bean Seed Fly, Narcissus Bulb Flies and Ants.

Azobenzene. Used as a smoke against the eggs of the Glasshouse Red Spider Mite. It is non-toxic to humans but is harmful to young plants in general and to gerbera, maiden-hair fern, pilea, schizanthus, and stephanotis. It should not be used on plants which are dry at the root.

BHC (*benzene hexachloride*) and *Gamma-BHC* (or *Lindane*). The insecticidal properties of this material were discovered shortly after those of DDT. It acts more quickly than DDT but is not so persistent. A contact and stomach poison of the chlorinated hydrocarbon group, it is also slightly volatile and was used as a soil insecticide but, because it imparts a musty flavour to edible plants, it has now largely been superseded by aldrin for that purpose. Gamma-BHC or lindane is a more potent form of BHC and its tainting properties are greatly reduced but, nevertheless, potatoes and other root crops should not be grown on lindane-treated soil for at least 18 months. Neither should BHC be used in any form on cucurbits (cucumber, marrow, etc.), currants, vines, or hydrangeas. Both BHC and lindane can be obtained as dusts, sprays and smokes. Do not pick edible crops during the 14 days following spraying or dusting.

Pests controlled include Woodlice, Symphylids, Millipedes, Springtails, Earwigs, Thrips, Aphids, adult Whiteflies, Leafhoppers, Capsids, Wireworms and many Beetles and Weevils, Root Flies, Gall Midges, Leaf Miners, Sawflies and Ants.

Chlorbenside. A Red Spider Mite ovicide used as a spray, which kills the summer eggs and immature stages of Fruit Tree and Glasshouse Red Spider Mites. It is persistent but not poisonous to humans and insects. It should not be used on cucurbits (cucumbers, marrows, etc.).

Chlorfenson (or *PCPCBS*). Another ovicide related to chlorbenside with similar properties and mode of action. It can, however, be used safely on cucurbits, but not on d'Arcy Spice apple. Fruit should not be sprayed within 3 weeks of picking.

DD (*dichloropropane-dichloropropene*). A liquid soil fumigant used mainly in glasshouses to control Root Knot Eelworm and Potato Root Eelworm. Its application requires a special injector which deposits the liquid 6–8 inches deep in the soil. Out-of-doors the treatment is not economic on large areas, except perhaps on light soils, but it may be worthwhile to treat small areas to check Potato Root Eelworm or Stem and Bulb Eelworm. No planting should be carried out for at least 6 weeks after treatment and the soil should be well cultivated 3 weeks after treatment to get rid of the fumes which would have adverse effects on the plants.

DDT (*dichloro-diphenyl-trichloroethane*). This was the first synthetic insecticide to be produced. It is very persistent, acting as a stomach and contact poison, and is used in the form of dusts, sprays or smokes. It can be used safely on almost all plants other than cucurbits (cucumber, marrow, etc.). With edible plants a period of 14 days should be allowed to elapse between treatment and harvesting.

Pests controlled include Thrips, Leafhoppers, Capsids, adult Whiteflies, Caterpillars, many species of Beetles and Weevils, Leatherjackets, Ants and Wasps. The emulsion form of DDT also kills many species of Aphids.

Demeton-Methyl (or '*Metasystox*').* A persistent contact and systemic poison of the organo-phosphorus group, but less toxic to humans than most systemic insecticides. It may be applied as a spray or by watering around the roots, the latter treatment being more effective, and will kill sucking insects up to 2 weeks after treatment. It should not be applied to edible crops within 4–6 weeks of harvesting, and should not be used on edible crops under glass.

Pests controlled include Red Spider Mites, Aphids, Woolly Aphid, Apple and Pear Suckers, Leafhoppers and Sawflies.

Derris. One of the older insecticides derived from the roots of certain plants, it is completely non-poisonous to humans and domestic animals and can be used on edible crops which are close to harvesting. It is however highly toxic to fish. It acts as a contact and stomach poison and is obtainable as a dust or a spray.

Pests controlled include Earthworms, Red Spider Mites (active stages), Cabbage Caterpillars, Sawflies. Derris will also give a partial control of Aphids and Thrips.

Diazinon. A recently-introduced organo-phosphorus insecticide, similar in its effects to parathion (q.v.), but much less toxic to humans and domestic animals. It should not, however, be used on edible crops within 2 weeks of harvesting. At present it is used only as a spray.

Pests controlled include Symphylids, Red Spider Mites (active stages), Aphids, Woolly Aphid, Suckers, Whiteflies, Scale Insects, Mealy Bugs and Capsids.

Dieldrin. Closely related to aldrin, this is also a persistent contact and stomach insecticide but with no fumigant action. It is non-tainting and is used in liquid form mainly on vegetables. These should not be eaten for 3 weeks after spraying.

Pests controlled include Pea and Bean Weevil, Flea Beetles, Leatherjackets, Narcissus Bulb Flies, Cabbage Root Fly, Onion Fly and Carrot Fly.

Dimethoate ('*Rogor*'). A new quick-acting organo-phosphorus spray which has a systemic action but which is much safer to handle than other systemics. Food-crops can be harvested 7 days after spraying. It should be used with caution on chrysanthemums, some varieties of which are damaged by the spray.

Pests controlled include Red Spider Mites (active stages), Aphids, and Suckers.

DNOC (*dinitro-ortho-cresol*) or *DNC*. Mixed with petroleum oil this material is applied to deciduous trees and bushes in the late dormant stage up to and including the breaking stage to kill the overwintering eggs and active stages of Fruit Tree Red Spider Mites, Aphids, Apple Sucker, Capsids and Winter Moth.

*Endrin.** A persistent contact and stomach poison allied to aldrin and dieldrin but much more toxic to humans and domestic animals. Crops should not be harvested for 6 weeks after being sprayed. It is used principally as an orchard spray.

Pests controlled include Aphids, Apple Sucker, Caterpillars, Apple and Plum Sawflies, Blackcurrant Gall Mite, Broad Mite and Strawberry Mite.

Fenson (or *PCPBS*). Another ovicidal spray related to chlorbenside and chlorfenson (q.v.) and similar in mode of action. It produces harmful effects, however, on cucurbits (cucumber, marrow, etc.), tomato seedlings, roses and a number of apple varieties, including Blenheim Orange, James Grieve, King of the Pippins, Lane's Prince Albert, Laxton's Epicure, Lord Derby, Lord Lambourne, Newton Wonder and Worcester Pearmain. Fruit should not be sprayed within 3 weeks of picking.

Fluoroacetamide. A liquid systemic poison which is used as a spray or a root drench. It is available in different concentrations, the higher of which are included in the Agriculture (Poisonous Substances) Regulations. The lowest concentration can be used with perfect safety on non-edible plants for the control of Aphids, and it has also been found effective against Blackcurrant Gall Mite on non-fruiting bushes.

HETP. See TEPP.

'*Kelthane*.' A new acaricidal spray of the chlorinated hydrocarbon group. It is slow-acting but non-poisonous and persistent, and controls both the eggs and active stages of Red Spider Mites.

Lead Arsenate. A liquid stomach poison used for many years but now generally superseded by DDT and other modern materials owing to its extreme toxicity to humans and domestic animals. It should not be used on edible crops within 6 weeks of harvesting.

Pests controlled include Earthworms, Caterpillars and Leatherjackets.

Lime Sulphur. Used mainly as a fungicidal spray this material is also effective against Gall Mites and Red Spider Mites.

Lindane. See BHC.

Malathion. An organo-phosphorus contact poison with a low mammalian toxicity. It is obtainable as a spray or a dust, and food-crops can be eaten 7 days after treatment. It should not be used on antirrhinums, crassula, ferns, petunias or sweet peas.

Pests controlled include Red Spider Mites (active stages), Thrips, Aphids, Leafhoppers, Whiteflies, Scale Insects and Mealy Bugs.

Metaldehyde. Mixed with a bait this is effective against Slugs and Snails, being both a contact and a stomach poison. It may also be used in spray form.

Metham sodium (*'Vapam'*, *'Vitafume'*, *etc.*). A new soil-sterilizing fumigant for the control of Root Knot Eelworm and Potato Root Eelworm under glass. It also controls Symphylids, soil fungi and germinating weed seeds. The liquid is applied in water 4–8 weeks before planting depending on the soil temperature, and the fumes are sealed in the soil by a further application of water. Before planting the soil should be well cultivated to disperse the fumes which can otherwise cause considerable damage to plants.

Nicotine. An old-established insecticide derived from the tobacco plant and obtainable as a spray, a dust or as 'shreds' for fumigation. It is a contact poison and has also a fumigant action if applied at temperatures of 65° F. or over. It is quick-acting but of short persistence and food crops can be safely eaten 48 hours after treatment.

Pests controlled include Springtails, Aphids, Capsids, Suckers and Sawflies.

Parathion.* An efficient but very poisonous contact insecticide of the organo-phosphorus group, it has the property of penetrating through the leaves of many plants. In the spray form it is very persistent, and edible crops should not be eaten for 4 weeks after treatment, but where smokes are used only a 24-hour interval is necessary except for lettuce where a 4-day interval should be allowed.

Pests controlled include Leaf and Bud Eelworms, Woodlice, Symphylids, Millipedes, Red Spider Mites (active stages), Thrips, Aphids, Woolly Aphid, Leafhoppers, Capsids, Suckers, Whiteflies, Scale Insects, Mealy Bugs, Leaf Miners and Sawflies.

Petroleum Oils. These are obtainable in two forms: (*a*) Winter Washes are suitable for use on dormant deciduous trees up to the breaking stage for the control of the overwintering stages of Red Spider Mites, Capsids, Scale Insects and Winter Moths. (*b*) Summer Washes may be used on growing plants with the exception of asparagus fern, bean, carnation, salvia, smilax and other oil-sensitive plants. They may be used as a wetter and spreader with derris, nicotine and other sprays. Among the pests controlled are Thrips, Red Spider Mites, Scale Insects and Mealy Bugs.

Phenkaptone. A recently introduced organo-phosphorus acaricide which kills the summer eggs and active stages of Red Spider Mites. It is a persistent spray with a good leaf-penetrating action. It should not be applied within 4 weeks of harvesting edible crops.

'*Phosdrin.*'* An organo-phosphorus insecticide with a contact, fumigant and systemic action. It gives a rapid kill and, although very poisonous to humans and domestic animals, it breaks down quickly after application so that treated food-crops can be consumed 3 days later.

Pests controlled include Aphids and Caterpillars.

Pyrethrum. Derived from the pyrethrum plant, this is a non-poisonous contact insecticide which soon loses its effectiveness when exposed to air. It has a rapid knock-down effect, however, which is utilized in mixtures with more persistent insecticides.

Tar Oils. Used as a winter wash on deciduous trees and bushes for many years, this material can only be applied when the trees are completely dormant and should not be allowed to come in contact with green foliage or young growth. In addition to killing the overwintering stages of many pests it cleans the bark of moss and lichens which shelter many hibernating pests.

Pests controlled include Aphids, Suckers, Scale Insects and Mealy Bugs.

TEPP (*tetraethyl-pyrophosphate*) or *HETP* (*hexaethyl tetraphosphate*).* These are virtually identical compounds, the active ingredient of HETP being TEPP. TEPP is an organo-phosphorus contact insecticide used as a spray. It is very poisonous in the concentrate form and when freshly made up, but breaks down rapidly in water. It can therefore be used on edible crops up to 48 hours before harvesting. It should not be used on Plumpton King or Stonor varieties of tomatoes, certain varieties of chrysanthemum and sulphur-shy gooseberries.

Pests controlled include Red Spider Mites (active stages), Springtails, Thrips, Aphids, Leafhoppers, Capsids, adult Whiteflies and Scale Insects ('crawlers').

The following rules should be carefully observed when applying chemical control measures.

(1) Read the label carefully, particularly with regard to the concentrations to be used and types of plants to be avoided. Concentrations higher than recommended may damage the plants.

(2) To safeguard bees and other pollinating insects avoid spraying open flowers.

(3) Some sprays and smokes cause damage to plants if applied in hot bright sunlight. Treatment should be given during dull weather or in the evening.

(4) Apply sprays during calm weather to avoid drift to open flowers or edible crops ready for harvesting.

(5) When using smokes ensure that the glasshouse is free from air leaks. The temperature should be at least 60° F. but better results are obtained at 70° F., particularly with Red Spider Mite and Whitefly. Never fumigate plants which are dry at the roots.

(6) Utensils which have been used for mixing and applying hormone weedkillers should not be used for insecticides.

BIBLIOGRAPHY

The following list of books is given for those who wish to acquaint themselves more fully with the subjects dealt with in this book.

AITKENHEAD, P. (Editor), 1958, 'Narcissus Pests' (M.A.F.F. Bull. No. 51), H.M.S.O., London.

BARNES, H. F., 1946–56, 'Gall Midges of Economic Importance', Vols. 1–7, London.

CHRYSTAL, R. N., 1937, *Insects of British Woodlands*, London.

DOWSON, W. J., 1957, *Plant Diseases due to Bacteria*, Cambridge.

FOX WILSON, G., 1953, 'Pests of Flowers and Shrubs' (Min. of Agric. Bull. No. 97), H.M.S.O., London.

GOODEY, T., 1933, *Plant Parasitic Nematodes*, London.

GRAM, E., and WEBER, A., 1952, *Plant Diseases*, London.

GREEN, D. E., 1946, *Diseases of Vegetables*, London.

HAYHURST, H., 1942, *Insect Pests of Stored Products*, London.

IMMS, A. D., 1942, *Outlines of Entomology*, London.

MARTIN, H., 1952, *Guides to the Chemicals used in Crop Protection*, Ontario.

MARTIN, H., 1959, *Scientific Principles of Crop Protection*, London.

MASSEE, A. M., 1954, *The Pests of Fruits and Hops*, London.

MILES, H. W., and M., 1948, *Insect Pests of Glasshouse Crops*, London.

MORETON, O. D., 1958, 'Beneficial Insects' (M.A.F.F. Bull. No. 20), H.M.S.O., London.

SMITH, K. M., 1931, *A Textbook of Agricultural Entomology*, Cambridge.

SMITH, K. M., 1957, *A Textbook of Plant Virus Diseases*, London.

Southey, J. F. (Editor), 1959, 'Plant Nematology' (M.A.F.F. Tech. Bull. No. 7), H.M.S.O., London.

Wallace, T., 1951, *The Diagnosis of Mineral Deficiencies in Plants*, London.

Wardle, R. A., 1929, *The Problems of Applied Entomology*, Manchester.

West, T. F., Hardy, J. E., and Ford, J. M., 1951, *Chemical Control of Insects*, London.

Wormald, H., 1955, *Diseases of Fruits and Hops*, London.

Attention is also drawn to the Advisory Leaflets on plant pests which are issued by the Ministry of Agriculture, Fisheries & Food and by the Forestry Commission.

CHAPTER TWO

Bulbs, Corms and Tubers

Bulbs and Corms Aphid-infested. Bulbs, Corms and Tubers Discoloured Externally. Bulbs Discoloured Internally. Bulbs Mite-infested. Bulbs, Corms and Tubers Tunnelled or Eaten.

THE direct effect of pest injury to bulbs, corms and tubers is that the large stocks of reserved food contained therein are considerably reduced and, consequently, the vigour of the plants is lowered. While the extent of the damage caused by the primary invader may be small, the resulting injury may be severe owing to the invasion of secondary organisms (e.g. free-living Nematodes and Millipedes, and weakly parasitic bacteria and fungi) which extend the initial damage. Early diagnosis is essential, otherwise the organism primarily concerned may be overlooked.

Many pests of bulbous, rhizomatous and tuberous-rooted plants are primarily root-attacking organisms, and are considered under 'Root Pests'.

The normal treatment meted out to bulbs, corms and tubers is that they are lifted annually and stored for a period of weeks, even months. It is desirable not only to reject all damaged bulbs before storage, but to keep a careful watch upon all stored bulbs to avoid both attacks of and an extension of injury by such pests as the Gladiolus Thrips (*Taeniothrips simplex* Mor.) on gladiolus, the Grey Bulb Aphid (*Dysaphis tulipae* B. de Fonsc.) on gladioli and tulips especially; and the Bulb Mite (*Rhizoglyphus echinopus* Fum. & Rob.) on hyacinth, narcissus and tulip bulbs and on dahlia tubers, especially on those damaged by mechanical means or by organisms, e.g. Eelworms, Bulb Fly larvae, bacteria and fungi.

A bulb is a modified bud, usually underground, and consists of a small stem upon which is arranged a number of thickened, fleshy scale leaves, which overlap more or less completely, e.g. hyacinth, lily, narcissus, onion, scilla, tulip and some species of iris.

A corm is a 'solid' bulb, consisting of a short, thick stem bearing a few thin, scaly leaves and with buds borne on its apex, e.g. colchicum, crocus, cyclamen and gladiolus.

A tuber is a fleshy, swollen, subterranean stem, beset with buds or 'eyes', in the axils of which may be found minute scaly leaves, e.g. dahlia, Jerusalem artichoke and potato.

BULBS AND CORMS APHID-INFESTED

The Grey Bulb Aphid (*Dysaphis tulipae* B. de Fonsc.), (Nov.–Feb.), may be found infesting the bulbs of tulip, iris, lily and scilla, and the corms of gladiolus and crocus. Under favourable conditions the aphids will reproduce throughout the winter in store, feeding in clusters under the outer scales. When the bulbs are planted out the growth is checked. The aphids feed on the young leaves which become distorted and, in severe cases, turn brown and die.

Control. (1) Immerse the infested bulbs when dormant for 5 minutes in a solution of lindane plus wetter, or in nicotine-soap solution, allowing them to dry gradually afterwards, or (2) fumigate the bulbs in an air-tight box with paradichlorobenzene. The crystals are sprinkled between two layers of sacking and a layer of bulbs placed on top. For only one layer 4 ounces of crystals per square foot are used, but for more than one layer the rate is reduced to 2 ounces. (3) Bulbs should be inspected before storing and infested ones kept isolated until treated. (4) Where young leaves become infested after planting spray with lindane plus wetter, nicotine-soap solution, or malathion.

BULBS, CORMS AND TUBERS DISCOLOURED EXTERNALLY

The Potato Tuber Eelworm (*Ditylenchus destructor* Thorne), (Aug.–Mar.), is a pest of potato crops in certain areas of eastern England. No indication of the infestation is apparent on the haulm and foliage but infested tubers show irregular discoloured and slightly sunken patches on the surface, similar to those produced by Potato Blight (*Phytopthora infestans*), but somewhat soft to the touch (Fig. 7). The affected areas become dried and cracked and in severe infestations the whole tuber dries up. If stored in clamps such potatoes start to rot down.

Control. (1) Slightly infested potatoes should not be stored but used or sold immediately after lifting. Severely damaged potatoes should be fed to chickens or animals after cooking. (2) Infestations can be considerably reduced by rotation and by the destruction of weed hosts such as Field Mint and Creeping Sowthistle. (3) Infested tubers should not be used as seed potatoes.

The tulip race of the Stem and Bulb Eelworm (*Ditylenchus dipsaci* (Kühn) Filipj.) has become a serious pest in some areas. The damage is not always evident in slightly infested bulbs but increases in store, appearing as greyish or brownish, spongy patches on the outer scales.

On the growing plant pale streaks appear on the upper stem and the flower, the epidermis often blistering and splitting. The flower may be bent over and the petals malformed. The leaves and lower stem are sometimes similarly damaged.

Control. (1) In light infestations rogue out all bulbs within 3 feet of infested plants, otherwise (2) destroy infested stocks immediately by burning or burying deeply. (3) Examine new bulbs carefully for signs of infestation. (4) Infested ground must be kept free of susceptible plants (See Appendix II, p. 209) for at least 3 years.

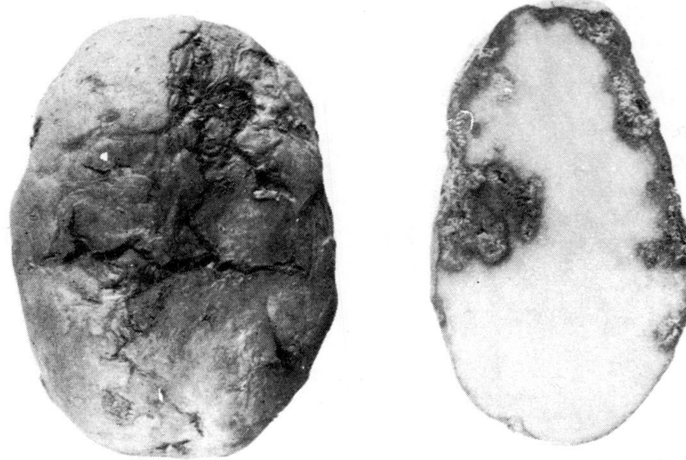

FIG. 7. External and internal damage on Potatoes infested with Potato Tuber Eelworm (*Ditylenchus destructor* Thorne). (*Crown Copyright Photograph.*)

The Gladiolus Thrips (*Taeniothrips simplex* Mor.) attacks the corms of gladioli in store, causing the formation of dry rough patches of a grey or brown colour on the surface tissue under the scales. The leaves and blooms of the growing plant are also attacked.

Control. See 'Foliage Mottled', p. 105.

The Lily Thrips (*Liothrips vaneeckei* Pries.), (Jan–Dec.), is occasionally a serious pest of lily bulbs and produces rust-coloured sunken feeding lesions in the basal regions of the outer scales. Severely attacked bulbs become flabby, the scales readily break away, which results in the invasion of secondary organisms (Bulb Mites, Millipedes, bacteria and fungi). The pest spreads from one bulb to another principally under storage conditions.

Control. (1) Destroy all mechanically injured and heavily infested bulbs. (2) Fumigate dormant bulbs with paradichlorobenzene in an air-tight container. The crystals should be sprinkled in the bottom of the container at the rate of 3 ounces per cubic foot of space. They should then be covered with a coarse cloth such as hessian and the bulbs laid on top. Leave for 60–96 hours according to the size of the bulbs.

BULBS AND TUBERS DISCOLOURED INTERNALLY

Some of the races of the Stem and Bulb Eelworm (*Ditylenchus dipsaci* (Kühn) Filipj.), (Jan.–Dec.), are serious pests of many bulbous plants (see Appendix II, p. 209), including hyacinth, iris, narcissus, snowdrop and scilla. The narcissus strain was at one time widely distributed, but infestations have considerably decreased since the adoption of hot-water sterilization of the bulbs by growers. The signs of attack are readily recognizable in the bulbs—some of the fleshy scale leaves show a distinct brownish colour and, when the bulb is cut horizontally, the infested areas take the form of concentric black or dark brown rings (Fig. 8). This damage is associated with swelling, stunting and distortion of the stems and leaves and late flowering (Fig. 84).

Control. (1) After lifting the bulbs burn all those which are severely infested or soft, together with withered foliage, etc. (2) The remainder, when completely dormant, should be subjected to hot-water treatment for 3 hours at a temperature of 110° F. (See Appendix I, p. 207). (3) Small areas of infested soil may be treated by fumigation with DD. (4) Plant hosts of the Eelworm (see Appendix II, p. 209) should not be grown in untreated infested ground for a period of at least 3 years. (5) A 3-yearly rotation should be practised where possible.

The Potato Tuber Eelworm (*D. destructor* Thorne) is responsible for internal discoloration and rotting of potato tubers (Fig. 7) (see 'Tubers Discoloured Externally', p. 31).

The Bulb Scale Mite (*Steneotarsonemus laticeps* Halb.), (Jan.–Dec.), is just visible to the naked eye and produces definite flecks and streaks of yellowish brown (in narcissus) or red (in amaryllis) on the inner scales and in the region of the neck of the infested bulbs (Fig. 9). The foliage may be distorted and flecked with yellow or red. Severe infestations result in either the death of the flower bud or in the production of weak, distorted or inferior blooms, often without foliage.

Control. (1) Dormant bulbs should be given hot-water treatment, immersing them for $1\frac{1}{2}$ hours at a temperature of 110° F. (see Appendix I, p. 207), or (2) expose dormant bulbs to frost. (3) Control

FIG. 8. *Above:* Narcissus bulbs infested with Stem and Bulb Eelworm (*Ditylenchus dipsaci* (Kühn) Filipj.).

FIG. 9. *Left:* Amaryllis bulb showing injury by Bulb Scale Mite (*Steneotarsonemus laticeps* Halb.).

on growing plants is difficult, but promising results have been achieved by spraying with systemic insecticides such as schradan, dimefox, or fluoroacetamide. (4) Bulbs should not be replanted in infested ground for at least one year. (5) Remove and sterilize the soil upon or in which infested pots have stood.

BULBS MITE-INFESTED

Apart from the above-mentioned Bulb Scale Mite, another species, the Bulb Mite (*Rhizoglyphus echinopus* Fum. & Rob.), (Jan.–Dec.), may be found on bulbs of eucharis, hyacinth, lily, narcissus and tulip. This mite which is globular, yellowish-white and easily visible to the naked eye, is not a primary pest but attacks bulbs which have been injured mechanically or by other pests and extends the damage.

Control. The mites can be killed by hot-water treatment as for the Bulb Scale Mite, but an attempt should also be made to establish and control the primary cause of the damage.

BULBS, CORMS AND TUBERS TUNNELLED OR EATEN

Slugs, especially the subterranean 'Keeled Slugs' (*Milax gracilis* Ley. and *M. sowerbyi* Fér.) and the Garden Slug (*Arion hortensis*

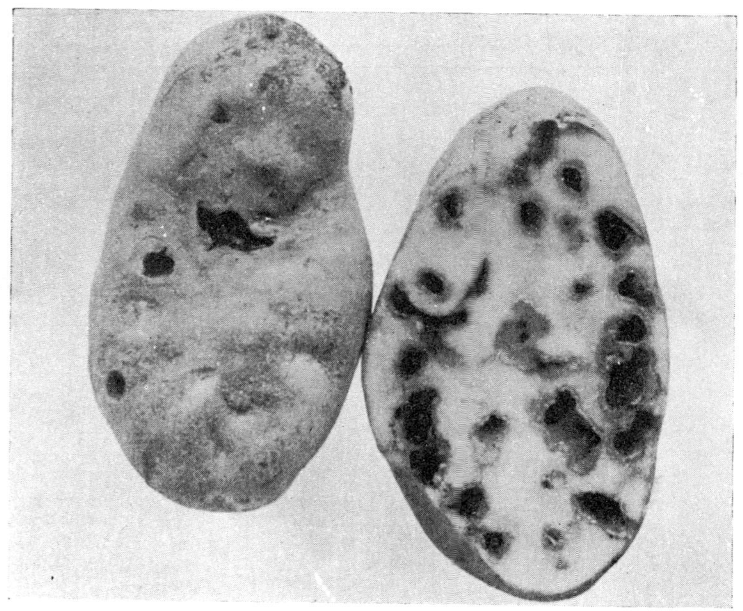

FIG. 10. Damage to Potato tubers by Keeled Slugs (*Milax* species).

Fér.), are well-known pests of a great variety of plants, including bulbs (e.g. tulip) and tubers (e.g. potato, Fig. 10), which are frequently completely destroyed by these pests. Slugs feed chiefly at night and, while the greatest damage is done during the late summer and early autumn (especially in potato crops), feeding may continue throughout the year when conditions are favourable.

Control. (1) Provide effective drainage—an overmoist soil being especially favourable to these pests. (2) Withhold annual heavy dressings of organic manures to ground of high humus content and substitute inorganic fertilizers for a year or so. (3) Handpick where outbreaks are small. (4) Lay down poison baits containing metaldehyde or Paris Green (see Appendix V, p. 216).

Millipedes of which the chief bulb-infesting species are the Spotted Millipede (*Blaniulus guttulatus* Bosc.) and the Flat Millipede (*Polydesmus angustus* Latz.), feed on a variety of vegetable matter including roots, bulbs (e.g. tulip) and tubers (e.g. dahlia and potato) (Fig. 11). They frequently follow an attack of subterranean Slugs and Wireworms, into the borings of which they penetrate and extend the

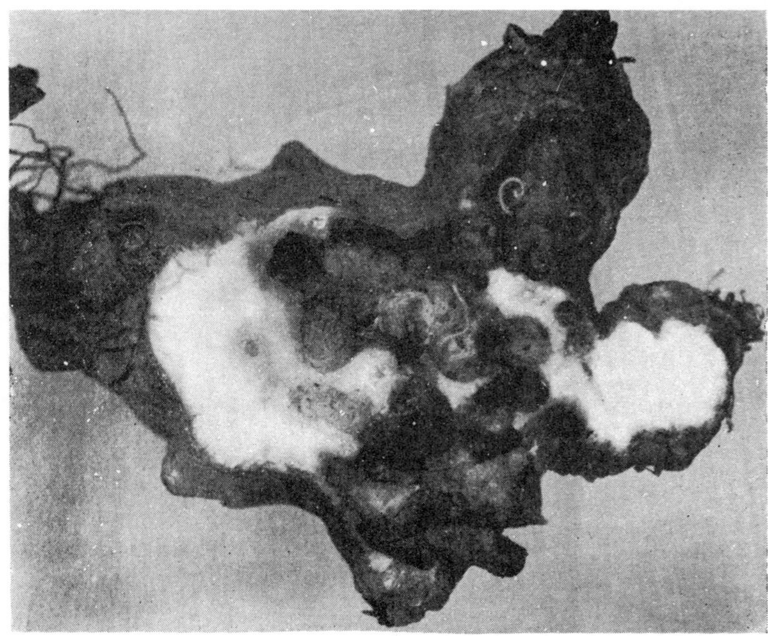

FIG. 11. Slug damage on Jerusalem Artichoke extended by Millipedes (*Blaniulus guttulatus* Bosc.). (*Shell Photograph.*)

initial injury. Under favourable conditions feeding continues throughout the year.

Control. (1) Ensure that the ground is well-drained—a damp soil being favoured by these pests. (2) Apply heavy dressings of lime to infested ground. (3) Apply a dressing of DDT, lindane[1] or aldrin dust, working it into the top 4 inches of soil.

The number of Lepidopterous pests of bulbs and tubers is not large, and among the more important are 'Surface Caterpillars' or 'Cutworms', and the larvae of Swift Moths.

The most destructive species of Cutworms are those of the Turnip (*Agrotis segetum* Schiff.), the Heart and Dart (*A. exclamationis* L.) and the Yellow Underwing Moths (*Triphaena pronuba* L.), (Aug.–Mar.). They feed at night on the underground portions and at the base of the stem and on the lower leaves of many cultivated plants, and are frequent pests of potato tubers.

Control. (1) Clean cultivation, and the destruction of weed hosts among and near cultivated beds. (2) Apply a surface dressing of lindane[1] or DDT dust, or (3) lay down a poison bait consisting of bran moistened with lindane or aldrin.

The Garden Swift Moth (*Hepialus lupulinus* L.), (Jan.–Dec.), is more common in gardens than the Ghost Swift (*H. humuli* L.). The caterpillars feed in various roots, corms (gladioli), bulbs, rhizomes (bearded iris) and tubers (potato). They, unlike 'Cutworms', are extremely active and have the power of wriggling backwards as well as moving forwards, a simple characteristic that enables the gardener to identify these white larvae from other soil-inhabiting creatures.

Control. (1) Clean cultivation, and the destruction of weed hosts (e.g. docks) in the vicinity of borders; (2) regular hoeing—these caterpillars occur more frequently in undisturbed soil than in cultivated beds and borders. (3) Apply a dressing of lindane[1] or aldrin dust, worked into the top 4 inches of soil.

The chief Coleopterous pests are Cockchafer grubs, Wireworms and certain Weevil larvae.

The Cockchafer (*Melolontha melolontha* L.), (Jan.–Dec.), is a serious pest during its larval stages, known as 'White Grubs', to the underground portions of a great variety of crops. The larvae often occur in vast numbers in the soil of gardens bordering woodland, and may be found tunnelling into potato tubers (Fig. 12).

Control. As for Swift Moth Caterpillars.

[1] Lindane should not be used on ground where potatoes and root crops are to be grown within 18 months.

Wireworms, which are the larvae of Click Beetles, are the best-known, most destructive and widely distributed of all soil pests. They are so familiar that injury caused by other soil pests is frequently attributed to them. The larvae of several genera and species of the family *Elateridae* are termed 'Wireworms', although not all so-called

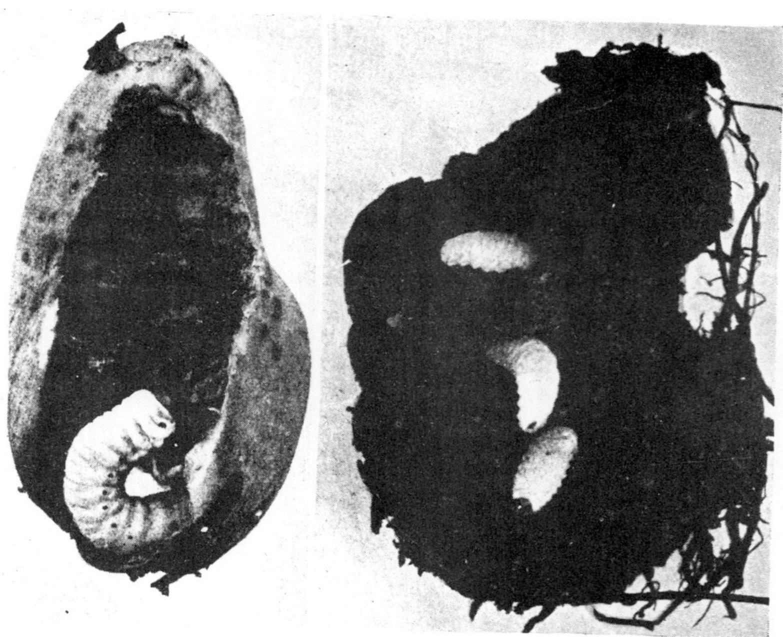

FIG. 12. Potato tuber attacked by Cockchafer larva (*Melolontha melolontha* L.).

FIG. 13. Begonia tuber attacked by Vine Weevil larvae (*Otiorrhynchus sulcatus* F.).

'Wireworms' are injurious to plants. The more common species are *Agriotes lineatus* L., *A. sputator* L., and *Athous haemorrhoidalis* F. (Jan.–Dec.), but several others occur throughout the country, though some are exceedingly local in their distribution. Their food comprises humus, decaying organic matter, and the roots, bulbs, corms, tubers and rhizomes of a great variety of plants, both cultivated and wild. Potato tubers are frequently completely riddled by these pests, especially in freshly-converted pasture and waste land (Fig. 14).

Control. (1) Clean cultivation and the destruction of weed hosts. (2) Hoe regularly to render soil conditions unfavourable to the larvae.

(3) Apply a dressing of lindane[1] or aldrin worked into the top 4 inches of soil. (4) Roll or tread seed beds before sowing to consolidate the ground. (5) On untreated ground harvest potatoes early (late August or early September) to avoid the peak feeding period of the larvae.

The Vine Weevil (*Otiorrhynchus sulcatus* F.), and to a lesser extent the Clay-coloured Weevil (*O. singularis* L.), (Aug.–Feb.), are destructive species both in their larval and adult stages. The Vine Weevil

FIG. 14. Potato tuber tunnelled by Wireworms (*Agriotes* species). (*Shell Photograph.*)

grub is a common pest of a variety of plants growing both in the open and under glass, more especially to cyclamen corms and to tuberous-rooted begonias (Fig. 13).

Control. (1) Clean cultivation, which in infested glasshouses should include an annual cleansing so that soil and plant débris be not allowed to collect beneath the staging, while the weevils must not be permitted to become established in ornamental rockeries and ferneries. (2) Dress the soil with aldrin or lindane dust, working it into the top 4 inches of soil, or mix these insecticides with the potting compost. (3) Growing plants which are infested should be repotted in treated soil when possible, otherwise water them with DDT, lindane, or parathion. (4) Trap the nocturnally active weevils in

[1] Lindane should not be used on ground where potatoes and root crops are to be grown within 18 months.

rolled-up paper or sacking, and inspect each morning. (5) Spray the hiding places of the adult weevils and damaged plants with DDT.

The most important Dipterous pests of bulbs are Leatherjackets, Bulb Flies and the Onion Fly.

Leatherjackets, which are the larvae of Crane Flies or Daddy-long-legs, are very destructive pests and are generally distributed throughout the country, being particularly abundant in the moister parts of England, Wales and Scotland. They feed on turf and are one of the chief pests of grass land, and attack roots and eat into bulbs and tubers. The species most abundant in gardens are *Tipula oleracea* L., *T. paludosa* Meig., and the yellow and black *Nephrotoma maculata* Meig. The larvae prefer damp soils and irrigated turf (e.g. lawns and greens), and speedily succumb when exposed to drought conditions.

Control. (1) Clean cultivation, and the destruction of weed hosts. (2) Hoe infested ground regularly. (3) Dress the soil with DDT or

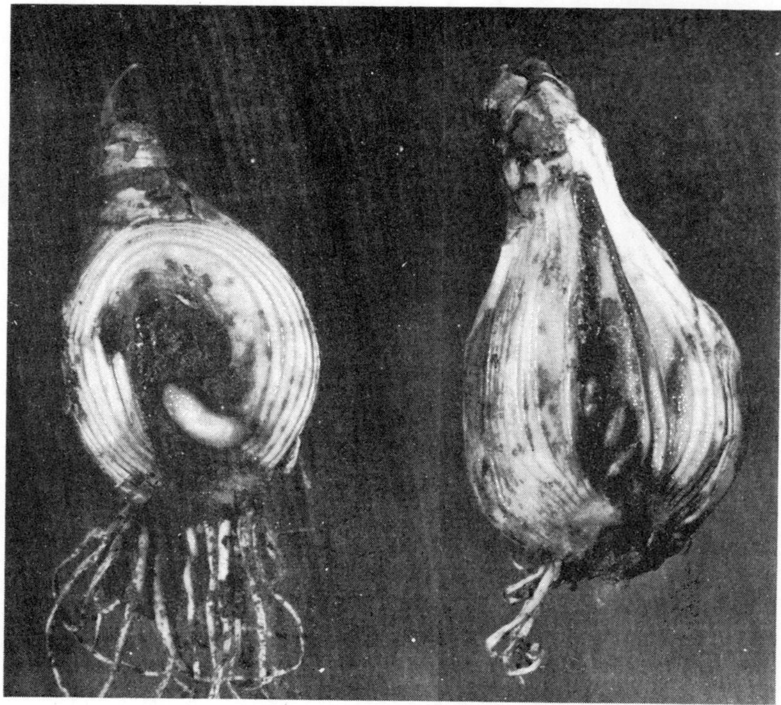

FIG. 15. Narcissus bulbs containing (*left*) larva of Large Narcissus Fly (*Merodon equestris* F.) and (*right*) larvae of Small Narcissus Fly (*Eumerus* species). (*Shell Photograph.*)

aldrin dust, working it into the surface, or (4) use poison baits consisting of bran moistened with DDT or lindane (5) On lawns water with a solution of DDT, or (6) apply a dressing of DDT or aldrin dust mixed with sand or fine soil for even distribution. (Note: Insecticides are best applied during mid-October to November or in April.)

The Large Narcissus Fly (*Merodon equestris* F.), (June–Mar.), is a serious pest of narcissus bulbs, the interiors of which are hollowed out by the large, fleshy, dirty white maggots (Fig. 15). Other bulbous plants are attacked, including amaryllis, hyacinths, scillas and lily. One larva only is usually found in a single bulb, though two or three may sometimes be found. Infested bulbs are detected by the injury to the basal plate from which exudes a wet mass of frass and, in the growing plants, by the presence of weak and distorted leaves or of gaps among the plants.

Control. (1) Lift and destroy all bulbs which fail to develop. (2) Reject all soft bulbs and subject the remainder, when dormant, to hot-water treatment for 1 hour at 110° F. (see Appendix I, p. 207), or (3) immerse dormant bulbs for 3 hours in a solution of lindane to which a wetter has been added. (4) To protect bulbs against attack dip them in a solution of aldrin or dieldrin for 15 minutes before planting out, or (5) dust the soil around the necks of the bulbs with lindane dust at fortnightly intervals from the end of April to the end of June. (6) Do not ripen bulbs in full sunshine where they attract egg-laying adults, but in a shed or in a shaded place.

The Small Narcissus Flies (*Eumerus strigatus* Flor. and *E. tuberculatus* Rond.), (June–Mar.), are associated with injury to bulbs similar to that caused by the Large Narcissus Fly. The chief hosts include narcissus, hyacinth and onion, though iris tubers are frequently attacked, while other plants are attacked when their roots or tubers are damaged by other pests. As many as 10-30 larvae may be found in a single bulb, and may occur in bulbs already infested with the larva of the larger fly (Fig. 15).

Control. The same methods of avoidance and treatment as those advocated for the Large Narcissus Fly.

The Onion Fly (*Delia antiqua* Meig.), (May.–Aug.), is the chief and most destructive pest of onions (Fig. 16), and will attack both leeks and shallots. The most severe damage is done during the seedling stage in spring and early summer, at which period the larvae travel from plant to plant along the rows and completely destroy the crop.

As many as 30 larvae may be found in a single large bulb, the result being that the leaves turn yellow, wilt and come away easily from the bulb when pulled. There may be three broods of flies during the season, but overlapping of the generations occurs.

FIG. 16. *Left*: Onion plants damaged by Onion Fly (*Delia antiqua* Meig.). *Right*: Infested onion. (*Shell Photographs.*)

Control. (1) Lift and burn attacked plants—care being taken to remove the larvae remaining in the soil as the bulbs are lifted. (2) Grow autumn sown plants, onion 'sets' or transplants raised under glass in spring in districts where the pest is abundant. (3) Apply a dieldrin seed dressing before sowing. (4) Dust the ground with aldrin at the 'loop' stage and again 10 days later, applying it in a 4-inch band along the rows. (5) Dust the drills with aldrin before planting sets.

CHAPTER THREE

Roots

Roots Aphid-infested. Roots Constricted. Roots Eaten. Roots with Frothy Masses. Roots Galled. Roots Over-developed. Roots Rusty. Roots Splitting. Roots Underdeveloped. Roots with Woolly Masses.

THE main functions of roots are fixation or anchorage and absorption. The root is an organ essential to the life of the plant, for the aerial portions are entirely dependent on the work of the root system for their water supply and mineral salts. The result of any injury to the roots by insects and other soil-inhabiting creatures and by bacterial, protozoal and fungal organisms, is that the entire plant is affected to a degree that depends upon the extent and nature of the injury.

While the death of the plant may not necessarily follow as a result of root injury, any reduction in the amount of water-absorbing tissue that may follow as a result of pest damage will so affect the plant that the foliage wilts and turns yellow as the amount of moisture absorbed will be insufficient to supply the loss through transpiration.

Several other factors are responsible for wilted foliage other than the presence of root-devouring insects, and it will be shown later (see 'Stems and Shoots Tunnelled', p. 82) that wilting is a symptom which arises from the attacks of stem-, shoot- and bark-boring insects. Again, such secondary signs of attack as wilting, yellowing and the premature falling of the foliage arise from the loosening of the soil around the root system by burrowing insects and by ants, which make their nests among roots so that these are exposed and death follows as a result of drought and exposure.

There is great variation in the size, shape and consistency of roots, while the area occupied by the root system will vary with the plant and with the soil in which it is growing. The root system consists of a primary or tap-root that grows vertically downwards, and a series of secondary or lateral roots that are produced and grow obliquely downwards, while tertiary or sublateral roots grow out from the laterals. The main work of absorption is performed by the root-hairs, which are situated near the tips of the roots.

It is not always easy to distinguish between the true root and the underground stem unless a critical examination is made of the cellular structure.

Some roots are succulent and are known as tuberous roots—these being distinct from tubers, which are fleshy underground stems. The aerial roots of certain orchidaceous plants will be considered only so far as they are subject to attack by certain pests, e.g. Woodlice, Cockroaches and Crickets.

ROOTS APHID-INFESTED

The presence of Aphids upon the roots of plants may be detected as a rule by loss of vigour, by wilting and discoloration of the foliage, and by premature leaf-fall. While some species of Aphids live permanently on the roots, e.g. the Artichoke Tuber Aphid (*Trama troglodytes* Heyd.), others live for a time on the roots and, sooner or later, a brood or specialized form appears that migrates to the stems, shoots or foliage either of some other plant (the alternate host), e.g. the Poplar-Lettuce Root Aphid (*Pemphigus bursarius* L.), or of the same plant, e.g. the Plantain Aphid (*Aphis plantaginis* Schrank.).

It is supposed that most of the subterranean species of Aphids have an alate (i.e. winged) phase that allows the insects to migrate to other (alternate) host plants, but information is not available as to the alternate hosts of many root-infesting species.

Many of these root-feeders are closely associated with ants, which seek them for their sweet exudations ('honeydew'). Some species of Aphids are exclusively myrmecophilous and there exists between these two widely-separated groups of insects a relationship that may be described as symbiotic. This close association is frequently of considerable economic importance, for infestations of certain species of Aphids may be checked by the destruction of the nests of their attendant ants.

It is not possible to discuss at length the many root-infesting species, but mention is made of the more common root pests of horticultural plants, viz.: (1) summer forms of *Aphis sambuci L.* on the roots of *Dianthus gratianopolitanus* and *D. plumarius*, perpetual-flowering carnations, and London Pride (*Saxifraga umbrosa*). (2) *Dysaphis tulipae* B. de Fonsc, on bulbs and corms (see 'Bulbs Aphid-infested', p. 31), and *Dysaphis crataegi* Kalt. on the roots of carrot and parsnip (see 'Roots Splitting', p. 59). (3) *Anoecia corni* F. on the roots of various grasses and cereals, groundsel, dandelion, docks and thistle, and, during late summer and autumn, on the leaves and shoots of the dogwood (*Cornus sanguinea*). (4) *Trama troglodytes* Heyd. is attended by ants, and may be found throughout the year on the tubers of artichoke and the roots of such plants as artemesia, hawkweeds, sowthistle and thistles. (5) *Aploneura lentisci* Pass. is a species that frequently swarms on grass roots growing in fields and garden paths. (6)

Smynthurodes betae Westw. often occurs in vast numbers on the roots of broad, French and runner beans. (7) *Pemphigus bursarius* L. is a serious pest of lettuces in late autumn and early spring, when colonies are found on the roots covered with white, flocculent 'wool'. It infests also the roots of sowthistle and wild *Chenopodium* (see 'Roots with Woolly Masses', p. 60). Winged forms appear

FIG. 17. Auricula roots infested with Root Aphid (*Pemphigus auriculae* Murr.).

and migrate to poplars upon which ultimately are produced 'pocket galls' on the petioles (leaf-stalks). (8) *P. auriculae* Murr., is the well-known Auricula Woolly Aphid (Fig. 17) (see 'Roots with Woolly Masses', p. 60). (9) *Eriosoma lanigerum* Hausm., the familiar 'Woolly Aphid' or 'American Blight' of apple trees (see 'Roots Galled', p. 56, and 'Stems with Woolly Masses', p 80), may occur in two forms upon apple roots, namely: (*a*) a form that overwinters on the underground stem, on 'suckers' and on exposed roots, and ascends the stem in spring to feed upon the shoots, and (*b*) a true subterranean form that persists on the roots throughout the year and is found as a root pest in Australia, New Zealand, South Africa and North America. (10) *Eriosoma ulmi* L. causes the leaves of elms (*Ulmus procera* and *U. glabra*) to curl, and later is a pest of some importance on the roots of currants and gooseberry (see 'Roots Splitting', p. 58).

Control. (1) Clean cultivation, including the destruction of weeds in headlands and ditches, in the immediate neighbourhood of borders and vegetable plots, and in fruit plantations—many weeds serving as alternate hosts of certain root-infesting Aphids. (2) Cultivate infested ground deeply, trenching so that the upper layer of soil is well buried. (3) Remove all crop remnants, e.g. lettuce stumps, to reduce the available food supply of these pests. (4) Practise crop rotation so that the crops serving as hosts to a particular species are not grown successively in infested ground. (5) Where practicable, repot or replant the infested plants in clean soil after washing the roots in nicotine-soap solution or spraying them with malathion; otherwise (6) give a root drench of parathion (non-edible plants only) or malathion, repeating the treatment 14 days later. (7) Destroy nests of ants in the vicinity of plants which serve as hosts to Root Aphids (see 'Foliage Wilting', p. 158).

ROOTS CONSTRICTED

The Pygmy Mangold Beetle (*Atomaria linearis* Steph.), (May–June), causes injury to young mangolds, beetroot and sugar beet by destroying the fine roots and feeding on the main root, often causing the formation of a black thread-like constriction just below ground level. Seedlings thus attacked usually die and readily snap off in the wind. The foliage and crowns of the plants may also be attacked.

Control. (1) Practise rotation of crops to avoid successive planting of susceptible crops in the same area. (2) Lindane seed dressings give a partial control. (3) Give a heavy rolling in the seedling stage.

Attacks by Springtails (*Collembola*) result in similar constrictions of the upper roots or lower stems of mangold and beetroot seedlings which are at or immediately above ground level (see 'Stems Gnawed', p. 72).

ROOTS EATEN

The several types of injury to roots included in this category are: (*a*) partial or complete girdling (e.g. Cockchafer larvae); (*b*) partial or complete severing (e.g. *Otiorrhynchus* larvae); and (*c*) tunnelling, e.g. Millipedes, Wireworm and Carrot Fly larvae in root crops.

While the cause of various root injuries arises from attacks of subterranean species of Slugs (*Milax*), Millipedes, Woodlice and the larvae of many Lepidopterous, Coleopterous and Dipterous insects, the effect in most cases is that the plants wilt—this being due to a partial or complete cessation of the normal functions of the roots and/or underground stems wherein the passage of water and nutrients is hindered.

The several pests here considered are primarily concerned in root injuries, but there are various secondary agents, including Millipedes and the larvae of such flies as Sciarids or Fungus Gnats and Anthomyids, that may follow an attack of a primary root pest and extend the initial injury. Bacterial and weakly parasitic fungal organisms are also implicated—entry to the healthy tissues being gained through feeding lesions and mechanical injuries.

Millipedes, (Jan.–Dec.), are responsible for both primary and secondary root injuries, more especially to carrots and strawberries, and to various bulbs, corms and tubers.

Control. See 'Bulbs Tunnelled', p. 36.

Several species of the *Symphyla*, in particular the Glasshouse Symphylid (*Scutigerella immaculata* Newp.), are serious pests in glasshouses in many parts of the country and also cause damage out-of-doors in S.W. England. They attack a great variety of plants including tomato, cucumber, lettuce, anemone, primula and sweet pea, destroying the small rootlets and burrowing into the larger ones (Fig. 18). Surface gnawings result in the formation of corky patches

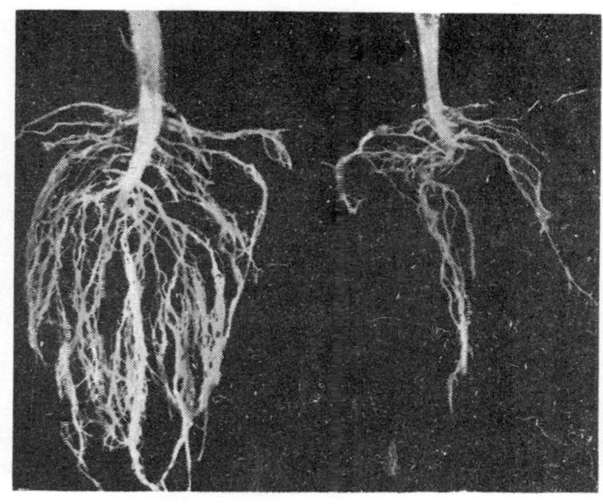

FIG. 18. *Right:* Tomato roots damaged by Glasshouse Symphylids (*Scutigerella immaculata* Newp.). *Left:* normal root system. (*Shell Photograph.*).

over the injured areas. Attacked plants wilt during the day, the lower leaves turning yellow and the upper leaves dark green.

Control. (1) Treat the soil with lindane dust within a month before planting, working it into the top 4 inches (lindane should not be used for cucurbits). (2) Dip the roots into parathion before planting out, or (3) water with parathion or lindane within 3 days of planting out. (4) Soil fumigation with DD will also give a good control.

Woodlice often occur in vast numbers in old and shaded gardens, in glasshouses and conservatories, and around compost and manure heaps. Most species are intolerant of dry conditions, so that high populations are associated with moist soils and with an overabundance of dead and decaying organic matter or humus. The species *Armadillidium nasatum* B.-L., *A. vulgare* Latr. and *Porcellio laevis* Latr. are chiefly pests in glasshouse borders attacking the roots of cucumber and tomato; while *Androniscus dentiger* Verh. frequently injures the aerial roots of orchids. The roots of adiantum and other ferns are injured to a great extent by Woodlice in ill-kept conservatories and in small greenhouses.

Control. (1) Destroy and dispose of all dead and decaying plant tissue, garden rubbish, decaying tree stumps, etc. (2) Remove rotting staging in glasshouses and decayed wooden edgings of paths. (3) Repoint brickwork where necessary. (4) Apply DDT or BHC as a dust or spray, or parathion to infested areas and hiding places.

Cockroaches, including the cosmopolitan American species, *Periplaneta americana* L., and Crickets (*Gryllulus domesticus* L.), (Jan.–Dec.), are particularly destructive in orchid houses where they devour with avidity the aerial roots of many species of orchids.

Control. See 'Flowers Eaten', p. 176.

Among the Order *Lepidoptera* are found several species of moths, the larvae of which are root-feeders, but mention is made of two groups only, namely: (*a*) Surface Caterpillars or Cutworms, and (*b*) Swift Moth larvae.

(*a*) While there are many species of *Agrotis* whose larval habits are similar to those considered here, the most destructive species in gardens have already been discussed (see 'Bulbs Tunnelled', p. 37). Cutworms are nocturnally active and, while they feed occasionally on the basal leaves of their host plants, their attacks are concentrated on the stems just above and immediately below ground level, and on the roots of a great variety of plants, notably root crops, e.g. beetroot, mangolds, swedes and turnips.

(*b*) Swift Moth caterpillars are primarily root-feeders, and attack the lateral roots, and later tunnel into the larger and thicker roots, of many cultivated and wild plants, including carrot, parsnip, strawberry and herbaceous plants, and such weeds as dandelion, dead nettles, docks and plantains. They are destructive to many bulbs, corms, rhizomes and tubers.

Control. See 'Bulbs Tunnelled', p. 37.

Of Coleopterous insects, there is a great number of species whose larval stages are passed in the soil; and, though many are beneficial by reason of their predacious habits, e.g. Carabid larvae, others are among the most destructive pests of plants, e.g. Chafer grubs, Wireworms and the larvae of certain *Curculionidae*.

Chafer beetles, of which the Cockchafer (*Melolontha melolontha* L.) is probably the most destructive in gardens. (Jan.–Dec.), cause considerable damage in their larval stages to the roots of grasses, cereals, forest and fruit trees, hedge plants, ornamental trees and shrubs, roses, strawberries, and to other agricultural and horticultural crops (Fig. 19). Not only are the roots severed by the 'White Grubs', but the lower part of the stem below ground level is barked. The larvae of the Garden Chafer (*Phyllopertha horticola* L.) and the Rose Chafer (*Cetonia aurata* L.) are primarily pests of pasture, though the larvae of the former species often abound at the roots of graminaceous plants in grass orchards.

Control. (1) Handpick the larvae during the operations of digging and trenching. (2) Provide a fine tilth for seed-beds and nursery beds, and heavy rolling before sowing and planting, to crush larvae and consolidate soil loosened by their workings. (3) Allow poultry a free run of infested ground during and after ploughing and trenching. (4) Trap the larvae in pieces of turf placed grass downwards on the soil surface. (5) Dress infested land with lindane[1] or aldrin dust, working it into the top 4 inches of soil. (6) Where established plants are attacked drench the roots with a solution of DDT with a spreader incorporated. (7) Roll infested lawns and greens heavily or water with DDT. (8) Destroy adult Chafers during their periods of activity (see 'Flowers Eaten', p. 169).

Wireworms are the most widely distributed of all soil pests, and

[1] Lindane should not be used on ground where potatoes and root crops are to be grown within 18 months.

attack the roots, bulbs, corms, tubers and rhizomes of a very great variety of plants (see 'Bulbs Tunnelled', p. 38). They feed also on the roots of wild plants, e.g. grasses, charlock, docks and many hedge- and ditch-side plants, so that the eradication of weeds in headlands and ditches, along cart-tracks and garden plots should be attempted to prevent migrations from such areas into neighbouring cultivated ground.

FIG. 19. Apple root girdled by Cockchafer larvae (*Melolontha melolontha* L.)

FIG. 20. Strawberry roots damaged by larvae of Vine Weevil (*Otiorrhynchus sulcatus* F.). (*Photograph by East Malling Research Station.*)

The most severe infestations occur upon crops that follow permanent pasture, and trouble with these pests invariably arises when grass and waste land is converted into arable. Wireworms are frequently introduced into glasshouse borders and into composts through the agency of loam. Crops particularly susceptible to attack include beetroot, carrot and other 'roots', carnation, lettuce and wheat. An uncommon form of injury occurs with chrysanthemum and tomato plants, in the stems of which the larvae tunnel for some distance above soil level. The term 'Black Wireworms' is applied to Millipedes, while such beneficial predacious soil creatures as Centipedes and the larvae of various Ground or Carabid beetles are frequently mistaken for Wireworms and destroyed.

Control. See 'Bulbs Tunnelled', p. 38.

The larvae of many Curculionid weevils are destructive to plant roots. Among the more important species are those belonging to the genus *Otiorrhynchus*, namely, *O. sulcatus* Fab. or Vine Weevil, and *O. singularis* L. or Clay-coloured Weevil (Aug.–Feb.). The number of host plants is considerable, and severe injury occurs both to hardy and to tender plants, e.g. crassulas, glasshouse ferns, primulas, polyanthus, saxifrages and other alpines. They are major pests of young forest trees in nursery beds, and to plants in alpine houses and frames and in indoor ferneries or conservatories (Fig. 20).

Control. See 'Bulbs Tunnelled', p. 39.

There are found among the *Diptera* (Flies) a large number of species whose larvae are root-feeders.

Leatherjackets are troublesome pests in many gardens, being particularly prevalent in the moister districts of the British Isles, and in badly-drained soils elsewhere. Their presence in glasshouse borders and potting composts arises from the use of infested loam and turf. They have a wide range of food plants, including both agricultural and horticultural—cereals and grasses, mangolds and potatoes (see 'Bulbs Tunnelled', p. 40), turnips, strawberries, primulas and other plants, including vegetables and ornamentals.

Control. See 'Bulbs Tunnelled', p. 40.

The Carrot Fly (*Psila rosae* F.), (June–Oct.), is the chief enemy of carrots both under garden and field cultivation. Other host plants include parsnip, parsley, celery and celeriac. It is most prevalent on light, dry soils, though it is widely distributed throughout the country. The larvae tunnel into the roots (Fig. 21), causing them to become 'rusty' and to decay as a result of the invasion of secondary organisms. The first indication of an attack is the death of seedlings, and then the reddish hue of the foliage of established roots. The larvae may continue to injure roots in clamps.

Control. (1) Where the fly is prevalent sow in late May or early June to escape the peak of the first generation of larvae. (2) Sow in exposed positions and destroy weed shelter. (3) Sow thinly to reduce the need for singling—the odour of crushed foliage attracts the flies. (4) After singling consolidate the soil by treading or watering. (5) Treat the seed, of early carrots in particular, with lindane or dieldrin seed dressing, or spray with lindane at the seedling stage.

(6) Spray with dieldrin or dust the rows with lindane in mid-May (earlies), early August and early September. (7) When transplanting celery dip the plant in lindane or dieldrin or drench with dieldrin after planting. (8) Destroy all infested plants. Never leave them in the ground during the winter.

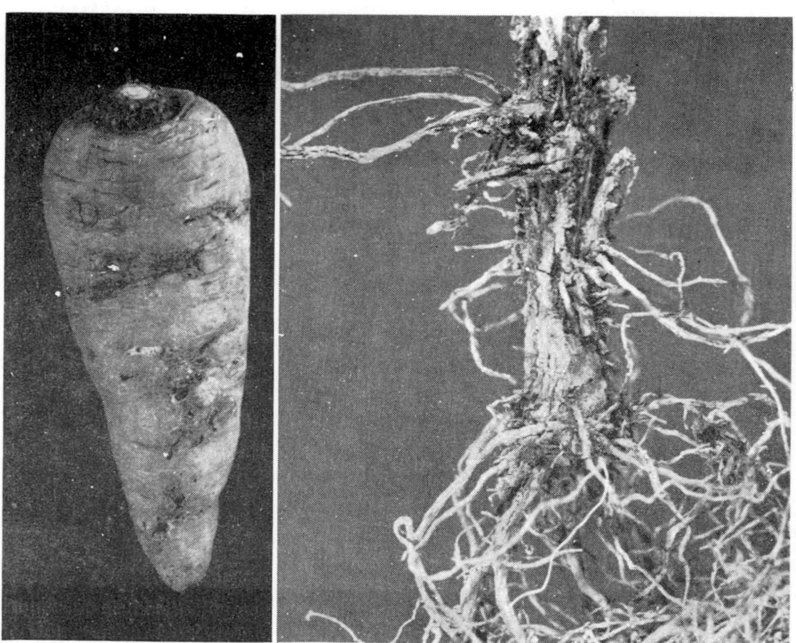

FIG. 21. Carrot injured by Carrot Fly (*Psila rosae* F.). (*Shell Photograph.*)

FIG. 22. Chrysanthemum stool showing damage by Chrysanthemum Stool Miner (*Psila nigricornis* Meig.). (*Shell Photograph.*)

The Chrysanthemum Stool Miner (*Psila nigricornis* Meig.), (Sept.–May), is an important pest of chrysanthemums grown under glass. The maggots feed on the roots and form long tunnels in the base of the stem and under the epidermis of the root stock. These tunnels later split open (Fig. 22). The effect of this damage is to impair the vigour of the plant, causing wilting of the shoots and reducing the number of shoots formed. Lettuces are also attacked particularly when they follow chrysanthemums.

Control. (1) Attacked stools should be watered copiously with demeton-methyl. (2) Attacks can be prevented by watering the soil around the plants with dieldrin in August and September or by working aldrin dust into the soil or compost before planting.

Several species of flies belonging to the Family *Anthomyidae* are known as 'root flies', and many are primary pests of plants. The larvae of many are saprophagous and, though not primarily responsible for root injuries, may extend the initial damage caused by soil-inhabiting pests of all kinds.

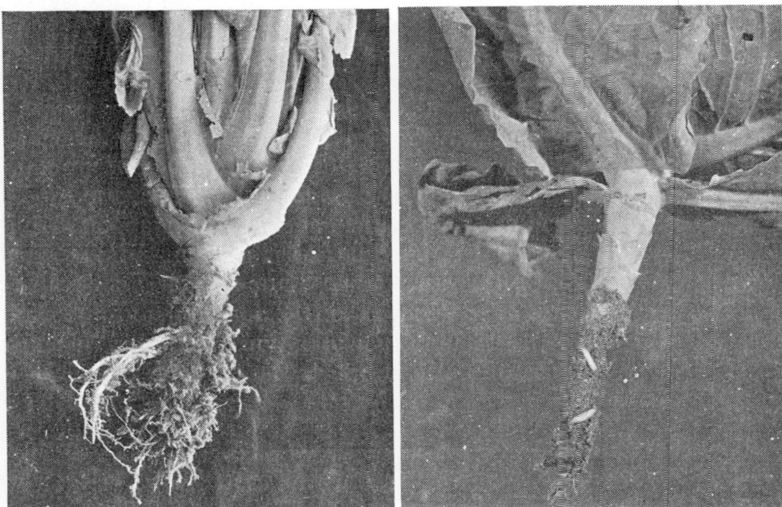

FIG. 23. Roots of Cabbage plants showing different degrees of damage by the Cabbage Root Fly (*Erioischia brassicae* Bouché). (*Shell Photographs.*)

The Cabbage Root Fly (*Erioischia brassicae* Bouché), (Apr.–Sept.), is the most destructive of all pests of brassicas, and causes great losses to cabbage and cauliflower in particular. It also attacks wallflower. The larvae may injure the plant in various ways, for instance, by eating the young roots and by tunnelling into the primary root and underground stem—the final result being a decayed, snag-like root (Fig. 23), by tunnelling into the fleshy roots of radish and turnip, and by invading the fleshy branches of the curds of cauliflowers. In Northern Scotland the species is accompanied by the Turnip Root Fly (*E. floralis* Fall.), (June–Oct.), whose larvae attack the same range of plants, and occasionally cause considerable losses of turnips and swedes.

Control. (1) Crop rotation, thereby avoiding successive cruciferous crops on infested land. (2) Lift and destroy severely attacked roots together with the larvae immediately surrounding them. (3) Apply aldrin dust to the seed drills before covering, or (4) apply aldrin or dieldrin in a band along the rows of seedlings. (5) When transplanting dip the roots in aldrin or dieldrin, or (6) drench with aldrin or dieldrin within 4 days of planting out.

ROOTS WITH FROTHY MASSES

While the presence of frothy masses or 'Cuckoo-spit' on leaves and shoots arising from Froghopper (Cercopid) infestations is well known, the fact that the roots of certain plants are similarly affected is not generally realized. The nymph of the Red and Black Froghopper (*Cercopis sanguinea* Geoff.) is found surrounded with frothy secretions on the roots of couch grass, bracken, docks and mint, but the amount of injury is negligible. Secondary infection by micro-organisms may, however, arise through the feeding lesions.

Control. (1) Clean cultivation, including the destruction of weed hosts in the vicinitv of mint beds. (2) Drench infested beds with parathion.

ROOTS GALLED

Galls may appear on such portions of the roots as the root-tip, root hairs, primary or tap-root, and secondary and tertiary lateral rootlets. The anatomical structure of gall formations has been studied by various workers, who have described in detail the several types of hypertrophy of root tissues which occur in plants as a result of attacks of various soil organisms. (The swellings or nodules on the roots of Leguminous plants due to the presence of nitrogen-fixing bacteria are frequently confused with galls arising from an infection of some root-parasitic species of nematode.)

Among the *Nematoda* which cause the formation of galls the most important species are the Root Knot Eelworms (*Meloidogyne* spp.) which chiefly affect glasshouse plants in this country, and galled roots are not uncommon upon such plants as begonia (Fig. 24), carnation, coleus, cucumber, plumbago and tomato. Over 800 host plants of these species have been listed by the United States Bureau of Plant Industry. Infested plants may be recognized by the pale lower foliage. The upper foliage tends to wilt in sunshine and in some cases surface roots grow from the base of the stem. The galls which are present on the original roots vary in size from the head of a pin to a walnut. On tomatoes they are hard and elongate while on cucumbers they are spongy and globular.

Control. (1) All infested soil should be subjected to steam sterilization. (2) Wash down the brickwork and staging with cresylic acid emulsion. (3) Sterilize plant pots and crocks. (4) To keep the eelworm in check during the years between steam sterilization soil injections of DD may be given. (5) If the infestation is noted during the growing period cover the surface of the soil with 1–1½ inches of peat to encourage new root growth.

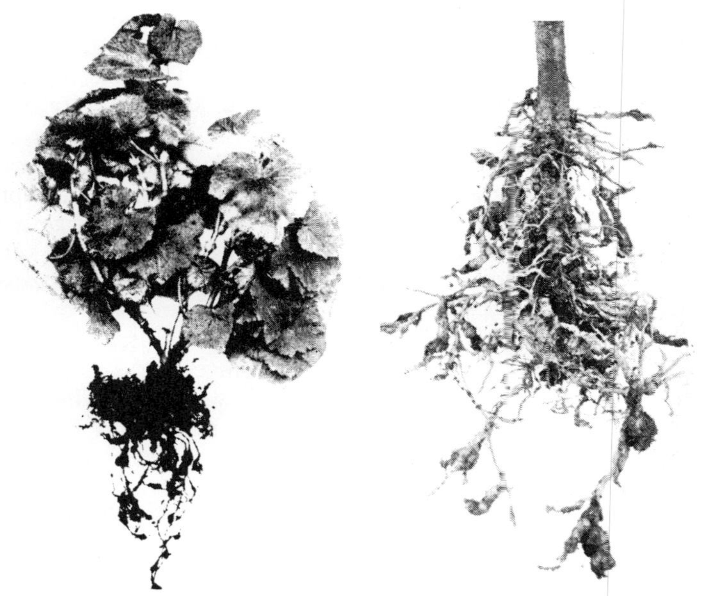

FIG. 24. Begonia roots (*left*) and Tomato roots (*right*) galled by Root Knot Eelworm (*Meloidogyne* species).

The Potato Root Eelworm (*Heterodera rostochiensis* Woll.) produces small nodule-like galls on the roots of tomatoes, particularly in glasshouses. Infested plants are retarded, wilt in sunshine, and the leaves turn dark green with a purplish hue on the undersides.

Control. (1) In glasshouses, as for Root Knot Eelworm (see above). (2) Out of doors, see 'Roots Underdeveloped', p. 59.

Among the more common Homopterous insects that form root galls are the Vine Louse and the Woolly Aphid.

The Vine Louse (*Phylloxera vastatrix* Planch.) is occasionally introduced to this country from abroad. There are forms producing galls on vine roots which decay as a result, and others produce galls on the leaves.

Control. If the presence of the Vine Louse is suspected it should be reported to the Ministry of Agriculture who will take appropriate action.

The Woolly Aphid (*Eriosoma lanigerum* Hausm.) is an important root pest of apples in Australia, New Zealand, South Africa and North America, but it is doubtful whether the true root form occurs in Britain. Sometimes, however, the aphids may be found at the base of the trunk below ground level or on roots exposed by cultivation, where they may form galls.

Control. See 'Stems with Woolly Masses', p. 89.

The most important Coleopterous root-galling pest is the Turnip Gall Weevil (*Ceuthorrhynchus pleurostigma* Marsh), (Aug.–Apr.). The damage is done by the larvae, which live in rounded galls on the roots of broccoli, brussels sprouts, cabbage, cauliflower, kales, swedes and turnips, and on charlock. Plants which are attacked when young are weakened and are less able to resist drought, especially on infertile soils. The galls are often confused with those arising from an infection of Club Root or Finger-and-Toe (*Plasmodiophora brassicae*). The weevil galls are hollow, each of which contains a legless grub (Fig. 25), while those due to Club Root are larger, more elongated and solid.

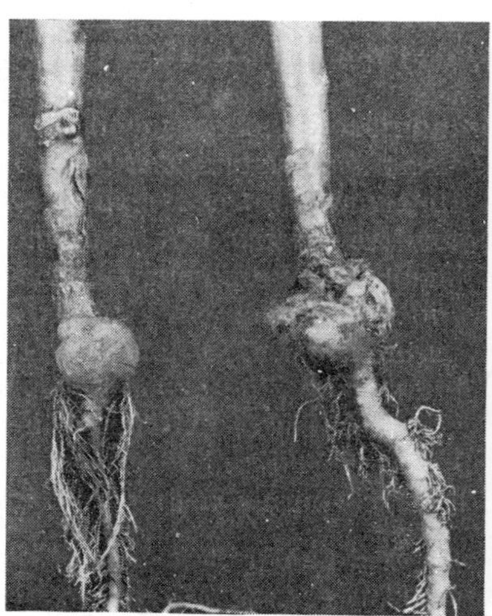

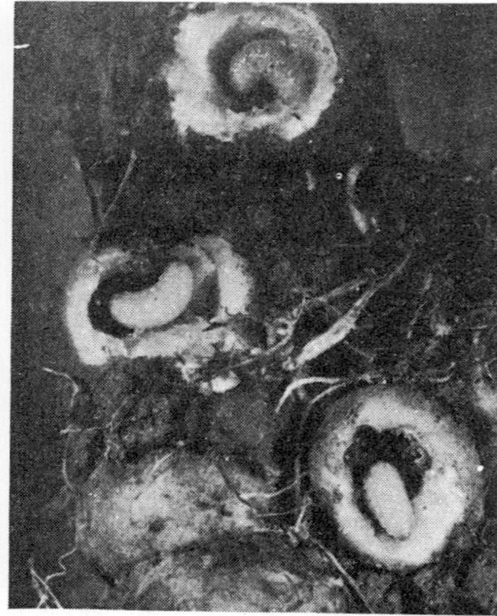

FIG. 25. *Left:* young Cabbage plants galled by the Turnip Gall Weevil (*Ceuthorrhyncus pleurostigma* Marsh). *Right:* galls cut open to show larvae. (*Shell Photographs.*)

Control. (1) Apply lindane dust in 2-inch bands along the rows of seedlings when they have two pairs of rough leaves. (2) Avoid transplanting galled seedlings. (3) Apply a quick-acting fertilizer to stimulate growth checked by the presence of galls on the roots. (4) Practise rotation. (5) All infested brassica stumps should be lifted and stacked loosely to dry them and prevent further development of the larvae. (6) Cultivate infested land deeply, burying the upper layer of soil to destroy the pupae.

There are certain Hymenopterous insects belonging to the Family *Cynipidae* or 'Gall Wasps' that form root galls. The most familiar is that found on the roots of oaks (*Quercus robur* and *Q. petrala*). These large, brownish, glabrous, sessile galls are noted when the roots of oaks are disturbed during the operations of digging and trenching in the immediate vicinity of these trees. The insects which cause these galls (*Biorrhiza pallida* Oliv.) are also responsible for the formation of the galls, known as 'oak-apples', on the shoots.

Control. These root galls have little deleterious effect upon the host tree, and their presence calls for no remedial measures.

ROOTS OVER-DEVELOPED

The Beet Eelworm (*Heterodera schachtii* Schmidt), (Jul.–Oct.), produces an excessive development of the lateral rootlets on sugar beet, beetroot, spinach and mangold. The presence of stunted plants showing yellowish, wilted and dying foliage usually indicates an infestation, which may be confirmed by examining the primary root, which, when attacked by this pest, is under-developed and whiskered owing to the development of 'hunger roots', to which are attached the encysted female nematodes.

The Cabbage Root Eelworm (*H. cruciferae* Frankl.), causes similar hypertrophy of the lateral roots of brassicas, turnips, etc. Infested plants make poor growth and the outer leaves wilt under dry conditions.

Control. (1) Practise rotation. Susceptible crops (see Appendix II, p. 211) should not be grown on clean land more than once in 4 years. Where the eelworm population is high, susceptible crops should not be grown for at least 5 years. (2) Clean cultivation to avoid the infestation being carried over on weed or 'bridging' hosts. (3) Washings from infested roots should be poured into main drains to avoid contamination of ground. (4) Prevent the spread of infested soil on implements, boots, etc.

The Root Knot Eelworm (*Meloidogyne* spp.), (Jul.–Dec.), is in this country primarily a pest of glasshouse crops (see 'Roots Galled', p. 54), but the use of infested soil as a top dressing in the vegetable garden may result in outbreaks in the open. The effect on root crops, e.g. carrot and parsnip, is similar to that produced on sugar beet by *H. schachtii*, and the excessive hairiness of the tap root is due to the need for additional water-absorbing root tissues to replace those galled by eelworms.

Control. Refrain from placing infected soil from glasshouse borders on the compost heap, and from incorporating it with soil in the open garden (see 'Roots Galled', p. 54).

ROOTS RUSTY

Rusty patches may be observed on the roots of plants and are due in certain instances to an infestation of some root pest. This symptom is more pronounced in the case of Carrots and Parsnips attacked by the Hawthorn-Carrot Aphid (*Dysaphis crataegi* Kalt.) (see 'Roots Aphid-infested', p. 44), and by the larvae of the Carrot Fly (*Psila rosae* Fab.) (see 'Roots Eaten', p. 51).

ROOTS SPLITTING

The splitting of roots is not necessarily symptomatic of insect attack, although some species of Aphids are primarily responsible for this type of injury. The fleshy roots of some plants, more especially carrots, split as a result of the pressure exerted by turgescent tissues on the strained epidermis and, being functional disorders in many

FIG. 26. Splitting of Carrots following attack by the Hawthorn-Carrot Aphid (*Dysaphis crataegi* Kalt.). (*Crown Copyright Photograph.*)

cases, occur as a result of: (*a*) the rapid absorption of water by the roots following a period of drought; (*b*) the continued high moisture content of the soil due in some instances to defective drainage; (*c*) an excessive amount of nitrogenous matter in the soil and a deficiency of potash and phosphates; and (*d*) roots remaining in the ground for some considerable period after they have reached maturity.

At least three species of Aphids give rise to root splitting, namely, (*a*) *Dysaphis crataegi* Kalt. may cause the roots of carrot to split (Fig. 26); (*b*) the Parsnip Root Aphid (*Anuraphis subterranea* Wlk.), which produces cracks on the roots of parsnip similar to those occurring on carrots; and (*c*) the Currant Root Aphid (*Eriosoma ulmi* L.), which congregates on the larger roots of currants and gooseberry and causes them to split. It is particularly harmful to young bushes in nurseries.

Control. See 'Roots Aphid-infested', p. 44.

ROOTS UNDER-DEVELOPED

The Potato Root Eelworm (*Heterodera rostochiensis* Woll.) is the most dangerous pest of potatoes. Infested plants are weak and stunted and the foliage is dull and unhealthy-looking, with a tendency to turn brown and wither (Fig. 27). The root system is poor and the tubers are greatly reduced in size and number. Tomatoes are also attacked and here too the root system is poorly developed and may

FIG. 27. Potato plant showing loss of lower foliage and poor yield due to infestation of Potato Root Eelworm (*Heterodera rostochiensis* Woll.). (*Shell Photograph.*)

be rotted. The foliage is pale green or purplish and the plants are stunted.

If the roots of infested plants are examined with a magnifying glass small whitish or brown cysts may be seen clinging to them. These contain the eggs which can remain viable for many years.

Control. (A) Potatoes. (1) Heavily infested land should be rested from potatoes for 5–8 years. (2) Practise crop rotation. Main-crop potatoes should be grown once in 4 years on medium to heavy soil, and once in 6–7 years on light soils. With early potatoes 2 successive crops may be grown every 5 years. (3) 'Groundkeepers', or self-set potatoes should be rogued out and weed hosts eradicated between crops. (4) Use only certified 'seed'. (5) Avoid the spread of infested soil on boots, implements, etc.

(B) Tomatoes. (1) Replace infested soil with steam sterilized soil. (2) Treatment with DD will keep the pest in check and can be used to lengthen the interval between steam treatments. (3) If the infestation is noticed on growing plants cover the surface of the soil with moist peat to the depth of 1–1½ inches and feed heavily.

ROOTS WITH WOOLLY MASSES

The presence of white, flocculent masses on the roots of many plants is of more frequent occurrence than is realized, and is often detected only after lifting the crop or attacked bushes. Their presence may not become apparent until the aerial portions of the infested plants exhibit symptoms of ill-health, e.g. wilted foliage, and yellowing and premature leaf-fall.

Two main groups of insects are responsible for the production of woolly masses on the roots of plants, viz.: (*a*) Root Aphids and (*b*) Root Mealy Bugs.

(*a*) The more common species of Aphids that are surrounded with flocculent material are: (i) the Lettuce Root Aphid (*Pemphigus bursarius* L.,), (Aug.–Mar.), on the roots of lettuce, sowthistle and *Chenopodium*; (ii) the Auricula Root Aphid (*P. auriculae* Murr.), on the roots of auricula (Fig. 17) and other species of primula, especially pot-grown plants (see 'Roots Aphid-Infested'); and (iii) the Currant Root Aphid (*Eriosoma ulmi* L.) (see 'Roots Splitting', p. 59).

Control. See 'Roots Aphid-Infested', p. 44.

(*b*) Some species of Mealy Bugs are subterranean in their habits, and live on the roots of several cultivated plants, especially ornamentals, and often in close association with Ants. The amount of white, powdery meal with which their bodies are covered varies with the species. Among the more common species of *Rhizoecus* which attack plant roots, more especially in glasshouses, are: (i) *R. falcifer* Künck. on abutilon, cassia, correa, dracaena, olearia and many other subjects grown in temperate houses; (ii) *R. dianthi* Green on *Dianthus gratianopolitanus*, *D. plumarius* and *D. barbatus* (sweet william), and pelargonium; (iii) *Pseudococcus mamillariae* Bouché, a particularly destructive pest on the roots of cacti and various succulents.

Control. (1) Wash the roots of infested plants in a solution of malathion or parathion. (2) Replant in clean soil and pots. (3) Sterilize infested soil with steam and scald pots and crocks. (4) Where it is not practicable to disturb the plants water copiously around the roots with malathion or parathion, repeating the treatment at 14-day intervals as necessary.

CHAPTER FOUR

Stems and Shoots

Stems and Shoots Aphid-infested. Shoots Distorted. Stems Dying Back. Stems Bearing Egg-masses. Stems with Frothy Masses. Stems Galled. Stems Gnawed or Rasped. Stems Gumming. Stems with Larval Colonies. Stems with Lesions. Stems Scaly. Stems Severed. Stems Tunnelled. Stems with Woolly Masses.

THE primary stem or axis is the leaf-bearing part of the plant, and is the main channel of communication between the roots and the aerial portions (buds, leaves, flowers, fruits and seeds). Branches and shoots are outgrowths from the stem and are termed secondary and tertiary axes. The types of stem are numerous, for they may be annual, biennial or perennial; erect, climbing, twining, creeping or floating aerial, surface (runners and stolons), or subterranean (bulb, corm, rhizome and tuber); woody, herbaceous or succulent; solid or hollow; straight or flexuose; cylindrical, angular, ribbed, flattened or winged; and smooth, hairy, prickly or warty.

The Biblical quotation (1 Cor. xii. 26): 'And whether one member suffer, all the members suffer with it', is particularly applicable to the stems of plants when injured by some animal or vegetable organism, for the main lines of communication between the water- and food-absorbing organs—the roots—and the food-manufacturing organs—the leaves—run along the main axis or stem. Injury by pests to the main stem interferes with the food and water supply and results in a reduction of conductive tissue, with subsequent wilting of the plant. Gumming and bleeding, the production of cankerous growths, and chlorosis are other effects that follow injury by stem-infesting insect pests.

While very many insects are capable of attacking healthy tissues and of penetrating through the bark and epidermis of stems, other insects attack only stems that have been injured mechanically, by bacterial and fungal organisms, and by climatic conditions (e.g. intense freezing, lightning, gales and prolonged drought), all of which produce lesions, wounds and bark-split, and allow such secondary agents to invade the damaged tissues and to extend the initial injury. Similarly, the wounds made by insects afford focal points of entry for disease organisms, thus allowing even weakly parasitic organisms to gain entrance and invade the tissues.

STEMS AND SHOOTS APHID-INFESTED

Many species of Aphids congregate in large colonies on the shoots and stems of plants, and their presence is readily detected by the most unobservant. These insects abstract the cell sap and tap the flow of plant food within the stem and shoot tissues, so that the vigour is lowered, wilting, yellowing and premature leaf-fall occur, and growth is checked. Many of these shoot-feeders are visited by Ants, which seek them for their sweet excretions or 'honeydew'.

The number of stem-infesting species of Aphids is large, and mention is made only of the more common plant pests, namely: (i) the black Bean Aphid (*Aphis fabae* Scop.), (May–Jul.), which infests a great variety of garden plants and weeds, on the foliage and petioles (Fig. 28) of which it clusters in vast numbers. It infests also the stems

FIG. 28. Broad Bean shoot infested with Bean Aphid (*Aphis fabae* Scop.). (*Shell Photograph.*)

FIG. 29. Rose stem infested with Rose Aphid (*Macrosiphum rosae* L.). (*Shell Photograph.*)

and shoots of plants, more especially, euonymus and broad bean. (ii) The Green Apple Aphid (*Aphis pomi* Deg.), (May.–Jul.), which clusters on the shoots of apple, pear, quince and hawthorn, and on certain of the ornamental *Pyrus* species. (iii) The Elder Aphid (*Aphis sambuci* L.), (May–Jul.), which is found on the stems of *Sambucus nigra*. (iv) The Chrysanthemum Aphid (*Macrosiphoniella sanborni*

Gill.), (Jul.–Nov.), forms large colonies on the shoots and stems of chrysanthemums out-of-doors in summer and persists on plants brought into glasshouses in autumn. (v) The Rose Aphids (*Macrosiphum rosae* L., and *Myzaphis rosarum* Kalt.), (Apr.–Aug.), which cluster thickly on the shoots of wild and cultivated roses, more especially on ramblers (Fig. 29). (vi) The Cypress Aphid (*Cinara cupressi* Buckt.), (Mar.–June), which is a shoot and stem feeder on *Cupressus macrocarpa*. (vii) The Willow Stem Aphid (*Tuberolachnus saligna* Gmel.), (June–Aug.), which is a large aphid found clustering in colonies on the stems of wild and ornamental species of *Salix*. (viii) The Woolly Aphid or American Blight (*Eriosoma lanigerum* Hausm.), (May–Aug.), which infests the shoots and stems of apple, ornamental species of *Pyrus*, hawthorn and *Cotoneaster horizontalis*.

Control. (1) Deciduous trees and bushes, when completely dormant, should be sprayed with a tar oil wash to destroy the overwintering stages, or (2) apply a DNC-petroleum wash in late winter. (N.B. The manufacturers' instructions should be read carefully before applying either of these washes.) (3) Infested shoots and stems should be sprayed with lindane, nicotine, TEPP, malathion, parathion, or with a systemic insecticide.

SHOOTS DISTORTED

The Stem and Bulb Eelworm (*Ditylenchus dipsaci* (Kühn) Filipj.), (Mar.–Aug.), causes the shoots of certain plants, more particularly clovers, lucerne and evening primroses (*Oenotheras*), to become angled, distorted and intertwined.

Control. See 'Foliage Narrowed', p. 152.

At least one species of Capsid Bug, the Common Green Capsid (*Lygus pabulinus* L.), (Apr.–Aug.), is concerned with the malformation of shoots of red currants, gooseberry, blackberry and loganberry.

Control. See 'Foliage Ragged', p. 153.

The Froghopper (*Philaenus leucophthalmus* L.), (May.–Jul.), during its larval or 'Cuckoo-spit' stage causes severe shoot distortion in plants, notably lavender (see 'Foliage with Frothy Masses', p. 144).

Aphids are frequently concerned with stem and shoot distortion, owing to the abstraction of sap and the injury to the cellular tissue so that growth takes place more rapidly on one side of the shoot than on the other. Among the more common species responsible for this type of damage are: (i) the Green Apple Aphid (*Aphis pomi* Deg.), which infests the small shoots of apple, more especially on young trees, and of hawthorn, and produces distortion (Fig. 30);

and (ii) the Chrysanthemum Aphid (*Macrosiphoniella sanborni* Gill.), which causes severe shoot distortion.

Control. See 'Stems Aphid-Infested', p. 63.

FIG. 30. Apple shoots distorted by Green Apple Aphid (*Aphis pomi* Deg.).

STEMS DYING BACK

The partial or complete dying back of shoots and stems is due to many factors other than insect attack, e.g. unfavourable weather, unsuitable soil and/or site, infections of disease organisms, and mechanical injury.

The stag-headed condition frequently observed in oak trees may be due to insect attack (e.g. Bark Beetles and Wood-Borers), but more often follows as a result of old age, unfavourable soil conditions, nutritional deficiencies, and bacterial and fungal invasions. The Papery-Bark disease of apple and pear trees is a somewhat similar disorder and is due primarily to unhealthy root action arising from waterlogging of the soil or following an extended period of drought.

The types of injury caused by insects and resulting in die-back of shoots, branches and stems are: (*a*) the partial or complete girdling of stems at ground level by Cutworms, and of shoots by twig-cutting Weevils (*Rhynchites*, *Caenorhinus* and *Anthonomus*); (*b*) the loss of sap due to its extraction by sucking insects, principally Aphids and Scale Insects; (*c*) the tunnelling in the bark by Bark Beetles; and (*d*) the boring of galleries by the caterpillars of Goat and Wood Leopard Moths, of Currant and other Clearwings, of Raspberry Shoot and Rosy Rustic Moths, and of the Larch and Pine-shoot Moths; by the larvae of Longhorn (*Cerambycid*) beetles, and by Shot-Hole Borers; by the larvae of the Carnation Fly; and so on, all of which are considered under the sectional headings of 'Stems Aphid-Infested', p. 63), 'Stems Gnawed' (p. 71), 'Stems Scaly' (p. 77), and 'Stems Tunnelled' (p. 82).

STEMS BEARING EGG-MASSES

A number of plant pests lay their eggs singly so that their presence frequently escapes the attention of the grower, while others deposit a mass of eggs and as such attract the attention of the untrained

FIG. 31. Eggs of Green Apple Aphid (*Aphis pomi* Deg.) on Apple shoots.

FIG. 32. Egg bracelet of March Moth (*Alsophila aescularia* Schiff.).

observer. Among the more obvious egg-masses on stems are those of: (i) the Fruit Tree Red Spider Mite (*Panonychus ulmi* Koch), (Nov.–Apr.), (p. 104), which lays a considerable number of reddish eggs on the stems, shoots and around the spurs of apple, pear, plum, damson, etc.; (ii) the Green Apple Aphid (*A. pomi* Deg.), (Oct.–Apr.), (p. 63), which deposits a number of black, shining eggs on the shoots of apple (Fig. 31), quince and hawthorn; (iii) the March Moth (*Alsophila aescularia* Schiff.), (Feb.–Apr.), (p. 132), which lays a complete bracelet of eggs, covered with hairs from the fan-like tail of the female (Fig. 32), on the shoots of many forest and fruit trees, more especially apple; and (iv) the Lackey Moth (*Malacosoma neustria* L.), (Aug.–Apr.), (p. 132), which lays a complete and regular band of eggs round the shoots of several forest, fruit and ornamental trees and shrubs. Reddish or purplish clusters of the algae-feeding Oribatid or 'Beetle Mites' are frequently found on the stems of fruit and ornamental trees and shrubs (e.g. lilac), and are mistaken for the eggs of the injurious Red Spider Mites.

Control. (1) Cut off and burn shoots bearing egg-masses, the presence of which are detected more readily during pruning operations in winter. (2) During the dormant season spray the stems and shoots of infested fruit trees, forcefully and thoroughly, with a tar oil wash or, if Fruit Tree Red Spider Mite is present, with DNC-petroleum. (3) During the growing season take control measures against the pest concerned.

STEMS WITH FROTHY MASSES

A mass of froth-like matter or 'Cuckoo-spit' on shoots, stems and leaves is well known—the spittle-like excretion being produced by the nymphs of Froghoppers (*Cercopidae*). The more common species associated with garden plants are discussed under the section 'Foliage with Frothy Masses', p. 144. The most abundant species in gardens is *Philaenus leucophthalmus* L., (June–July), which is frequently a pest of no mean importance on apple, rose, geum, lavender,

FIG. 33. The frothy exudation of the Cuckoo-spit Froghopper (*Philaenus leucophthalmus* L.) on *Achillea* species. (*Shell Photograph.*)

solidago and numerous other plants, both cultivated and wild (Fig. 33).

Control. See 'Foliage with Frothy Masses', p. 144.

STEMS GALLED

The production of gall-formations is discussed under 'Foliage Galled'. True galls, such as those arising from attacks of Gall Midges (*Cecidomyidae*) and Gall Wasps (*Cynipidae*) are due to a set of chemical and physiological reactions on the part of the host plant, which is stimulated by the larva of the gall-maker, which, by its presence as a moving body, by its feeding, or by its excretion of irritating fluids, sets up hypertrophy of cellular tissues. The term 'gall' is, however, applied by some authorities to any abnormality in growth, e.g. leaf-curl, etc.

Galls on stems may arise as a result of (*a*) the feeding of a sucking insect, e.g. the tumour-like galls produced by Woolly Aphid; (*b*) the insect itself which produces irritation resulting in rapid local cellular growth and cell division; and (*c*) the mechanical wounding of plant tissues during oviposition resulting in extremely local irritation. It has been suggested that the inter-relationship between the gall-producer and the plant is parasitic—the initial action of the larva being counteracted by tannin production on the part of the plant (especially in oaks) and that the effect is one of inter-compensation.

FIG. 34. 'Pineapple' galls on Spruce formed by the Spruce Gall Adelges (*Adelges abietis* L.). (*Photograph by R. P. Scase.*)

The types of galls on stems are so varied in their size, shape, colour and consistency that it is possible only to mention some of the more common types found in and around gardens.

Gall Mites (*Eriophyidae*) are among the organisms responsible for the production of those curious and familiar malformations on trees known as 'Witches' Brooms'. Such abnormal outgrowths comprise a dense mass of twigs crowded together on the shoots and branches and resemble large birds' nests. The commencement of a 'Witches' Broom' is a swollen bud, while further development of the lateral buds produces marked proliferation.

Some 'Witches' Brooms' are caused by Gall Mites, e.g. *Eriophyes rudis* Can. on birch, and *E. triradiatus* Nal. on willow shoots; others by fungi, e.g. *Taphrina* (*Exoascus*) *turgidus* on birch; while others are in the nature of hereditary monstrosities, especially those occurring on coniferous trees, e.g. *Abies*.

Control. The growth of the trees suffers little as a result of these galls and, apart from cutting out and burning them when they are unsightly, no control measures are necessary.

Among the *Hemiptera*, the chief culprit is the Woolly Aphid, which

FIG. 35. Galling of Apple shoot caused by Woolly Aphid (*Eriosoma lanigerum* Hausm.). (*Shell Photograph*.)

FIG. 36. Chrysanthemum stem galled by Chrysanthemum Midge (*Diarthronomyia chrysanthemi* Ahlb.).

produces tumour-like galls on the shoots (Fig. 35) and stems of apple, certain ornamental species of *Pyrus* (*Malus*) and *Pyracantha*, and on hawthorn. It is not uncommon to find the galls eaten out by birds—not for the insects which abound on them, but for the succulent tissues within such swellings.

The Spruce Gall Adelges (*Adelges abietis* L. and *A. laricis* Vall.) form pineapple-shaped galls on the shoots of spruce (Fig. 34), while the galls formed by the Douglas Fir Adelges (*A. cooleyi* Gill.), also on spruce, are longer and narrower.

Control. See 'Stems with Woolly Masses', p. 89.

With Dipterous insects, members of the Family *Cecidomyidae* are associated with gall-formation—members of this group of insects being referred to as Gall Midges. The most important of the species which form galls on stems is the Chrysanthemum Midge (*Diarthronomyia chrysanthemi* Ahlb.), (Jan.–Dec.). In severe attacks the larvae form small cone-shaped galls on the stems as well as on the leaves. The stems may become severely distorted (Fig. 36).

Control. See 'Foliage Galled', p. 146.

Other common gall-forming Cecidomyids are: (*a*) the Raspberry Stem Gall Midge (*Lasioptera rubi* Heeg.), which produces walnut-like swellings on the shoots of raspberry and on wild and cultivated blackberries; and (*b*) the Shot-Hole Gall Midge (*Helicomyia saliciperda* Duf.), which, though not a true gall-former, lives in the stems of willows, *Salix* species, and produces a 'shot-hole' effect. Birds rip up the bark in search of the larvae—the result being a canker-like tumour.

Control. See below.

The only Hymenopterous insects that require special mention are members of the Superfamily *Cynipoidea,* known as Gall Wasps or Gall Flies, which produce galls on all parts of the plant from the roots to the flowers and fruits. The oak is the chief host of Cynipids, and it is estimated that 80 per cent. of the known species produce galls on *Quercus* and are confined to that genus. Specimen trees in arboreta and gardens may be rendered unsightly by the presence of such persistent galls as 'Marble Galls', but little permanent injury is done to infested trees as a result of their attacks, with the exception of some check in growth following infestations on apical and lateral buds.

A gall-maker of special interest in gardens is the Bedeguar Gall Wasp (*Rhodites rosae* L.), (Jul.–Apr.), the larva of which causes the condition called Robin's Pincushion on the shoots of wild and cultivated roses. These galls consist of a mass of moss-like filaments surrounding a cluster of woody cells that harbour the larvae (Fig. 37).

Control. (1) Prune off and burn galled shoots—this being applicable only to raspberries, blackberries and to roses. (2) Cut out or pare over galls on willow branches due to the Willow Stem Gall Midge, and paint over wounds with white lead paint or Stockholm tar. (3) Remove and burn galled shoots on wild plants, e.g. *Rubus* and *Rosa*, growing in close proximity to cultivated plants of the same genera.

FIG. 37. 'Robin's Pincushion' gall formed on Rose by Bedeguar Gall Wasp (*Rhodites rosae* L.). (*Shell Photograph.*)

STEMS GNAWED OR RASPED

In this category are included injuries caused by the gnawing and rasping of the stem both above and below soil level. The result is that the stem is partially or completely girdled and supplies of water may be interrupted or completely cut off thereby producing wilting, premature defoliation, and subsequent death of the plants.

Many soil-inhabiting creatures, other than insects, e.g. Slugs, Snails, Millipedes and Woodlice, are frequently destructive to the underground stems of plants, more especially to herbaceous subjects. Also, the succulent aerial and subterranean stems of many garden plants are rasped by Slugs and Snails, which scrape off the epidermis and feed on the soft tissues immediately beneath. This type of injury is particularly marked on the underground stems of potato and on many herbaceous plants.

Control. See 'Bulbs Tunnelled', p. 35.

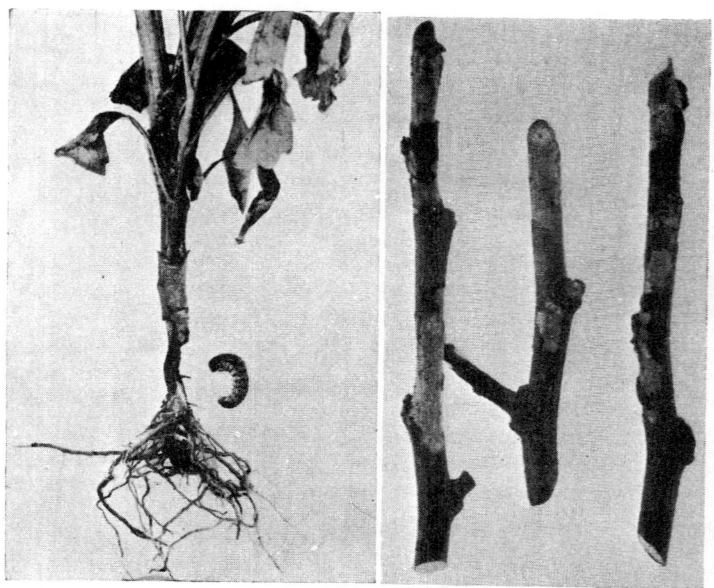

FIG. 38. Stem of Annual Aster girdled by Cutworm (*Euxoa* species).

FIG. 39. Apple shoots damaged by Clay-coloured Weevil (*Otiorrhynchus singularis* L.). (*Photograph from A. M. Massee, 'Pests of Fruits and Hops'.*)

Springtails (*Collembola*) can be serious pests in glasshouses, particularly where the soil is moist and acid. *Tomocerus longicornis* Müll. and *Onychiurus stachianus* Bagn. are commonly found rasping holes in the stems of young seedlings which in consequence make poor growth and often die. The germinating seeds, pseudobulbs and aerial roots of orchids are severely damaged by *Orchesella* spp. *Hypogastrura armata* Nic. tunnels deeply in the stalks and caps of mushrooms.

Control. (1) Keep the soil well drained and counter the acidity by liming. (2) Wash down the staging, etc., with cresylic acid emulsion. (3) Apply lindane or aldrin dust to the soil within a month before planting, forking it into the top 4 inches of soil. (4) Water infested seedlings with lindane, aldrin, nicotine or TEPP when the soil temperature is high and the insects are near the surface.

Among the *Lepidoptera* are found two particular groups of pests whose larvae feed on the stems of garden plants, viz.: (*a*) Surface Caterpillars or Cutworms, *Euxoa* and *Agrotis* spp., which feed at and below soil level (Fig. 38); and (*b*) Swift Moth larvae, *Hepialus* species, which feed below ground (see 'Bulbs Tunnelled', p. 37).

The larvae of a Tortricid Moth (*Ditula angustiorana* Haw.), (May–June), is frequently destructive to specimen trees and hedge plants of yew, the shoots of which are girdled causing the tips to turn brown and to die-back—the result of an infestation being often attributed to frost.

Control. (1) Cut off and burn the dead and dying shoots of yew. (2) Spray or dust infested plants with DDT in May and June.

Among Coleopterous insects responsible for stem-gnawing are certain Weevils and Chafers.

(*a*) The Clay-coloured Weevil (*Otiorrhynchus singularis* L.), (June–May), in both its larval and adult stages is responsible for this type of injury. The larvae girdle the stems below soil level of a great variety of plants, more especially hard-wooded subjects, e.g. virginia creeper (*Parthenocissus*), *Vitis* species and coniferous seedlings. The nocturnally-active adult weevils congregate in considerable numbers in the debris under hedges, shrubs and fruit trees from which they emerge after dark to feed on the plants, the base of the stems of which are partially or completely girdled (Fig. 39).

Control. See 'Bulbs Tunnelled', p. 39.

(*b*) Weevils of the genus *Strophosomus* occasionally gnaw the stem epidermis of azaleas and rhododendrons.

Control. See 'Foliage with Epidermis Eaten', p. 139.

(*c*) Both adults and larvae of the Asparagus Beetle (*Crioceris asparagi* L.), (May–Sept.), gnaw away the epidermis of the fronds of asparagus and also cause extensive defoliation thus weakening the roots (Fig. 40). Earlier in the year some damage may also be done to the young shoots which are rendered unsaleable by gnawing and contamination with the black fluid excreted by the larvae.

Control. When the damage is seen, spray with DDT or, if within 14 days of cutting, with derris.

(*d*) Chafer Beetles, including: (i) the Cockchafer (*Melolontha*

melolontha L.), which in its larval stages is particularly destructive to the roots and underground stems of many plants, including bedding plants (chrysanthemums, dahlias, pelargoniums and zinnias) and hard-wooded subjects (fruit trees and roses); (ii) the Summer Chafer (*Amphimallus solstitialis* L.) and (iii) the Brown Chafer (*Serica brunnea* L.) are two important pests in forest nurseries.

Control. See 'Roots Eaten', p. 49.

FIG. 40. Girdling and defoliation of Asparagus by Asparagus Beetle (*Crioceris asparagi* L.). (*Photograph by P. Becker.*)

FIG. 41. Young Apple tree barked by Hares. (*Photograph by P. Becker.*)

Wasps (*Vespula* spp.), (Jul.–Sept.), are frequently destructive to dahlias, the succulent petioles and stems of which are rasped by these insects. Their purpose is to obtain food and nest material, though occasionally moisture is required as the epidermal and sub-epidermal layers may be discarded. Hornets will ring the bark of ash and alder in a similar manner, and carry off the pieces for use in nest construction.

Control. (1) Destroy all nests in the vicinity of the flower beds (see

'Fruits Eaten Away', p. 177). (2) If necessary, spray the stems and foliage with DDT but avoid spraying the flowers.

Mammalian pests such as rabbits, hares, squirrels, voles and occasionally mice cause severe damage to the stems and trunks of bushes and trees of many types, particularly in winter when other food is short. The bark is gnawed away and young trees may be completely ringed and killed (Fig. 41).

Control. (1) Trees and bushes can be protected by painting the trunks or stems when dormant with a repellant made up by dissolving 1 lb. of commercial resin (colophony) in 1 pint of denatured ethyl alcohol. Proprietary repellants are available and tree-banding grease has also been used successfully. (2) The trunks of trees may be surrounded by wire netting turned over at the top to prevent it being climbed. (3) Where rabbits or squirrels are numerous the advice of the Ministry of Agriculture should be sought and a drive made to eradicate them or to reduce the population. (4) Warfarin baits may be used against mice and voles (see Appendix IV, p. 215).

STEMS GUMMING

The terms 'Gummosis', 'Resinosus', and 'Bleeding' are applied to plants, especially trees, suffering from a loss of gum, resin and sap. The effect may be due to mechanical injuries, wounds and severe pruning, especially in stone fruits; to sap under pressure owing to functional disorders—the term 'weeping' trees being applied to those whose stems 'bleed' and from which Slime Flux exudes; to infections of bacterial organisms (e.g. Bacterial Canker in plums) and fungal organisms; and to attacks of wood-boring insects and Bark Beetles.

Gummosis occurs commonly in stone fruits, e.g. almond, cherry, peach and plum, and excessive gumming may accompany an attack of Shot-Hole Borer Beetles (*Anisandrus dispar* F.), which are occasionally drowned in their galleries before they can emerge from their 'flight holes' (Fig. 55). Resinosus occurs in coniferous trees, and frequently follows attacks of Pine Shoot Moths and Bark Beetles.

The chief pests concerned are considered under the section 'Stems Tunnelled', p. 82.

STEMS WITH LARVAL COLONIES

The larvae of certain species of Moths and Sawflies are gregarious and live in colonies on the stems and shoots of plants. Some live in webs or 'nests' and are commonly known as 'Tent Caterpillars'.

The more important plant pests in this country whose larvae live in 'tents' on shoots and branches are: (*à*) the Lackey Moth (*Malacosoma neustria* L.), (June–Jul.), which forms nests on apple, pear and other fruit trees, on some forest trees, and on roses (Fig. 43). (*b*) The Ermine Moths, namely, *Yponomeuta cognatella* Hübn., (May–June), on *Euonymus japonicus* and other ornamental species of spindle tree;

FIG. 42. Apple shoot webbed by small Ermine Moth caterpillars (*Yponomeuta* species). (*Shell Photograph.*)

FIG. 43. Colony of Lackey Moth caterpillars (*Malacosoma neustria* L.) on Rose.

Y. euonymella L., (June), on bird cherry (*Prunus padus*); *Y. padella* L. and its biological race *Y. malinella* F., (May–June), on hawthorn and blackthorn, and on apple respectively (Fig. 42); and *Y. rorella* Hübn., (May–June), which often swathes the stem and branches of willows with its webbing. (*c*) The Hawthorn Webber (*Scythropia crataegella* L.), (May–June), on hawthorn and cotoneaster. (*d*) The Juniper Webber (*Dichomeris marginella* F.), (May–June), on juniper. (*e*) The Social Pear Sawfly (*Neurotoma saltuum* L.), (July–Aug.), on pear, cherry and plum.

Control. (1) If possible, cut out the 'tents' when the larvae are inside, i.e. at night, during unfavourable weather, or when hibernating during the winter, or (2) burn away the 'tents' after dark with a blowlamp. (3) Spray the foliage with DDT. In the case of fruit routine sprays should suffice to check infestations but if it is necessary to spray after blossom an acaricide should be added to control Fruit Tree Red Spider Mite.

STEMS WITH LESIONS

The lesions to which reference is made are those that are produced either as a result of the feeding of a sucking insect, more especially Aphids, or oviposition punctures made by such insects as Capsid Bugs, by Stem Sawflies (*Cephidae*), and by certain species of true Sawflies (*Tenthredinidae*).

Many species of Aphids produce lesions in the soft tissues of both hardy and tender plants, and discoloration may follow as a result of the death of the cells and from the invasion of weakly parasitic organisms. The damage is then frequently mistaken for either virus, bacterial or fungal infections. Again, the lenticels (breathing-pores) on green shoots of fruit trees have been confused with Capsid oviposition punctures by untrained observers.

Among the several species of Capsid Bugs which oviposit in the stems and shoots of plants are: (*a*) the Apple Capsid (*Plesiocoris rugicollis* Fall.), (Jul.–Apr.), and (*b*) the Common Green Capsid (*Lygus pabulinus* L.), (Jul.–Apr.), both of which lay their eggs in fruit trees and, in the latter species, in soft fruits and in the shoots of many hard-wooded plants.

Control. See 'Foliage Puckered', p. 122.

Of the Hymenopterous insects the Large Rose Sawfly (*Arge ochropus* Gmel.), (June–Aug.), makes rows of incisions on the young shoots and flower stalks of roses in each of which an egg is laid. The injured part becomes discoloured and often distorted. When the larvae hatch out they commence feeding on the foliage and, unless control measures are taken, may cause severe defoliation.

Control. (1) Prune off and burn shoots in which eggs have been laid. (2) Keep a watch for the green caterpillar-like larvae and, if present, spray the bush with DDT or BHC.

STEMS SCALY

The stems of a great variety of plants, both under glass and in the open, are encrusted with scale insects or Coccids. The presence of large numbers of these insects on the stems renders the plants unsightly, reduces the amount of available food supply within the plant by the abstraction of sap, and results in checked growth, lowered vigour, wilting and premature leaf-fall. The plants are also rendered unsightly by their presence and by the honeydew which they excrete and which provides a medium for the growth of sooty moulds.

The most satisfactory control is obtained after the eggs hatch and the active larvae are walking over the shoots and foliage before settling down to a sedentary existence. For this reason the dates given below are those during which hatching takes place in outdoor species, though they may vary somewhat with climatic conditions. Under glass, if the temperature is suitable, hatching may occur at any time.

Among the more common outdoor stem-infesting species are: (*a*) The Oystershell Scale (*Quadraspidiotus ostreaeformis* Curt.), (June), which is found on the bark of apple, pear, peach, plum, birch, poplar and horse-chestnut: (*b*) the Willow Scale (*Chionaspis salicis* L.), (May–June), on the stems of alder, broom, elm, lilac and willow

FIG. 44. Nut Scale (*Eulecanium coryli* L.) on Pyracantha.

FIG. 45. Woolly Currant Scale (*Pulvinaria vitis* L.) on Red Currant.

—these two species are often so numerous on the stems that they have the appearance of having been whitewashed; (*c*) the Brown Scale (*Eulecanium corni* Bouché), (Aug.–Sept.), occurs on the stems and foliage of apricot, currant, peach and vine, and on ornamental trees and shrubs such as carpentaria, ceanothus, cotoneaster, pyracantha and robinia; (*d*) the Yew Scale (*E. pomeranicum* Kaw.), (Aug.–Sept.), on the leaves and foliage of yew; (*e*) the Nut Scale (*E. coryli* L.), (Aug.–Sept.), on the stems of apple, pear, hazel, hawthorn and pyracantha (Fig. 44); (*f*) the Scurfy Scale (*Aulacaspis rosae* Bouché), (Aug.–Sept.), on the stems of wild and cultivated roses (Fig. 48); (*g*) the Woolly Currant Scale (*Pulvinaria vitis* L.), (June–July), on the shoots and stems of alder, birch, hawthorn, red currant and vine (Fig. 45); (*h*) the Mussel Scale (*Lepidosaphes ulmi* L.), (May), on the stems and branches of apple and of ornamental shrubs, e.g. ceanothus, cotoneaster, *Pyrus* spp., etc.; (*i*) the Beech Scale (*Cryptococcus fagi* Bär.), (Aug.–Sept.), on the stems and branches of beech, being more partial to the green than to the copper varieties (Fig. 46). Some of these scales are also found in glasshouses.

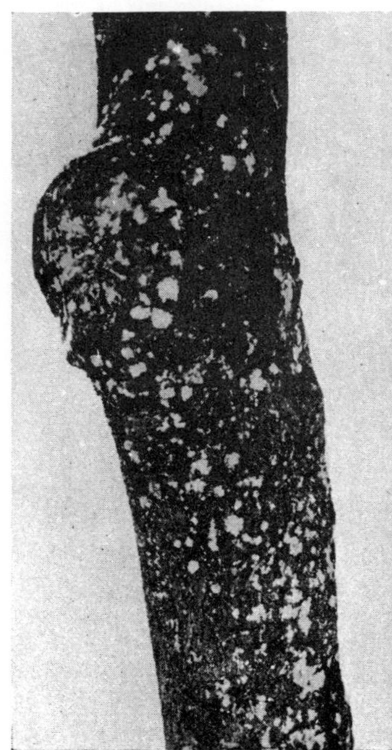

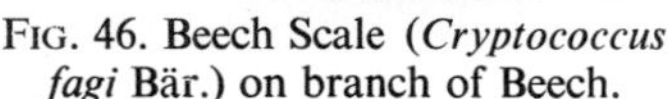

FIG. 46. Beech Scale (*Cryptococcus fagi* Bär.) on branch of Beech.

FIG. 47. Fluted Scale (*Icerya purchasi* Mask.) on Mimosa.

Scale insects which are generally found only under glass in this country include (*j*) the Oleander Scale (*Aspidiotus hederae* Vall.) on the leaves and shoots of oleander, acacia, Japanese laurel, ornamental asparagus, etc. (Fig. 106); (*k*) the Aspidistra Scale (*Hemichionaspis aspidistrae* Sign.) on the leaves and stems of palms, aspidistra and some ferns; (*l*) the Fig Mussel Scale (*Lepidosaphes ficus* Sign.) on the foliage and stems of figs; (*m*) the Fluted Scale (*Icerya purchasi* Mask.) on the stems and leaf bases of acacia and citrus trees (Fig. 47); (*n*) the Glasshouse Orthezia (*Orthezia insignis* Doug.) feeds on the stems and foliage of a wide range of plants in temperate and tropical houses; (*o*) the Cushion Scale (*Pulvinaria floccifera* Westw.) is found in greenhouses and conservatories on the leaves and stems of camellias and orchids (Fig. 109); (*p*) the Hemispherical Scale (*Saissetia coffeae* Wlk.) is a polyphagous species particularly injurious to ornamental asparagus, ferns, fig, oleander, etc.

FIG. 48. Scurfy Scale (*Aulacaspis rosae* Bouché) on Rose.

FIG. 49. Apple shoot severed by Apple Twig Cutter (*Rhynchites coeruleus* Deg.). (*Photograph from A. M. Massee, 'Pests of Fruits and Hops'.*)

Control. (1) Where practicable, e.g. on ornamentals, wash the plants with dilute nicotine-soap solution, using a sponge, brush or scraper to remove the scales. (2) Prune out heavily-infested shoots and branches. (3) Spray 2 or 3 times at 14-day intervals with malathion, parathion, or a nicotine-white oil emulsion (see Appendix V, p. 216). (With orchids it is advisable to test the spray on a specimen of each type or on a single leaf before applying it generally. Malathion has been used successfully on cymbidiums. Nicotine-white oil can be used on all orchids with the exception of cattleyas.) (4) On deciduous trees and shrubs a tar oil wash should be applied when the plants are completely dormant.

STEMS SEVERED

The type of injury to which reference is made here is exemplified by (*a*) the Apple Twig Cutter (*Rhynchites coeruleus* Deg.), (May–June), a weevil which partly or completely severs the shoots of apple,

FIG. 50. Injury to stems of Strawberry blossom trusses by Strawberry Rhynchites (*Caenorhinus germanicus* Herbst.). (*Photograph by East Malling Research Station.*)

pear and plum after ovipositing in the upper portion. This hangs down and eventually falls to the ground carrying within it the tunnelling larva (Fig. 49). (*b*) The Strawberry Rhynchites (*Caenorhinus germanicus* Herbst.), (May–June), is occasionally a serious pest in strawberry plantations where it lays eggs in the stems of leaves and blossom trusses. These are then gnawed below the egg-laying site and they wither and break off (Fig. 50). The weevil also attacks helianthemum, geum, blackberry, loganberry and raspberry in a similar fashion. (*c*) The Strawberry Blossom Weevil (*Anthonomus rubi* Herbst.), (Apr.–May), severs the bud stalks of strawberry and *Rubus* species after laying its eggs in the flower buds.

Control. (1) Collect and burn all shoots, etc., severed by the weevils. (2) Spray or dust with DDT at the pink bud stage (apples), when the first flower truss is formed (strawberry), when the green flower buds develop (raspberry, blackberry, etc.). Repeat the treatment 14 days later if severe attacks are expected.

STEMS AND SHOOTS TUNNELLED

The number of insect species that bore into the stems and shoots of plants is very large, and space will permit only the briefest review of the more important pests of garden plants.

The damage due to stem-borers is that the amount of conductive tissue is reduced, with subsequent wilting, bleeding and gumming.

The underground as well as the aerial portions of the stems of plants are tunnelled, and the wounds thus made are invaded by secondary agents (e.g. Millipedes below ground), and bacterial and fungal organisms both below and above ground, all of which extend the initial injury and may mask the effect of the primary agent.

Among the *Lepidoptera* are found a host of Moth species, the larvae of which bore galleries in stems, e.g. (*a*) the Goat Moth (*Cossus cossus* L.), which attacks the trunks of fruit trees, especially apple and cherry, and many broad-leaved trees, e.g. ash, beech, elm, poplar and willow; (*b*) the Wood Leopard Moth (*Zeuzera pyrina* L.), which is a more serious fruit pest, attacking the branches of apple, cherry, pear and plum, and a number of forest and ornamental trees, e.g. ash, birch, oak, lilac and rhododendron (Fig. 51); and (*c*) the Hornet Moth (*Sesia apiformis* Clerck), which attacks a number of trees, more especially poplar, burrowing in the trunk and main roots. The activities of these caterpillars result in wilting and death of the affected tree or branch, but an infestation may sometimes be noticed before great damage is done by the appearance of frass and wood-dust on the ground under the entrance of the tunnel.

Control. (1) Where practicable prune badly-attacked branches back to undamaged wood and burn the prunings. (2) If the trunk is severely damaged grub out the tree and burn it. (3) Where the attack is slight the caterpillar may be hooked out or stabbed by a pointed wire thrust into the tunnel, or (4) may be killed by placing in the holes crystals of paradichlorobenzene, a piece of sodium cyanide or cotton wool soaked in carbon disulphide, plugging the entrance afterwards with clay or putty.

The larvae of the Pith Moth (*Blastodacna atra* Haw.), (Aug.–June), burrow into the stems of the blossom trusses, young shoots and spurs of apple. The damage is usually first noticed in May and June when the leaves and flowers on attacked shoots wither and die. Weak lateral shoots may be produced as a result of the death of the terminal shoot.

Control. (1) Burn all prunings. (2) Hand-pick and burn all infested shoots and blossom trusses. (3) Spray with DDT in mid-July and again at the beginning of August, adding an acaricide to prevent a build-up of Fruit Tree Red Spider Mite.

FIG. 51. Caterpillar of Wood Leopard Moth (*Zeuzera pyrina* L.) tunnelling in Rhododendron.

FIG. 52. Black Currant shoots tunnelled by caterpillars of Currant Clearwing Moth (*Aegeria tipuliformis* Clerck).

FIG. 53. Pine shoots tunnelled by caterpillars of the Pine Shoot Moth (*Rhyacionia buoliana* Schiff.).

The Currant Clearwing (*Aegeria tipuliformis* Clerck), (Aug.–May), is a common pest of currants, especially blacks in old plantations where the larvae tunnel in the shoots causing them to die (Fig. 52).

Control. (1) Prune off and burn all wilted shoots in the summer. (2) In winter bend the shoots over carefully. Those weakened by tunnelling will snap and should be cut back to clean wood and burned. (3) Spray with DDT in late May or early June to kill the moth while egg-laying. (4) On young non-fruiting plantations parathion may be applied from mid-June to early July to kill the eggs.

The Currant Shoot Borer (*Lampronia capitella* Clerck), (Apr.–May), makes tunnels in the young shoots of currants in the spring.

Control. See 'Buds Tunnelled', p. 98.

The Raspberry Shoot Moth (*Lampronia rubiella* Bjerk.), (Apr.–May), is occasionally a destructive pest of raspberries and blackberries. The larvae feed at first in the plug of the fruit, but cause little injury at this period. They then overwinter in cocoons among rubbish around the stools, and in cracks in support-canes, and in spring crawl up the canes and burrow into the shoots causing them to wither.

Control. (1) Pick off and burn all infested shoots as they appear in spring. (2) Clear all rubbish from the stools, cut out old canes and burn them, and discard cracked and decayed supports. (3) In late February apply an 8 per cent. tar oil wash thoroughly to the soil along the rows and to the bases of the canes and supports. (4) If tar oil treatment is omitted spray the canes with DDT in early April.

The Pine-Shoot Moth (*Rhyacionia buoliana* Schiff.), (May–Aug.), is a disfiguring pest on Scots and some other pines by reason of the shoot-tunnelling caterpillars, which burrow into the buds and cause them to wilt and shrivel (Fig. 53). Injury to the 'leader' results in the production of a profusion of small shoots giving the tree a 'witches' broom' type of deformation, and completely spoils the shape of specimen trees.

Control. (1) Remove and burn all wilted shoots while the larva is within the tunnel. (2) Spray or dust with DDT at the beginning of August and again 3 weeks later to destroy the young caterpillars before they enter the buds.

Such methods are practicable only with small specimen trees.

The Rosy Rustic Moth (*Gortyna micacea* Esp.), (May–July), occurs periodically in certain localities, especially on potatoes grown in newly-converted grass and waste land. The larvae tunnel in the haulms of potato and in the stems of tomato, rhubarb, raspberry and iris, as well as in many weeds, e.g. docks, plantains and various sedges.

Control. (1) Clean cultivation, and the control of weed hosts in and around cultivated areas; and (2) collecting and burning infested haulms and stems.

Of Coleopterous insects, there are numerous species that, in their larval and/or adult stages, either bore into the stem (e.g. Longhorn Beetles and Shot-Hole Borers) or confine their attention to the bark and cambium (e.g. Bark Beetles).

Wireworms are primarily subterranean feeders, but they on occasion tunnel into the stems, both above and below ground, of carnations, chrysanthemums and tomatoes.

Control. See 'Bulbs Tunnelled', p. 38.

The Cabbage Stem Flea Beetle (*Psylliodes chrysocephala* L.), (May–Sept.), attacks cruciferous crops, chiefly brassicas. The larvae tunnel in the stems and succulent mid-ribs of cabbage and cauliflower causing the plants to wither and die.

Control. (1) Practise rotation to avoid growing successive brassica crops in infested ground. (2) Destroy stumps and any cruciferous weeds in the vicinity of the plot. (3) Lift and destroy the infested plants as soon as wilting is observed. (4) Spray or dust young plants in autumn with lindane. (5) Infested ground should be dressed with aldrin dust when preparing it for the next crop.

Another pest which tunnels in the stems of brassicas and also wallflowers is the Cabbage Stem Weevil (*Ceuthorrhyncus quadridens* Panz.), (May–June). The damage done is similar to that caused by the Cabbage Stem Flea Beetle.

Control. (1) Spray or dust seedlings with lindane at 14-day intervals from early April onwards to kill the adults, or (2) dip infested plants in lindane before planting out.

The Longhorn or Cerambycid Beetles are all stem-borers, some attacking broad-leaved trees (especially oak), some confining their attacks to conifers (especially pine), while others are chiefly important as pests of seasoned timber. In the majority of cases the trees attacked are already unhealthy due to faulty root action, fungus attack, etc., the species usually found attacking trees in gardens are: (*a*) the Small Poplar Borer (*Saperda populnea* L.), which gives rise to gall-like swellings on the branches and stems of young poplars, and (*b*) the Wasp Beetle (*Clytus arietis* L.), whose larvae tunnel into oak, beech and, occasionally, wistaria.

Control. Cut out and burn infested branches, and paint over with Stockholm tar wounds made by the boring grubs.

The Bark Beetles (*Scolytidae*) are extremely important pests of a great variety of trees and shrubs, both deciduous and evergreen. The Family is divided into two groups, viz.: (I) the true Bark Beetles or 'Engraver Beetles'—so named on account of the intricate patterns of their galleries—and (II) the 'Ambrosia', Pinhole or Shot-Hole Borer Beetles.

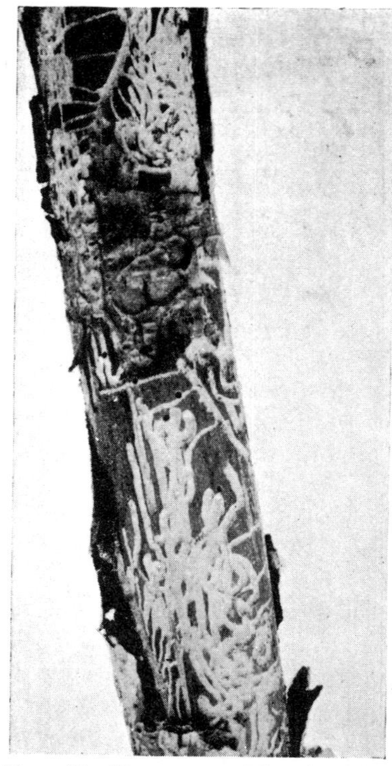

Fig. 54. Damage to Pine by Pine Shoot Beetle (*Myelophilus piniperda* L.).

(I) Bark Beetles are in most instances secondary agents and attack trees that are unhealthy and have lost vigour as a result of one or more of the following factors: unsuitable soil and/or site, unfavourable climatic conditions, mechanical injuries, careless and too drastic pruning operations, lightning damage and fire scorch, severe defoliation due to leaf-eating insects, and to infections of bacterial and fungal organisms. Attention should be paid to maintaining trees and shrubs in health by practising correct cultural operations — direct, nutritional and mechanical.

The chief pests of fruit and ornamental trees and shrubs are: (*a*) the Large Elm Bark Beetle (*Scolytus scolytus* F.), which is a destructive pest of elms, both specimen, avenue and park trees; (*b*) the Large and Small Fruit-tree Bark Beetles (*S. mali* Bech. and *S. rugulosus* Ratz.), which are both pests of fruit trees, more especially apple, and may be distributed with trees from infested areas; and (*c*) the Pine Shoot Beetle (*Myelophilus piniperda* L.), which is the commonest and one of the most important of the Pine Bark Beetles attacking Scots pine (Fig. 54).

(II) The Ambrosia Beetles are so named on account of the presence of the Ambrosia fungus that grows in their galleries, and without which the beetles are unable to exist. The two common species are: (*a*) the Shot-Hole Borer (*Anisandrus dispar* F.), which is chiefly found attacking apple and plum trees (Fig. 55), in which the beetle and larval galleries extend throughout the wood; and (*b*) the Flat-Celled

FIG. 55. Exit holes (*left*) and internal damage (*right*) of Shot-Hole Borer (*Anisandrus dispar* F.) on Plum.

Shot-Hole Borer (*A. saxeseni* Ratz.), which usually bores into the sapwood and the gallery terminates in a large chamber.

Control. The following principles of plant protection should be applied to orchards, arboretums, shrub borders and pinetums to avoid outbreaks of Bark Beetles. (1) Provide adequate and effective drainage in damp and heavy soils. (2) Mulch trees that are growing in dry, light soils subjected to drought conditions. (3) Supply plants with complete food requirements to prevent nutritional disorders. (4) Remove cleanly, and burn, all dead and dying limbs and shoots, and collect and burn all prunings. (5) Paint over all cut surfaces with white lead paint. (6) Bark all large branches and stems after cutting. (7) Keep trees and shrubs free from infection of disease organisms, and control infestations of sucking insects and leaf-defoliators. (8) Paint infested areas of trunks and branches with 10 per cent. tar oil, ensuring that this material does not come in contact with leaves and young growth.

Among Dipterous insects are found a large number of Flies whose larvae are destructive to the underground and aerial stems of garden plants.

Leatherjackets, like Wireworms, are mainly root-feeders, but they also attack the underground stems of a great variety of plants, both vegetables and ornamentals.

Control. See 'Bulbs Tunnelled', p. 40.

The larvae of the Frit Fly (*Oscinella frit* L.), (May–June), attack sweet corn, burrowing into the succulent tissues of the growing point, which results in the formation of stunted and twisted leaves, darker in colour than the normal leaves. In severe attacks the growth of the main shoot is stopped altogether.

Control. (1) Spray with DDT when the plant has two or three leaves. (2) Where the fly is regularly troublesome attacks can be avoided by sowing early under cloches which can be removed in the latter part of May, or by sowing in pots in a greenhouse and planting out at the end of May. Also, plants sown out of doors at the end of May are less liable to attack.

The Carnation Fly (*Delia brunnescens* Zett.), (Apr.–Oct.), is during its larval stage destructive to the leaves and stems of carnations and sweet williams, both under glass and in the open. The larvae at first mine the leaves, later burrowing down into the stem and devouring the pith. The attacked plant wilts and finally dies.

Control. (1) Pick off and burn all mined leaves as soon as the presence of the pest is detected. (2) Remove and burn all heavily infested plants. (3) Spray or dust with DDT or BHC in September and October to kill egg-laying females.

The Bean Seed Fly (*D. cilicrura* Rond.), (May–June), tunnels in the developing stem of bean seedlings, destroying the plumules and making them blind and snake-headed. Attacked seedlings usually collapse and die.

Control. See 'Seeds attacked after Sowing', p. 199.

The Cabbage Root Fly (*Erioischia brassicae* Bouché), (Apr.–Sept.), is a primary pest of brassicas, principally cabbage and cauliflower. The larvae are chiefly root-feeders, but they also tunnel up the stems below and above soil level.

Control. See 'Roots Eaten', p. 53.

Of Hymenopterous insects, the stem-feeding groups are found in certain Sawflies and in the Siricid and Xiphydriid Wood-Wasps. The larvae of the latter group are wood-borers and, like Bark Beetles, generally choose trees weakened in health.

STEMS WITH WOOLLY MASSES

The presence of dense, white, woolly patches on the stems and branches of fruit and ornamental trees, and on various conifers, indicates the presence of some member of the *Hemiptera*.

Certain species of *Adelges* form woolly patches on the stems and shoots of conifers, where they destroy the foliage and lower the vitality of the plants. These include (*a*) *A. abietis* L., (Apr.–May), on spruce and larch; (*b*) *A. nordmannianae* Eck., (Apr.), and (*c*) *A. piceae* Ratz. on silver fir; (*d*) *Pineus pini* Börn., (Apr.–May), on Scots pine; (*e*) *P. strobi* Macq., (Apr.–May), on Weymouth pine. *A. abietis* is also responsible for the formation of 'pineapple' galls on the shoots of spruce in the early summer.

Control. (1) Spray with BHC during the first week of April, repeating the application 3 weeks later if necessary. (2) Remove and burn galls on spruce before July.

The Woolly Aphid (*Eriosoma lanigerum* Hausm.), (Apr.–Sept.), produces dense masses of woolly material on the stems of apple, *Pyrus* species, hawthorn and *Cotoneaster horizontalis* (Fig. 56). Grafts and pruned surfaces are particularly liable to attack and areas where colonies have fed may become abnormally swollen and split.

Control. (1) Spray at the pink bud stage with BHC to which a succinate spreader has been added. (2) Where infestations develop after petal fall spray with malathion, demeton-methyl, rogor or diazinon. (3) Isolated colonies may be eradicated by painting with 10 per cent. tar oil or BHC. (4) As an alternative to spraying the fruit grower may wish to introduce the Woolly Aphid Parasite (*Aphelinus mali* Hald.) into infested orchards.

Certain other pests produce wool-like masses on stems, for instance, the Beech Scale (*Cryptococcus fagi* Bär.), which infests the stems and main branches of beech trees (Fig. 46). Little damage to the tree results where the pest is lightly distributed, but high populations of the insects may kill a tree over a period of years—the effect being cumulative owing to the constant abstraction of sap.

FIG. 56. Colonies of Woolly Aphid (*Eriosoma lanigerum* Hausm.) on Cotoneaster.

FIG. 57. Colony of Glasshouse Mealy Bug (*Planococcus citri* Risso) on Codiaeum. (*Shell Photograph.*)

Control. (1) Spray forcibly or brush thoroughly the infested stems and branches during the dormant season with a tar oil wash. (2) In spring spray with malathion, parathion, or a nicotine-white oil emulsion (see Appendix V, p. 216).

Other Scale Insects which produce woolly material on stems are: (*a*) the Cushion Scale (*Pulvinaria floccifera* Westw.) (Fig. 109); (*b*) the Woolly Currant Scale (*P. vitis* L.) (Fig. 45); (*c*) the Fluted Scale (*Icerya purchasi* Mask.) (Fig. 47) and (*d*) the Glasshouse Orthezia (*Orthezia insignis* Doug.).

Control. See 'Stems Scaly', p. 77.

Mealy Bugs are closely related to Scale Insects but, instead of being protected by a scale, their bodies are covered with white woolly-looking wax. They are also active throughout their entire life-cycle, and suck the sap from the stems and leaves of a wide variety of plants, mainly in greenhouses. These pests also have a habit of hiding within curled leaves, in the leaf-sheaths and in the bud axils. They excrete honeydew which covers the leaves and attracts Sooty Moulds. Infested plants lose vigour and their leaves may turn yellow and drop off. The more important species are: (*a*) the Currant Mealy Bug (*Pseudococcus fragilis* Brain) which feeds on a wide variety of greenhouse plants and may also occur out-of-doors on flowering currants, ceanothus, laburnum and other plants; (*b*) the Glasshouse Mealy Bug (*Planococcus citri* Risso) which is very common in greenhouses on ferns, ornamental asparagus, palms, vines, etc. (Fig. 57); (*c*) the Vine Mealy Bug (*P. maritimus* Ehrh.) which feeds on azaleas, amaryllis, vines, etc.

Control. (1) On deciduous woody plants (vines, peach, etc.) apply a tar oil wash in December. Vine rods should be scraped beforehand. (2) On growing plants spray with malathion, parathion or nicotine-white oil emulsion 2 or 3 times at 14-day intervals. (3) Small isolated groups which are hidden from sprays may be painted with a solution of malathion or nicotine-white oil.

CHAPTER FIVE

Buds

Buds Rendered Blind. Buds Eaten. Buds Galled. Buds Proliferated. Buds Swollen. Buds Tunnelled.

A BUD is a rudimentary shoot, leaf or flower, and any injury that it receives will result in checking the growth of the plant in some form or another and in reducing the production of foliage leaves and flowers. The buds in most woody plants are covered with budscales which protect the growing point from severe weather conditions and against loss of water. Beneath these scales shelter is afforded to such microscopic pests as Gall Mites (e.g. Pear Leaf Blister Mite, *Eriophyes piri* Nal. on pear).

While some pests attack the terminal bud, others injure the axillary or side-buds, with the result that the buds are rendered 'blind' or growth is stimulated to such a degree that lateral growth is encouraged to an abnormal extent, resulting in proliferation and in such outgrowths as 'witches' brooms'.

The designation 'Bud Pests' includes some creatures not primarily concerned in bud injuries, though buds may be injured by them during some part of their life-cycle, e.g. the Pine Shoot Moth and other shoot-borers that commence as bud-borers and develop into stem- and shoot-tunnellers. The Black Currant ('Big Bud') and Hazel Gall Mites and the Apple Bud Weevil are true bud-feeders, while the Clay-coloured Weevil and the Earwig, for instance, are not dependent upon buds as they feed on other parts of plants.

Attention is drawn to the Ministry of Agriculture's Fruit Tree Spraying Charts, Bulletin 137, which illustrate the various stages of bud development in hardy fruits, and serve as a guide to the fruit-grower and enable him to avoid injury to buds by choosing the correct periods of growth for the application of spray fluids.

BUDS RENDERED BLIND

Arrested development is the outcome of 'blindness' in buds, which may be due to a definite injury (mechanical or biological, i.e. pest damage), to some nutritional or functional disorder, or to a general hereditary weakness in the stock.

The chief pests concerned with this type of damage are:

(*a*) The Black Currant Gall Mite (*Cecidophyopsis ribis* Nal.), (Apr.–May), though giving rise to the condition known as 'Big Bud' in black currants, causes little enlargement in the buds of red and white currants and in gooseberry, which turn brown and shrivel up, and is often thought to be due to small birds 'working' the buds.

Control. See 'Buds Swollen', p. 96.

(*b*) Blindness of the buds of black currant may also be caused by the Leaf and Bud Eelworm (*Aphelenchoides ritzema-bosi* (Schwartz) Stein.) which invades the buds during the growing season. These buds usually die or develop very feebly the following spring. Serious damage is, however, confined to one or two varieties.

Control. No satisfactory control is known. Cuttings should not be taken from infested bushes.

(*c*) The Rhododendron Leafhopper (*Graphocephala coccinea* Forst.), (Apr.–Oct.), is an introduced insect which has increased in numbers in recent years. This increase has been accompanied by a rise in the incidence of 'Bud Blast', a disease of rhododendrons caused by the fungus *Pycnostysanus* (*Sporocybe*) *azaleae*, which causes the flower buds to turn brown and die. It is claimed that there is a significant association of the disease with the insect but the manner of transmission of the spores has not yet been demonstrated. Very little direct damage is done as a result of the insects feeding on the foliage.

Control. While the connection between the Rhododendron Leafhopper and 'Bud Blast' has not been conclusively established it has been shown that the spread of the disease can be checked by spraying with DDT emulsion at 14-day intervals from August to October, thereby eliminating the Leafhopper.

(*d*) The Tarnished Plant or 'Bishop' Bug (*Lygus rugulipennis* Popp.), (July–Oct.), pierces the flower buds of chrysanthemums and dahlias with its stylets and renders many blind. Those buds that are able to develop further result in malformed, one-sided blooms.

Control. See 'Flowers Distorted', p. 164.

(*e*) The Swede Midge (*Contarinia nasturtii* Kieff.), (June–Oct.), is a key pest of many brassicas, especially cabbage, turnip and swede, and gives rise to different types of injury, e.g. blind buds 'crinkle' or 'crumple' leaf, and 'many-necked' condition.

Control. (1) Practise crop rotation and keep land clear of cruciferous weeds. (2) Lift and destroy attacked plants as soon as detected.

(3) Spray the soil with aldrin or dieldrin at the end of May to kill emerging flies, or (4) spray the plants with DDT or lindane in early June to kill them before they lay their eggs. (5) Swedes may be planted around the edge of fields as a trap-crop, to be lifted and destroyed as soon as they are well infested. (6) In areas where the midge is prevalent sow late to avoid the worst attack in the early summer.

BUDS EATEN

The European Earwig (*Forficula auricularia* L.), (Aug.–Oct.), is frequently destructive to the buds of chrysanthemums, especially in glasshouses. It is a nocturnal feeder, hence its activities are often overlooked.

Control. See 'Flowers Eaten', p. 166.

The Nut Bud Moth (*Panoplia penkleriana* Fisch. v. Rösl.), (Sept.–May), attacks hazel, the buds and catkins of which are damaged by the caterpillars.

Control. (1) Apply an 8 per cent. tar oil wash in December or early January, or (2) spray with DDT when the damage is first seen.

Chafer Beetles, in particular the Garden Chafer (*Phyllopertha horticola* L.), (May–June), often do considerable damage by eating the flower buds of roses and other plants (Fig. 119).

Control. See 'Flowers Eaten', p. 169.

The Clay-coloured Weevil (*Otiorrhynchus singularis* L.), (Apr.–June), is partial in its adult stage to young apple grafts, which may be killed following the destruction of the buds, leaving the graft blind.

Control. (1) Apply a grease-band to the trunk to prevent the wingless weevils climbing up. (2) Paint the grafts with lead arsenate paste. (3) Other control measures are given under 'Bulbs Tunnelled', p. 39.

Birds, in particular bullfinches, chaffinches, tits and sparrows cause a great deal of damage by destroying the flower buds of fruit trees and bushes, especially pear, plum, damson, peach, cherry and gooseberry. The outer scales of the buds are usually stripped off and dropped on to the ground and the tender inner part picked out and eaten. Many ornamental plants are stripped in the same manner. These include forsythia, wistaria, ornamental *Prunus* and sweet pea.

Control. It is very difficult to prevent this type of damage. Some suggestions are given in Appendix III, p. 213.

BUDS GALLED

The Arabis Gall Midge (*Dasyneura alpestris* Kieff.), (June–Sept.), causes characteristic galling of the terminal bud of *Arabis albida* (Fig. 58). The effect is that side branches arise, or the flowering branch is malformed.

FIG. 58. *Arabis albida* with buds galled by Arabis Midge (*Dasyneura alpestris* Kieff.).

Control. (1) Spray with parathion in early June and again in early July. (2) Remove and burn galled buds as they appear. (3) Dress the soil with aldrin dust after lifting infested plants.

BUDS PROLIFERATED

The production of a profusion of buds on such plants as strawberry and phloxes is generally associated with eelworm attack. The condition known as 'Cauliflower' disease of strawberries is the result of an infestation by Leaf and Bud Eelworms (*Aphelenchoides fragariae* (Ritz. Bos) Christie or *A. ritzema-bosi* (Schwartz) Stein.) in association with the bacterium *Corynebacterium fascians* Dow. The leaf and flower stalks are severely stunted and swollen and the leaf blades are suppressed, finally to give the plants a cauliflower appearance (Fig. 59).

Control. See 'Foliage Puckered', p. 120.

FIG. 59. 'Cauliflower' disease symptoms on Strawberry. (*Photograph by East Malling Research Station.*)

The Stem and Bulb Eelworm (*Ditylenchus dipsaci* (Kühn) Filipj.) may be indirectly concerned with proliferation of the basal buds on herbaceous oenotheras and phloxes.

Control. See 'Foliage Puckered', p. 120.

BUDS SWOLLEN

The Black Currant Gall Mite (*Cecidophyopsis ribis* Nal.), (July–May), produces the condition known as 'Big Bud' (Fig. 60), and is the best known and most widespread pest on black currants. The infested buds swell to about twice the size of normal buds and are almost globular. Usually the buds dry up and shrivel, but if only lightly infested they may produce small distorted leaves. Infested bushes may also suffer from the disease 'Reversion' which is transmitted by the mites.

Control. (1) Bushes affected by 'Reversion' should be grubbed out and destroyed. (2) As the first flower opens, spray non-fruiting bushes with a fluoroacetamide or endrin solution to which has been added a succinate wetter. Repeat the treatment 3 weeks later. (3) To keep the mite in check during subsequent years spray with 2 per cent. lime sulphur just before blossom and with a 1 per cent. solution 3 weeks later. (4) In western districts where the bushes are less able to tolerate sulphur, and in the case of 'sulphur-shy' varieties, applications of 2 per cent. refined petroleum oil plus a wetter are

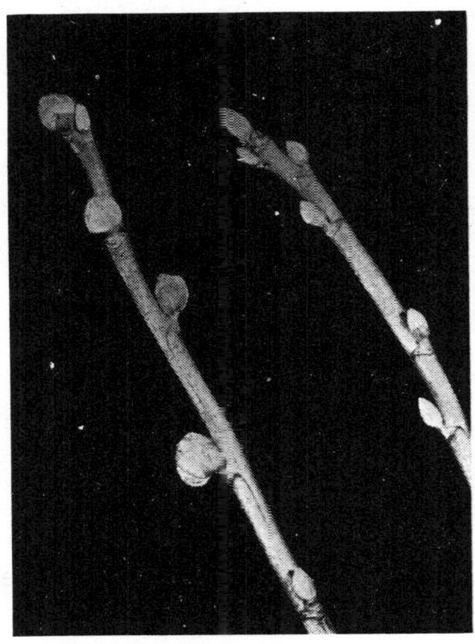

FIG. 60. *Left:* Swollen Black currant buds due to Black Currant Gall Mite (*Cecidophyopsis ribis* Nal.). *Right*: Healthy shoot. (*Shell Photograph.*)

claimed to be effective. (5) Ensure that cuttings come from clean stock. *Caution.* Both fluoroacetamide and endrin leave poisonous residues in fruit. If the former is used in private gardens the fruit should be stripped off to prevent it being eaten by children and animals.

The Nut or Hazel Gall Mite (*Phytoptus avellanae* Nal.), (Aug.–May), which is distinct from the previous species, causes the buds of cob nut and hazel to swell, but there is no evidence that its presence has any adverse effect on the crop.

Control. When the attack has become very severe spray with wettable sulphur at weekly intervals from mid-May to mid-June.

The Yew Gall Mite (*Cecidophyopsis psilaspis* Nal.), (May–Oct.), causes similar injury to the buds of yew. The terminal buds are infested and a great amount of damage may be done to young hedge plants and to nursery plants.

Control. (1) Handpick and burn enlarged buds in mid-May. (2)

Burn all prunings from infested plants. (3) Spraying in late April with endrin or fluoroacetamide may give control, but so far these substances have not been tested against this mite.

BUDS TUNNELLED

The larvae of the Bud Moth (*Spilonota ocellana* F.) burrow into the buds of many fruits usually in the early spring, apple, cherry and blackberry being the chief plants affected. The attacked buds usually fail to open. Later the larvae feed on the developing leaves and blossom trusses, which are spun together.

Control. (1) Spray with DDT at the green cluster stage. (2) Where damage is noted after blossoming hand-pick and destroy the infested blossom clusters, or (3) spray with DDT, adding an acaricide to prevent a build-up of Fruit Tree Red Spider Mite.

The Raspberry Shoot Moth (*Lampronia rubiella* Bjerk.), (Apr.–May), produces damage resembling that of the Currant Shoot-Borer. The larvae feed at first in the young fruit, but the injury at this time is negligible. Following hibernation they bore into the shoots, which wither and die. Both raspberries and blackberries are attacked.

Control. See 'Stems Tunnelled', p. 84.

The Pith Moth (*Blastodacna atra* Haw.), (Nov.–June), is not a true bud pest, although the entrance holes of the larvae are found frequently in the region of apple buds. The larvae feed beneath the bark and destroy the growth and blossom trusses, so that the injury is apparent in spring when the wilted shoots and shrunken trusses are noted.

Control. See 'Stems Tunnelled', p. 83.

The Red Bud Borer (*Thomasiniana oculiperda* Rübs.), (Aug.–Oct.), is frequently destructive to the buds of newly-budded apples and roses. The small red maggots of this Gall Midge live between the two layers of cambium, feeding on the sap.

Control. An attack may be avoided by thoroughly coating the buds, after tying, with petroleum jelly.

CHAPTER SIX

Foliage

Foliage Aphid-infested. Foliage Blistered. Foliage Coated with Honeydew and Sooty Moulds. Foliage Discoloured: I—Black or Brown Areas; II—Bluish; III—Bronzed; IV—Mottled; V—Reddish Discoloration; VI—Rusted; VII—Silvered; VIII—Spotted; IX—Veins Discoloured; X—Yellowed. Foliage Distorted: I—Bloated; II—Curled; III—Puckered; IV—Rolled; V—With Swellings; VI—Twisted. Foliage Dropping. Foliage Eaten: I—Clean-cut Holes; II—Epidermis Eaten; III—Perforated; IV—Notched. Foliage Excessively Hairy. Foliage with Frothy Masses. Foliage Galled. Foliage Mined. Foliage Narrowed. Foliage Ragged. Foliage Scaly. Foliage Scarred. Foliage Severed. Foliage Spun Together. Foliage Wilting. Foliage with Woolly Masses.

A TYPICAL leaf consists of the blade or lamina, the stalk or petiole —absent in sessile leaves—and the leaf base which connects the leaf to the stem. Great variations exist in the form, size and structure of foliage leaves. The chief function is that of food manufacture, while the subsidiary functions are those of respiration and transpiration.

The structure consists of a layer of assimilatory cells bounded by a protective epidermis and supported by vascular tissue in the form of a mid-rib and a framework of veins. The epidermis, which is composed of thick-walled cells, is perforated by pores or stomata to allow the free interchange of gaseous and water vapours.

All other parts of the plant subsist on the work of the leaf, food production taking place in the chlorophyll-filled palisade tissue situated beneath the upper epidermis.

The effect on the plant by leaf-infesting pests varies according to the type of injury, for instance:

(1) When the amount of assimilative tissue is reduced, food formation and growth is hindered, with the result that the vigour of the plant is lowered through the strain exerted upon the host in its effort to produce new growth. Leaf-eating insects (e.g. *Phyllobius* Weevils, and the larvae of Moths and Sawflies), leaf-rollers and leaf-tyers (e.g. the larvae of many Tortricid Moths) and leaf-curlers (e.g. the Cherry, Peach and Plum Leaf-curling Aphids) are responsible for this type of damage.

(2) The passage of elaborated food materials within the leaf is hindered or ceases altogether, and assimilative tissue is reduced, by leaf-mining insects, belonging to the Orders *Coleoptera* (Beetles and

Weevils), *Lepidoptera* (chiefly Tineid Moths), *Diptera* (Agromyzid, Phytomyzid and Anthomyid Flies), and *Hymenoptera* (certain Sawflies).

(3) There is an accumulation of elaborated food materials due to excessive stimulation set up by gall-forming mites and insects (e.g. Gall Midges and Gall Wasps or Cynipids).

(4) Cell sap and chlorophyll are abstracted, with the result that the leaf wilts, or becomes discoloured or mottled, or falls prematurely. This is apparent on plants attacked by Red Spider Mites, Capsid Bugs, Leafhoppers, Aleyrodids, Aphids and Coccids.

(5) The flow of available food is reduced through the severance of the veins and mid-rib or the petiole, and the tapping of the conductive and vascular tissue of the leaf by Capsid Bugs and Aphids.

(6) The amount of assimilatory tissue is reduced by the presence of honeydew excreted by Aleyrodids, Aphids and Coccids, this falling on the leaf and choking the stomata, thus preventing the normal functions of respiration and transpiration.

(7) The growth of seedlings is checked by insects (e.g. Aphids on carrot and Flea Beetles on various cruciferous crops), which feed on the cotyledons. The seed-leaves act either as store-houses for the food of the growing plant, or as ordinary foliage leaves by carrying on the work of assimilation.

FOLIAGE APHID-INFESTED

Aphids will attack the leaves and shoots of most plants. Apart from the harm they do by sucking the sap these pests may also transmit virus diseases, and bacterial and fungal organisms can gain entry to the plant tissues through the feeding wounds. Infested leaves may become distorted or galled, and the stomata may be blocked up by the honeydew excreted by the aphids. Honeydew also encourages the growth of sooty moulds which, though harmless, detract from the appearance of the plants (Col. Fig. II). The principal species responsible for these conditions are discussed under the appropriate headings (see 'Foliage Blistered', p. 101; 'Foliage Discoloured', p. 102; 'Foliage Coated with Honeydew', p. 101; 'Foliage Curled', p. 117).

Control (1) Spray the infested plants, if possible, before the leaves become distorted, with DDT emulsion, lindane, nicotine, TEPP, malathion, parathion, or a systemic insecticide. On fruit trees applications of lindane or DDT emulsion should be made early, between the bud-burst and green cluster stages. Currants should be sprayed at the grape stage with DDT emulsion. On other plants spray as soon as an infestation is seen. (2) Over-wintering eggs can be killed on deciduous trees and shrubs by spraying during the dormant season with tar oil or up to the bud-break stage with DNC-petroleum.

FOLIAGE BLISTERED

The Pear Leaf Blister Mite (*Eriophyes piri* Nal.), (Apr.–Aug.), produces small yellow or reddish pustules in the upper surface of pear leaves (Col. Fig. I) and, in severe infestations, on the fruitlets and their stalks, causing malformation and premature dropping of the fruit. The old blisters turn brown or black later in the season and are sometimes confused with Pear Scab. This species may also attack the foliage of apple, cotoneaster, mountain ash (rowan), white beam and wild service trees.

Control. (1) Where practicable hand-pick and burn the infested leaves as soon as they are detected. (2) Spray with lime-sulphur at the end of March.

There are several species of Gall Mites (*Eriophyidae*) which produce blisters similar to those on pear, on the leaves of such plants as elm (*Ulmus procera*), mountain ash (*Sorbus aucuparia*), maple (*Acer campestre*) and others. The pustules are considered unsightly when they occur on specimen trees, but they are economically unimportant. Such infestations are readily controlled, if desired, by lime-sulphur applications in February or March as for the Pear Leaf Blister Mite.

Several species of Aphids produce not only leaf-curl (see 'Foliage Curled', p. 117), but also blistering of the foliage. The more common species are: the Rosy Leaf-curling Aphid (*Dysaphis devecta* Wlk.), (May–July), and the Currant Blister Aphid (*Cryptomyzus ribis* L.), (May–June), which cause red blistering on the leaves of apple and currants respectively.

Control. See 'Foliage with Reddish Discoloration', p. 110.

The leaf-mining larvae of certain Anthomyiid Flies and the larvae of some Tineid Moths (e.g. *Coleophora* Casebearers) are stated to produce blistered foliage, but, as the term is not applicable to the type of injury set up by these larvae, they are considered under the heading 'Foliage Mined' (p. 150).

FOLIAGE COATED WITH HONEYDEW AND SOOTY MOULDS

It is frequently noticed that the foliage of plants infested with Aphids (Plant-lice), Psyllids (Suckers), Aleyrodids (Whiteflies) and

Coccids (Scale Insects and Mealy Bugs) becomes sticky and, later, covered with a growth of non-parasitic fungi, known as Sooty Moulds (Col. Fig. II). Such insects excrete quantities of honeydew, so that the upper surfaces of the leaves are drenched, resulting in a marked reduction in the normal functions of the leaves, namely, assimilation and respiration. This type of injury is especially prevalent under glasshouse conditions, and melon and tomato plants in particular when infested with Glasshouse Whitefly (*Trialeurodes vaporariorum* Westw.) suffer as a result of the continual excretion of honeydew by the larvae or 'scales', and the subsequent growth of Sooty Moulds.

Many Aphids produce similar damage on plants, and such plants as broad beans infested with 'Black Fly' (*Aphis fabae* Scop.) are found to have the foliage coated with honeydew and Sooty Moulds.

Again, numerous species of Scale Insects and Mealy Bugs are responsible for this fouling of the foliage. The Soft Scale (*Coccus hesperidum* L.) excretes vast quantities of honeydew, which falls on the leaves of various citrus (orange-trees) and vines, and on many other plants grown in temperate and hot-houses. The European Brown or Peach Scale (*Eulecanium corni* Bouché) is responsible for such injury to the foliage of *Cotoneaster horizontalis*, currants, gooseberry, peach and other plants, while the Yew Scale (*E. pomeranicum* Kaw.) fouls the foliage of yew hedges with honeydew and its attendant growth of black moulds.

Control. See 'Foliage Aphid-infested', p. 100 (Aphids); 'Flowers Withered', p. 171 (Suckers); 'Foliage Mottled', p. 108 (Whiteflies); 'Stems Scaly', p. 77 (Scale); 'Stems with Woolly Masses', p. 91 (Mealy Bugs).

FOLIAGE DISCOLOURED

Discoloration of the leaves of plants may be the result of (*a*) unbalanced nutrition, such as a deficiency of manganese, too much lime, etc.; (*b*) functional disorders such as a faulty or unhealthy root system; (*c*) infection by viruses, fungi, or bacteria; (*d*) feeding by insects and other pests.

I—Black or Brown Areas

The Leaf and Bud Eelworm (*Aphelenchoides ritzema-bosi* (Schwartz) Stein.), (Jul.–Dec.), is a widespread pest of chrysanthemums both under glass and in the open. It invades the leaf tissue by climbing up the stem and entering the stomata. The lower leaves are attacked first, yellowish green blotches appearing between the veins (Col. Fig.

III). These later turn brown or black and the leaves wither and drop off (Fig. 61). The infestation travels upwards and the eelworms may

FIG. 61. *Chrysanthemum rubellum* showing lower foliage attacked by Leaf and Bud Eelworm (*Aphelenchoides ritzema-bosi* (Schwartz) Stein.).

FIG. 62. Leaf of Pteris fern showing symptoms of attack by Leaf and Bud Eelworm (*Aphelenchoides fragariae* (Ritz. Bos) Christie).

invade the flower buds resulting in blindness or in deformed undersized blooms. If the terminal buds are invaded the leaves around them may be misshapen and show brownish scarred areas generally near the petiole, caused by external feeding on the young leaves. *A. fragariae* (Ritz. Bos) Christie causes similar symptoms on a variety of plants including begonia and ferns (Fig. 62). For other hosts of both species see Appendix II, p. 212.

Control. (1) Collect and burn all withered leaves. (2) Infested plants should be subjected to hot-water treatment (see Appendix I, p. 207). (3) Do not plant any of the host plants (see Appendix II, p. 212) in infested ground for at least 3 years. (4) In greenhouses, soil, pots, boxes, etc., should be steam-sterilized and the humidity reduced as much as possible. (5) The stems of valuable plants may be banded with Vaseline to prevent eelworms climbing them. This should be done early in the season and renewed as the plant grows. (6) In nurseries the use of parathion will reduce infestation on chrysanthemums. The spray should be applied when the stools are boxed up and at 14-day intervals until the cuttings have been taken.

When the cuttings are established 3 applications should be given at 14-day intervals.

The terminal leaves of black currants turn black after having been twisted and curled by the larvae of the Black Currant Leaf Midge (*Dasyneura tetensi* Rübs.).

Control. See 'Foliage Curled', p. 118.

Blackening of foliage may also be caused by the growth of Sooty Moulds (*Cladosporium* spp. and *Capnodium* spp.) on the surface (Col. Fig. II). These moulds, though not pathogenic to the plant, may injure it by blocking the stomata. The moulds grow on honeydew which is deposited on the upper surfaces of the leaves by various insect pests infesting the plant. The insects concerned include Aphids, Whiteflies, Apple and Pear Suckers, Mealy Bugs and Scale Insects.

Control. (1) On valuable plants sponge off the Sooty Mould where possible with water in which soft soap has been dissolved. (2) Eradicate the insects responsible (see 'Flowers Withered', p. 171 (Suckers); 'Stems Aphid-infested', p. 100 (Aphids); 'Foliage Mottled', p. 108 (Whiteflies); 'Stems Scaly', p. 77 (Scales); 'Stems with Woolly Masses', p. 91 (Mealy Bugs).

II—Bluish

Abnormally blue foliage is usually an indication that the roots of the plant are affected, and the discoloration may be accompanied by wilting. The Cabbage Root Fly may be responsible for this condition in brassicas (see 'Roots Eaten', p. 53). On tomato plants the leaves develop a bluish tint when the roots are attacked by Symphylids, Woodlice, Wireworms, etc. (see 'Roots Eaten', p. 47), or by Potato Root and Root Knot Eelworms (see 'Roots Underdeveloped', p. 59, and 'Roots Galled', p. 54). Bluish discoloration may also occur as a result of exposure to cold or faulty hardening off.

III—Bronzed

The leaves of fruit trees, e.g. apples, plums, damsons and pears, which are infested by the Fruit Tree Red Spider Mite (*Panonychus ulmi* Koch), (May–Sept.), first become a dull yellowish green and then, in July and August, a brownish green with a silvered appearance (Col. Fig. IV). Badly attacked trees lose their leaves prematurely.

Control. (1) To kill over-wintering eggs on apple, plum, or damson, but *not* pear, apply a DNC-petroleum wash as late as possible up to the breaking stage. (2) If the mites are present in the early summer spray after petal fall with malathion arapthion, demeton-methyl, phenkaptone, TEPP or derris. Later infestations can be controlled with a summer ovicide such as chlorbenside, fenson (PCPBS) or chlorfenson (PCPCBS) applied in mid-June and again 3 weeks later, or with phenkaptone applied in the latter half of June and repeated if necessary.

Note: Owing to the risk of the development of resistance to any one type of insecticide it is advisable to vary the treatment, applying a summer ovicide one year and an organo-phosphorus compound, such as malathion, phenkaptone, or demeton-methyl, the next year. Late-summer applications of malathion or demeton-methyl should be given about the third week of June and again 10–14 days later.

The Spruce Mite (*Paratetranychus ununguis* Jac.) causes the foliage of spruce, cypress and other conifers to take on a bronze hue during the latter part of the summer (Col. Fig. VII).

Control. See 'Foliage Mottled', p. 106.

IV—Mottled

The destruction of the epidermal and sub-epidermal cells and the palisade tissue by mites (e.g. Red Spiders) and sucking insects (e.g. Aphids and Leafhoppers) results in a distinctive mottling of the foliage.

FIG. 63. Typical mottling by Glasshouse Red Spider Mite (*Tetranychus telarius* L.) on leaf of Dwarf Bean. (*Crown Copyright Photograph.*)

The Glasshouse Red Spider Mite (*Tetranychus telarius* L.), (Jan.–Dec.), produces a fine marbling of the leaf-surface through the punctures made by its mandibular stylets. This type of injury may be seen on many plants, especially cucumber, French beans, peach and potato, roses (especially Polyanthas), salvia, tomato, tropaeolum and violet, and on many weeds, especially convolvulus and dead-nettle (Fig. 63 and Col. Fig. VIII).

Control. (1) General cleanliness in the glasshouse including the sterilization of support canes in which the mites hibernate. (2) Where temperatures are 70° F. or above fumigate with azobenzene, repeating the treatment in 5–10 days, or with parathion, repeating after 10 days, or (3) spray once with phenkaptone; twice with a 14-day interval with TEPP, parathion or a summer ovicide; or 3 times at 7-day intervals with derris or summer white oil. (4) Eradicate or spray plants and weeds growing near the glasshouse.

The Spruce Mite (*Paratetranychus ununguis* Jac.), (June–Sept.), may be responsible for mottling on the needles and foliage of spruce, some *Pinus* species, juniper, cypress and other conifers (Col. Fig. VII). The foliage of infested plants becomes marked with yellow or orange-yellow spots which converge on one another, and later become reddish or brown in colour. Heavily attacked plants assume a greyish brown appearance and the needles are easily shed. The mites also spin copious webbing which covers the shoots.

Control. Spray with phenkaptone, demeton-methyl, malathion or parathion, repeating 14 days later and again if necessary.

Different strains of the Gooseberry Red Spider Mite (*Bryobia ribis* Thom.) also cause mottling on the leaves of ivy and other ornamental plants (see 'Foliage Yellowed', p. 114).

Thrips or 'Thunder-flies', of which there are numerous species, produce a pale mottling of the foliage on many hardy and tender garden plants. They also feed on flower petals, causing the petals to become mottled with white spots, and some species are responsible for the transmission of virus infections. (*a*) The Greenhouse Thrips (*Heliothrips haemorrhoidalis* Bouché) is common throughout the year on a wide variety of plants including azalea, palms, fuchsia, rose, orchids, arum, etc. It can be recognized by the fact that it deposits on the undersides of the leaves globules of reddish liquid which later turn black. (*b*) The Onion Thrips (*Thrips tabaci* Lind.) is a serious pest of many plants, both under glass and in the open, and feeds upon the foliage and flowers of cineraria, cucumber, tomato and other plants. It is also important as the chief vector of the virus which causes 'Spotted Wilt'. (*c*) The Gladiolus Thrips (*Taeniothrips simplex*

Mor.), (June–Sept.), is becoming a common pest on gladiolus in the home counties and appears to be increasing elsewhere. The insects hibernate on the stored corms (see 'Bulbs Discoloured Externally', p. 32) and are present on the shoots when they break through the soil. The leaves later become mottled with silvery white spots and streaks (Col. Fig. V). The flowers are also attacked, resulting in a white mottling of the petals (Fig. 112), and in severe infestations they may wither and fail to open. Numerous other plants suffer from infestations of Thrips, e.g. begonia, cyclamen, citrus, fuchsia, peas, broad beans, privet, roses, tobacco, tropaeolum, vines and amaryllis (or hippeastrum). In the last mentioned, the red stain on the foliage due to anthocyanin pigment is a symptom that may be readily recognized.

Control. Gladiolus Thrips only. (1) Dust or spray with lindane at weekly intervals as soon as the damage is seen. (2) Store corms at a

FIG. 64. Leaves of Pelargonium and Primula mottled by Glasshouse Leafhopper (*Erythroneura pallidifrons* Edw.).

temperature not above 50° F. and dust with DDT or flaked naphthalene.

Other Thrips. Spray with DDT, lindane, parathion or malathion, or apply any of the first three as smokes. Repeat the treatment 10–14 days later.

Leafhoppers or Jassids produce a distinctive mottling of the foliage, and infestations of these insects are apparent to the most casual observer by the presence of irregular, yellow areas on the leaves. Some plants, e.g. Labiates, are specially favoured hosts of these insects. The more important species are: (*a*) *Typhlocyba froggatti* Bak., (July–Sept.), which is a common pest on apple, plum and other trees. (*b*) The Glasshouse Leafhopper (*Erythroneura pallidifrons* Edw.), (Jan.–Dec.), is the most destructive species in glasshouses, attacking plants in their seedling and mature stages, including annuals of all kinds, French beans, chrysanthemums, fuchsias, *Nicotiana*, pelargoniums, primulas, salvias and tomatoes (Fig. 64). (*c*) The Rose Leafhopper (*Typhlocyba rosae* L.), (Apr.–Aug.), renders unsightly the foliage of bush and climbing roses on account of the extensive mottled and marbled areas, and causes premature leaf-fall (Col. Fig. VI). (*d*) *Cicadella melissae* Curt., (May–Oct.), produces severe leaf-mottle on chrysanthemums, and is partial to sage. (*e*) *C. aurata* Liv., (May–Oct.), often abounds on potato foliage and attacks chrysanthemums and such weeds as nettles, which serve as wild hosts to this species. (*f*) *Typhlocyba tenerrima* H.-S., (June–Oct.), causes severe leaf mottling on blackberries.

Control. (1) Spray with DDT, lindane, malathion, TEPP or parathion, repeating the application 14 days later. The ground under the plants should also be treated to kill any insects which drop off. On apples and other fruit spraying should be done in early July. (2) In greenhouses DDT, lindane, or parathion may be used as smokes.

The Rhododendron Bug (*Stephanitis rhododendri* Horv.) causes a yellow mottling on the upper surfaces of the leaves of rhododendrons (Fig. 65) as well as rusty or chocolate-brown marks on the under surfaces (see 'Foliage Rusted', p. 110).

Whiteflies (*Aleyrodidae*) feed as adults and nymphs on the undersides of the leaves of their host plants causing yellow spotting and mottling of the upper surfaces (Fig. 66). Apart from this damage the scale-like nymphs excrete copious honeydew which covers the upper leaf surfaces and provides a medium for the growth of Sooty Moulds. The most harmful species in this country are (*a*) the Glasshouse

Whitefly (*Trialeurodes vaporariorum* Westw.), (Jan.–Dec.), which attacks a very wide variety of plants under glass and is also found out of doors during the summer on weeds and cultivated plants. (*b*) The Rhododendron Whitefly (*Dialeurodes chittendeni* Laing), (June–Sept.), is found mainly in southern England on rhododendrons, especially *R. catawbiense*. *R. caucasicum*, *R. ponticum* and their

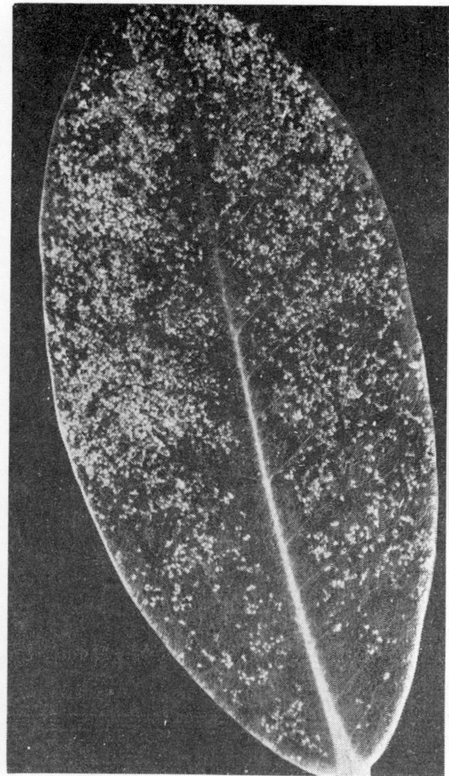

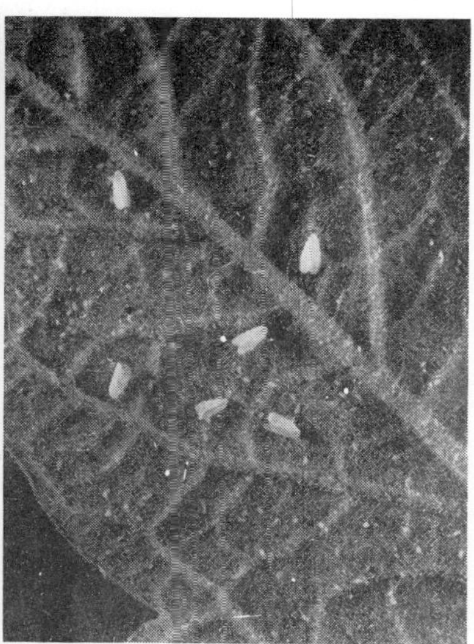

FIG. 65. *Left:* Damage by Rhododendron Bug (*Stephanitis rhododendri* Horv.) on upper surface of Rhododendron leaf. (*Shell Photograph.*)

FIG. 66. *Above:* Glasshouse Whitefly (*Trialeurodes vaporariorum* Westw.). Adults and immature 'scales' on underside of Tomato leaf. (*Shell Photograph.*)

hybrids. (*c*) The Cabbage Whitefly (*Aleyrodes brassicae* Wlk.), (May–Sept.), feeds on many varieties of brassicas.

Control. (1) If it is obtainable, the introduction of the Whitefly Parasite (*Encarsia formosa* Gah.) into infested greenhouses will efficiently control the Glasshouse Whitefly. (2) Alternatively, fumigate with DDT, lindane, or parathion smokes, 2 or 3 treatments being given at 14-day intervals. (3) On individual plants or out of doors, spray the undersides of the leaves fortnightly with DDT, lindane, malathion, or parathion until the infestation is eradicated. On rhododendrons spraying is best done during June and July. (4) During March any parts of rhododendron bushes which are badly infested by the young stages should be drastically pruned.

V—Reddish Discoloration

Redness of the leaves of strawberries may be caused by a decline of the plants due to faulty husbandry. In some varieties, however, particularly 'Royal Sovereign', infestations by the Leaf and Bud Eelworms (*Aphelenchoides fragariae* (Ritz. Bos) Christie and *A. ritzema-bosi* (Schwartz) Stein.) may sometimes give rise to unnatural reddening of the leaf stalks (see 'Foliage Puckered', p. 120).

Reddening of foliage is also caused by the feeding activities of some species of aphids. The more important of these are, (*a*) the Rosy Leaf-curling Aphid (*Dysaphis devecta* Wlk.), (May–July), which causes curling of the leaves of apple, the damaged areas becoming a bright red colour (Col. Fig. X). This species occurs generally on isolated trees and, though a persistent pest on them, does not become generally distributed throughout a plantation. (*b*) Similar damage to hawthorn is caused by *Dysaphis crataegi* Kalt.

Control. (1) Spray between the burst and green cluster stages with lindane or DDT emulsion. (2) Where leaf-curling has already commenced spray with malathion, parathion, diazinon or demeton-methyl.

(*c*) The Red Currant Blister Aphid (*Cryptomyzus ribis* L.), (May–June), infests the leaves of red and white currants where it produces blisters bright red to brownish red in colour (Col. Fig. IX). On black currants, which are occasionally attacked, the blisters are yellowish green.

Control. (1) Spray at the late grape stage with DDT emulsion. (2) Later attacks may be eradicated by spraying with malathion, parathion, diazinon or demeton-methyl.

Carrots attacked by the Carrot Fly (*Psila rosae* F.), (June–Oct.), may often show a reddening of the leaves (see 'Roots Eaten', p. 51).

VI—Rusted

Rust-coloured or chocolate-brown discoloration on the undersides of the leaves of rhododendrons is typical of the damage caused by the Rhododendron Bug (*Stephanitis rhododendri* Horv.), (May–Sept.). This serious pest is now generally distributed throughout England

and Wales and is particularly harmful to *Rhododendron catawbiense*, *R. caucasicum*, *R. fastuosum* and their hybrids. The upper surfaces of the leaves become discoloured by yellow mottling (Fig. 65).

Control. (1) Spray the undersides of the leaves with DDT, nicotine or TEPP, one application in mid-June and a second 3 weeks later. (2) Where the infestation is severe prune drastically in March and burn the infested branches.

VII—Silvered

The true silvering of foliage is found in plums and some other plants affected with 'Silver Leaf' fungus (*Stereum purpureum*), and is due primarily to the partial separation of the mesophyll cells from one another and from the epidermis. Owing to the abnormally large air spaces formed, the quality of light reflected from the leaf surface is changed, with the result that the leaves appear silvery. The silvering of leaves due to mite and insect infestations is due to the removal of sap from the tissues immediately below the epidermis, and to the laceration of the surface tissues resulting from the feeding of Thrips.

The Fruit Tree Red Spider Mite (*Panonychus ulmi* Koch), (June–Sept.), during heavy infestations causes the leaves of certain trees, especially apples, plums and damsons, to turn yellow and later a greenish-white.

Control. See 'Foliage Bronzed', p. 104.

The Glasshouse Red Spider Mite (*Tetranychus telarius* L.), (June–Oct.), when present in large numbers on the lower surface of the foliage of such plants as peach, strawberry, vine and violet, produces a silvering of the leaves.

Control. See 'Foliage Mottled', p. 105.

The Glasshouse Thrips (*Heliothrips haemorrhoidalis* Bouché) produces intense silvering of the foliage of half-hardy rhododendrons grown in temperate houses. Silvering is also caused by the feeding of the Privet Thrips (*Dendrothrips ornatus* Jabl.) on privet and lilac (Col. Fig. XI), and the Gladiolus Thrips (*Taeniothrips simplex* Mor.) on the leaves and flowers of gladioli (Col. Fig. V).

Control. See 'Foliage Mottled', p. 106.

Leafhoppers or Jassids produce a type of silvering on the leaves of such plants as apple, damson and plum (Jul.–Sept.).

Control. See 'Foliage Mottled', p. 108.

The Mealy Plum Aphid (*Hyalopterus pruni* Geoff.), (June–Aug.), is a common pest on damsons and plums, and occasionally on apricots, peaches and ornamental species of *Prunus*. No leaf-curl is produced despite the large numbers of Aphids that are massed on the lower leaf surface. Honeydew in quantity is produced, and this falls on to the lower leaves and fruits. An infested tree is readily recognized by the intense silvering of the foliage due to the copious wax that covers the bodies of these insects (Fig. 67).

Control. (1) Spray infested trees during the dormant season with a tar oil wash. (2) During the summer spray the undersides of infested leaves with malathion, parathion, BHC or a systemic insecticide.

VIII—Spotted

Discoloured spots on the foliage arise from (i) some nutritional deficiency (see Wallace); (ii) functional disorders and physiological

FIG. 67. Plum leaves infested with Mealy Plum Aphids (*Hyalopterus pruni* Geoff.). (*Shell Photograph.*)

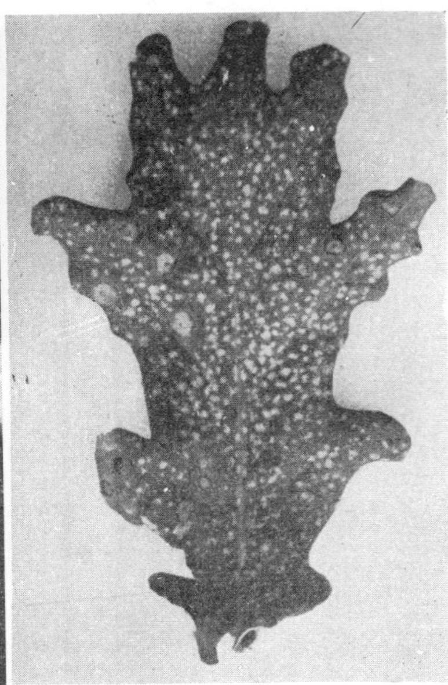

FIG. 68. Spotting of Oak leaf by Oak Phylloxera (*Phylloxera quercus* Planch.).

disturbances which may be localized; (iii) infections of bacterial and fungal organisms; (iv) infestations of mites and insects; and (v) other factors that affect the normal functioning of the leaf-cells. Owing to the great variation that exists in the type of spotting according to the factor concerned, to the nature of the invading organism, and to the reaction of the cellular tissue to local irritants, it is manifestly unwise to depend solely upon these characteristics for the determination of the primary cause. While recognizing that the colour, shape and size of the spots will vary considerably, it is possible to arrange a simple classification of leaf-spots based on their coloration. The pests responsible are considered in more detail elsewhere.

Black Spots. The lower surface of the leaves of indoor azaleas infested with the Glasshouse Thrips (*Heliothrips haemorrhoidalis* Bouché) will be found to have their lower surface sprinkled with black spots, due to the excretion by these insects, of tiny globules of red liquid, which darken after exposure to light (see p. 106).

Brownish Spots. (*a*) The Bulb Scale Mite (*Steneotarsonemus laticeps* Halb.) gives rise to reddish-brown and yellowish-brown spots on the inner scales and at the base of the flower-stalks of narcissus (see p. 33). (*b*) The Pear Leaf Blister Mite (*Eriophyes piri* Nal.) causes the formation of yellowish-green blisters on the upper surfaces of pear leaves (Col. Fig. I). These later turn red and finally dark brown (see p. 101). (*c*) Capsid bugs produce brown spots on the leaves of their several host plants, especially marked in the case of Common Green Capsid on potato (see p. 153). (*d*) Casebearers or Coleophorid Moths are responsible for brown spotting of the foliage (see p. 150). (*e*) Drought symptoms on rhododendrons are often characterized by definite spotting in the region of the stomata.

Reddish Spots. (*a*) The Pear Leaf Blister Mite (*E. piri* Nal.) (see above), (*b*) the Bulb Scale Mite (*S. laticeps* Halb.), (see p. 33), the Glasshouse Red Spider Mite (*Tetranychus telarius* L.), (see p. 105), and Thrips (see p. 106) give rise to distinctive red spots on the foliage of amaryllis due to the presence of anthocyanin pigment. (*c*) The Apple Capsid (*Plesiocoris rugicollis* Fall.) in particular produces reddish-brown spots on apple foliage (see p. 122).

Whitish Spots. Red Spider Mites, Thrips and Leafhoppers are chiefly responsible (see 'Foliage Mottled', p. 105).

Yellowish Spots. (*a*) Many Aphids (see p. 100), Whiteflies (see p. 108), Leafhoppers (see p. 108) and Scale Insects (see p. 77) produce local yellow spotting around their feeding lesions. (*b*) The Pear Leaf Blister Mite (*E. piri* Nal.), (see p. 101). (*c*) The Oak Phylloxera (*Phylloxera quercus* Planch.) produces distinctive yellow spotting on oak leaves (Fig. 68). (*d*) The female Chrysanthemum Leaf

Miner (*Phytomyza atricornis* Meig.) punctures the leaves of chrysanthemums with its ovipositor and feeds on the sap causing small bleached areas (Col. Fig. XII), (see p. 148).

IX—Veins Discoloured

In this category discoloration is confined to the mid-rib and/or the veins. This occurs in some plants following an attack by sucking insects, especially Capsid Bugs (*Calocoris norvegicus* Gmel. and *Lygus pabulinus* L.) and Aphids (*Myzus persicae* Sulz.) on potato foliage. Vein discoloration due to Capsids usually occurs rapidly after the infestation, and discoloured veins are associated with the presence of lacerated tissue in the form of pits. Such discoloration following Aphid attacks, however, develops after some days have elapsed since the initial infection, and the damage is not associated with lacerated tissue.

Some Scale insects are responsible for vein discoloration on such plants as aspidistra, ferns, orchids and palms.

Control. See 'Foliage Ragged', p. 153 (Capsids); 'Foliage Aphid-infested', p. 100 (Aphids); 'Stems Scaly', p. 77 (Scale).

X—Yellowed

Yellowing or chlorosis can be caused by several factors other than pest attack, including: (*a*) nutritional deficiencies of iron and manganese and over-sufficiencies of lime, manganese and nitrogen; (*b*) functional disorders, e.g. an unhealthy root system due to defective drainage causing waterlogged conditions; and (*c*) virus infections, e.g. Bean Mosaic.

The chief pests concerned with this condition are Red Spider Mites and Aphids.

The Fruit Tree Red Spider Mite (*Panonychus ulmi* Koch), (May–Sept.), causes the foliage of apple, plum, damson and pear to turn a yellowish green in the early stages of attack.

Control. See 'Foliage Bronzed', p. 104.

The Glasshouse Red Spider Mite (*Tetranychus telarius* L.), (May–Dec.), where present in large numbers, may cause complete yellowing of the foliage in many plants.

Control. See 'Foliage Mottled', p. 105.

The Gooseberry Red Spider Mite (*Bryobia ribis* Thom.), (April–June), gives rise to a severe chlorotic condition of gooseberry foliage, particularly during periods of drought in May and June. As a result the fruit is undersized and fails to mature. Various races of this mite also occur on apple, pear, hawthorn, ivy and grasses.

Control. Spray after the flowering stage with demeton-methyl, malathion, TEPP or derris, repeating the application 10 days later. If a summer ovicide is added to these materials, or if phenkaptone is used, one application may be sufficient. Special attention should be paid to the centre of the bushes.

Among the Aphids which produce yellowing on foliage is the Mealy Plum Aphid (*Hyalopterus pruni* Geoff.), (Aug.–Sept.), which infests plums and damsons.

Control. See 'Foliage Silvered', p. 111.

The Peach-Potato Aphid (*Myzus persicae* Sulz.) produces severe yellowing of the foliage of potatoes, especially on first earlies.

Control. See 'Foliage Aphid-infested', p. 100.

Insects that in their larval and/or adult stages bore and tunnel in the stems and shoots of plants (e.g. the larvae of Goat, Wood Leopard and Clearwing Moths, and Bark Beetles and Shot-Hole Borers) frequently produce symptoms that may be described as chlorotic. The foliage turns a yellowish green, later becoming yellow and wilting, whereas leaves suffering from normal chlorosis do not wilt. Again, insects that attack either the roots and underground portions of plants (e.g. Wireworms, Chafer and Weevil larvae and Leatherjackets—see 'Roots Eaten', p. 51) or the lower portion of the stem (e.g. Cutworms—see 'Stems Gnawed', p. 73) may give rise to similar symptoms.

Severe yellowing of the leaves of peas may often be the result of an infestation of the Pea Root Eelworm (*Heterodera göttingiana* Lieb.). Badly attacked plants are stunted, have poor root systems and may die before the pods ripen. Broad beans are also attacked and show similar symptoms though chlorosis is not so pronounced.

Control. Peas and broad beans should not be grown on infested land more than once in 4 years, or longer if possible.

FOLIAGE DISTORTED

Many pests cause the malformation of the leaves of their host plants, this being in most cases a direct result of their feeding activities. The malformation may be caused by injury to the leaf while it is still growing. Alternatively the injection of salivary juices by sucking insects, or the release of poisonous products by eelworms, may cause local or general irritation of the plant tissues which respond by abnormal growth or development. In the case of the Gall Midges and Leaf-rolling Sawflies the condition is initiated by the female insect laying her eggs on the leaf whereas among some Tortricid Moths it is the young larvae which are responsible.

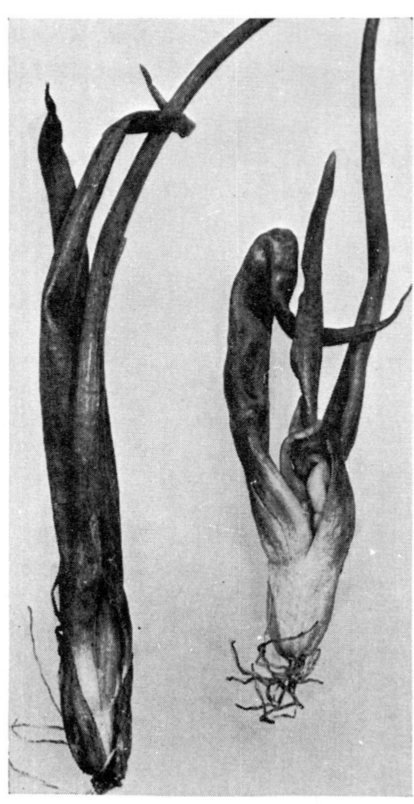

FIG. 69. Onion 'Bloat' due to infestation of Stem and Bulb Eelworm (*Ditylenchus dipsaci* (Kühn) Filipj.). (*Shell Photograph.*)

Where external feeders are concerned the rolling and curling of leaves serve a useful purpose by affording excellent protection from would-be predators. Similarly these pests are protected from many insecticides and for that reason chemical control measures should be applied before distortion commences or be directed against the more vulnerable stages in the life-cycle such as the egg-laying female.

I—Bloated

The Stem and Bulb Eelworm (*Ditylenchus dipsaci* (Kühn) Filipj.), (June–Aug.), gives rise in onion bulbs to the condition known as 'bloat', the leaves being malformed and swollen at the base (Fig. 69). Shallots, chives, garlic and leeks may be similarly affected. The biological race responsible is the same as that which attacks narcissus (see 'Bulbs Discoloured Internally', p. 33).

Control. (1) Burn all infested plants and debris. (2) Keep infested land clear of possible plant hosts for 3 years (see Appendix II, p. 209). (3) Practise a 3-yearly rotation. (4) Sow only seed taken from eelworm-free plants or which has been fumigated.

II—Curled

The presence of many species of Aphids is clearly recognized by the characteristic curling of the foliage. This symptom must not be confused with blistering (see 'Foliage Blistered', p. 101). In heavy infestations, the leaves shrivel and fall off. The more common species concerned with leaf-curl are: (*a*) the pink and green Potato Aphid (*Macrosiphum euphorbiae* Thos.), (Apr.–July), which has a wide

FIG. 70. Curling of Apple foliage by Rosy Apple Aphid (*Dysaphis plantaginea* Pass.). (*Shell Photograph.*)

FIG. 71. Foliage of Plum distorted by Damson-Hop Aphid (*Phorodon humuli* Schrank). (*Shell Photograph.*)

range of host plants and may be found throughout the year on certain glasshouse plants. These Aphids are found clustering on the growing points and terminal leaves, and give rise to leaf-curl on young plants of antirrhinums, annual asters and other ornamentals, and on lettuce and potato. (*b*) The Glasshouse Potato Aphid (*Aulacorthum solani* Kalt.), (May–Oct.), produces serious leaf-curl on potatoes and (*c*) the Shallot Aphid (*Myzus ascalonicus* Donc.), (May–July), causes curling of strawberry leaves. There are many other species of Aphids which curl the leaves of plants, but it is among fruit and ornamental trees that this type of injury is most pronounced. (*d*) The Blue Bug or Rosy Apple Aphid (*Dysaphis plantaginea* Pass.), (May–July), causes the leaves of apple to curl and crumple (Fig. 70). (*e*) The Rosy Leaf-curling Aphid (*Dysaphis devecta* Wlk.), (May–July), also causes severe leaf-curling on apple accompanied by bright red blistering (see 'Foliage Blistered', p. 101). (*f*) The Gooseberry Aphid (*Aphis grossulariae*

Kalt.), (Apr.-June), lives on the tips of the shoots and causes the leaves of gooseberry and, to a lesser extent, those of currants to form into a tightly-crumpled mass. (*g*) The Cherry Black Fly (*Myzus cerasi* F.), (May-July), curls the young leaves of fruiting cherries, particularly Morellos on walls, and of ornamental *Prunus* species. This aphid excretes large quantities of honeydew, which falls on to the foliage and checks the normal functions of the leaves, and attracts numbers of Ants which ascend the stems of trees attacked by this pest. (*h*) The Peach Aphids (*Appelia schwartzi* Börn. and *Myzus persicae* Sulz.), (Apr.-July), are serious pests of indoor and outdoor peaches and nectarines. (*i*) The Leaf-curling Plum Aphid (*Brachycaudus helichrysi* Kalt.), (Apr.-July), is a widespread pest of plum and damson (Col. Fig. II), and frequently produces unsightly damage on certain ornamental species, e.g. *Prunus mexicana*. (*j*) The Pear-bedstraw Aphid (*Dysaphis pyri* B. de Fonsc.), (May–July), is often found causing severe leaf-curl on pears, especially at the tips of young shoots. (*k*) The Bean Aphid (*Aphis fabae* Scop.), (Apr.–May), causes leaf-curl on its primary hosts—wild and cultivated forms of spindle (*Euonymus*). (*l*) The Viburnum Aphid (*Aphis viburni* Schr.), (Apr.–June), curls the leaves of viburnums, especially *V. carlesii*. (*m*) The Elm-currant Aphid (*Eriosoma ulmi* L.), (Apr.-July), distorts the foliage of the common elm (*Ulmus procera*) and the wych elm (*U. glabra*) (see 'Roots Splitting', p. 59).

Control. See 'Foliage Aphid-infested', p. 100. Treatment should be given early in the season before leaf-curling becomes severe, otherwise malathion, parathion, diazinon, or a systemic insecticide should be used.

The Box Sucker (*Psylla buxi* L.), (Apr.-June), is a fairly common insect in some parts of the country where it infests the common box. The young nymphs feed on the new leaf buds causing curling of the opening leaves which results in a disfiguring cabbage-like appearance of the young shoots (Fig. 72).

Control. (1) Where practicable, hand-pick and burn the curled shoots before the end of April. (2) To prevent egg-laying the infestation should be eradicated before the beginning of August. Sprays of TEPP, BHC or malathion should be applied 2 or 3 times at 14-day intervals during June and early July.

The Black Currant Leaf Midge (*Dasyneura tetensi* Rübs.), (May–Aug.), is a serious pest of black currants in many parts of the country. Certain varieties, e.g. Goliath, Seabrook's Black, Baldwin and Triple X, are particularly susceptible to attack. The larvae feed in the folds of the young leaves of the terminal shoot causing them to become curled, puckered and twisted, and finally to turn black (Fig. 73).

Control. (1) To prevent infestations spray with DDT at the grape stage and again 6 weeks later, directing the spray to the tips of the young growth. (2) Bushes which are already infested may be sprayed with parathion and the application repeated 10 days later, but do not use parathion within 4 weeks before picking.

FIG. 72. Curling of terminal foliage of Box by Box Sucker (*Psylla buxi* L.). (*Shell Photograph.*)

FIG. 73. Distortion of Black Currant leaves by Black Currant Leaf Midge (*Dasyneura tetensi* Rübs.). (*Crown Copyright Photograph.*)

The Broad Mite (*Hemitarsonemus latus* Banks) attacks a wide range of glasshouse plants and causes the leaves of some of them to curl downwards and to become brittle. This type of injury occurs on aubergine, begonia, dahlia, fuchsia, gerbera, tomato and other plants (Fig. 74).

Control. (1) Dust the infested plants with finely divided sulphur, or spray with parathion, 2 or 3 applications being given at 4- or 5-day intervals, or (2) spray once only with endrin.

Note: The minute mites fall readily to the ground when the plant is moved so that treatment should be given before the plants are removed to fresh sites.

The Strawberry Mite (*Steneotarsonemus pallidus* Banks) also attacks greenhouse plants which exhibit similar symptoms to those caused by the Broad Mite.

Control. The Strawberry Mite is more difficult to control than the

FIG. 74. Curling of Begonia foliage by Broad Mite (*Hemitarsonemus latus* Banks).

Broad Mite. Hot-water treatment, as used for Strawberry runners (see 'Foliage Puckered', below) can only be used on a few greenhouse plants. Successful control by kelthane, endrin and toxaphene sprays has been reported. Other commonly used chemicals are not effective.

III—Puckered

An infestation of the Stem and Bulb Eelworm (*Ditylenchus dipsaci* (Kühn) Filipj.) on strawberry plants gives rise to severe puckering and distortion of the leaves, especially in the spring and autumn (Fig. 75). The edges of the leaves are turned downwards and on the undersides near the petiole the main veins are often pale and enlarged. The stalks of the leaves and flowers are frequently swollen and may show a brown core when cut lengthwise.

The Leaf and Bud Eelworms (*Aphelenchoides ritzema-bozi* (Schwartz Stein.) and *A. fragariae* (Ritz. Bos) Christie) also cause puckering of strawberry leaves but this is less severe and more local than is the case with the Stem and Bulb Eelworm. A distinguishing feature is the presence of rough greyish scars on the upper surfaces of the leaves near the petiole caused by external feeding while the leaves are still folded in the bud (Fig. 110). Infested leaves often have almost hairless stalks.

FIG. 75. Strawberry infested with Stem and Bulb Eelworm (*Ditylenchus dipsaci* (Kühn) Filipj.) showing puckered leaves. (*Photograph by East Malling Research Station.*)

FIG. 76. Symptoms on Strawberry of infestation of Strawberry Mite (*Steneotarsonemus pallidus* Banks). (*Photograph by East Malling Research Station.*)

Control. (1) Lift and destroy stunted plants in the spring. (2) Subject infested runners to hot-water treatment (see Appendix I, p. 208), or (3) dip the runners in a solution of parathion before planting out. (4) Avoid planting strawberries or other susceptible plants (see Appendix II, p. 209) in infested ground for at least 3 years. (5) If possible use only wheat or barley straw for strawing.

The Strawberry Tarsonemid Mite (*Steneotarsonemus pallidus* Banks), (May–Nov.), also produces a puckered effect on strawberry. The almost microscopic mites live in the folds of the young unexpanded leaflets, and cause the leaves to lose colour and to become brittle and crinkled (Fig. 76).

Control. Subject infested runners to the hot-water treatment in spring or autumn—an immersion for 7 minutes at a constant temperature of 115° F. is effective (see Appendix I, p. 208).

The Apple Capsid (*Plesiocoris rugicollis* Fall.), (Apr.–Aug.), is one of the most common pests of apple, and has become established in many orchards in this country. The young Capsids puncture the foliage causing puckering and the development of small reddish-brown marks which later turn blackish (Fig. 77). The young shoots may also be attacked causing stunted or forked growth. After petal-fall the insects feed on the developing fruit, making brown marks which enlarge as the fruit grows to form raised, rough, corky patches. Pears, currants and gooseberries are also attacked.

Control. Spray with DDT, BHC, or parathion at the green cluster stage.

On currants, gooseberry, and pear the most destructive Capsid is the Common Green Capsid (*Lygus pabulinus* L.), (Apr.–Aug.). This species also causes puckering of the leaves together with tearing round the feeding areas (Fig. 78), (see 'Foliage Ragged', p. 153).

The Apple Sucker (*Psylla mali* Schmid.), (Apr.–May), may also cause some puckering of apple leaves which is accompanied by severe damage to the blossoms (see 'Flowers Withered', p. 171).

IV—Rolled

The leaves of many plants are rolled either loosely or tightly, completely or partially, upwards (Pear Leaf-Curling, Violet and Bat-Willow Gall Midges) or downwards (Leaf-Rolling Rose Sawfly) as a result of mite and insect infestations. This folding over of the leaf or leaflet is not only unsightly, but the normal functions are prevented and the affected foliage withers and dies.

A few species of Gall Mites are responsible for leaf-roll, but are not considered here as their attacks are confined chiefly to wild and hedge plants, e.g. Hawthorn.

The larvae of many Tortrix Moths, of which there are very many, are responsible for a great amount of damage to the leaves of fruit, forest and ornamental trees and shrubs, and to many decorative

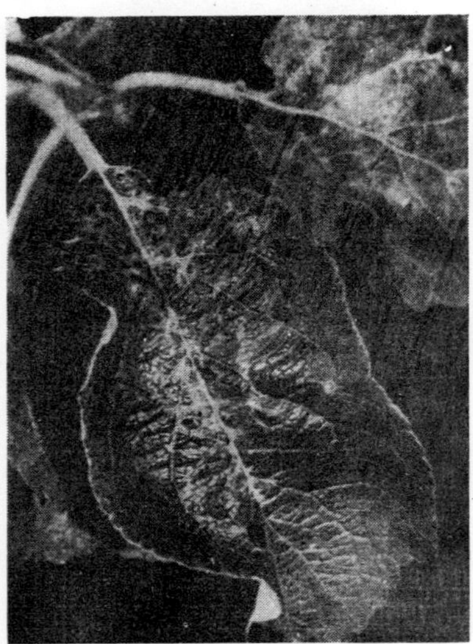

FIG. 77. Puckering of Apple leaf due to Apple Capsid (*Plesiocoris rugicollis* Fall.). (*Shell Photograph.*)

FIG. 78. Hydrangea showing puckering and tearing of the leaves due to Capsid attack. (*Photograph by P. Becker.*)

garden plants. The larvae feed on the young leaves which they roll and secure together with silken threads (see 'Foliage Spun Together', p. 157). The more common species are:

(*a*) The Green Oak Tortrix Moth (*Tortrix viridana* L.), (May–June), the larvae of which, together with other species, often cause complete defoliation of oak trees in early summer. The larvae frequently descend from the oak and prepare pupation quarters by rolling the leaves of rhododendrons and other shrubs which are grown as undergrowth in oak woods.

(*b*) The Fruit Tree Tortrix Moth (*Archips podana* Scop.), (May–June), occurs on oak, but is a common leaf-roller on fruit trees, including apple (Fig. 79), apricot, pear, plum and, indoors, attacks vines.

(*c*) *A. rosana* L., (May–June), is one of the rose-infesting species and causes disfiguring leaf-roll on bush and climbing roses.

(*d*) The Fruit Tree Tortrix Moth (*Ditula angustiorana* Haw.), (May–June), is a common pest on many fruit trees and attacks, also, the developing fruitlets.

(*e*) The Flax Tortrix Moth (*Cnephasia virgaureana* Treits.), (May–June), rolls the leaves of many herbaceous plants, including heleniums, phloxes, solidagos, and rudbeckias (Fig. 80).

FIG. 79. Apple leaves rolled and tied by caterpillars of Fruit Tree Tortrix Moth. (*Crown Copyright Photograph.*)

(*f*) The Apple Leaf Skeletonizer (*Anthophila pariana* Clerck), (May–Sept.), is sometimes common in the southern counties. The young larvae feed on the leaf epidermis and roll the leaves of apple, pear, hawthorn and ornamental *Pyrus*.

Control. (1) Hand-pick or crush the caterpillars within the rolled leaves when there are light attacks on roses and other ornamentals. (2) Spray the foliage *before* leaf-rolling commences with DDT. (3) Dust the foliage with nicotine dust at air temperatures above 65° F. *after* rolling has occurred.

The leaf-rolling habit is found among certain Weevils, the females of which cut the leaf to the mid-rib, and then roll one or both sides to form a tube in which the larvae live and feed. Species which roll the entire leaf are: (*a*) the Hazel Leaf Roller Weevil (*Byctiscus betulae* L.) on hazel and other trees, but especially on young birches; and (*b*) the Poplar Leaf Roller (*B. populi* L.) which causes similar leaf-rolling on poplar and young aspens. Other Curculionids roll only

FIG. 80. Leaves of Dogwood (*Cornus*) rolled and tied by caterpillars of the Flax Tortrix Moth (*Cnephasia virgaureana* Treits.).

the upper portion of the leaves, when the female weevils cut down to the mid-rib about half-way down the blade and roll up the severed portions, as with: (*c*) *Apoderus coryli* L. on beech, hazel and oak; and (*d*) *Attelabus nitens* Scop. on young oaks. The larvae of these several Weevils live in tunnels formed of leaves rolled by the adults.

Control. (1) Hand-pick and burn the rolled leaves of specimen trees where their presence may be considered unsightly. Spray small trees with DDT.

Several Gall Midges are responsible for leaf-roll, and among the more important are:

(*a*) The Pear Leaf Midge (*Dasyneura pyri* Bouché), (June–Oct.), which causes the edges of the foliage of pear to curl upwards and inwards, and in severe attacks, the leaf margins meet along the centre of the mid-rib (Fig. 81). The infested leaves eventually blacken, become brittle, and die.

Control. (1) Where possible hand-pick the infested leaves or summer-prune infested trees and burn the prunings. (2) Spray with parathion when the leaf-rolling commences and again 10 days later, or (3) spray with DDT at fortnightly intervals from late May to late June to kill the adults.

FIG. 81. Pear foliage damaged by Pear Leaf Midge (*Dasyneura pyri* Bouché). (*Shell Photograph.*)

FIG. 82. Distortion of Violet leaves by Violet Leaf Midge (*Dasyneura affinis* Kieff.). (*Crown Copyright Photograph.*)

(*b*) The Violet Leaf Midge (*Dasyneura affinis* Kieff.), (June–Dec.), is a serious pest of cultivated violets and occurs on wild plants. The leaves and frequently the sepals and petals, become swollen and the margins are rolled tightly upwards (Fig. 82).

Control. (1) Hand-pick and burn the infested leaves and flowers—this operation being confined to small batches of plants and those in frames. (2) Spray or dust with DDT or BHC before the peak egg-laying periods, i.e. in late April, early July, mid-August and mid-

October as necessary. (3) On a commercial scale spray with systox and dust with DDT at the above times.

One important species of Sawfly that causes leaf-roll is the Leaf-rolling Rose Sawfly (*Blennocampa pusilla* Klug.), (May–July), which is a common pest in roseries. The leaves of both wild and cultivated roses are subjected to a lateral rolling over of the margins (Fig. 83). Certain varieties are more susceptible to attack than others.

FIG. 83. Damage to Rose foliage by Leaf-rolling Rose Sawfly (*Blennocampa pusilla* Klug.).

Control. (1) Hand-pick and burn the folded leaves as soon as they are seen in spring. (2) Spray susceptible varieties with DDT or BHC at 10-day intervals from mid-May. (3) Dust rolled leaves with nicotine dust to destroy the larvae within the curled leaf margins. (4) Thoroughly wash the roots of newly-introduced bushes before planting to remove any pupae that may be entangled in the matted roots.

V—With Swellings

The appearance on the growing leaves of narcissi and snowdrops of small swellings or 'spickles' is an indication that the plants are infested by the Stem and Bulb Eelworm (*Ditylenchus dipsaci* (Kühn) Filipj.), (Jan.–Dec.). The swellings are usually noticeable by their unhealthy yellow colour, but in slight infestations they may remain green.

Control. See 'Bulbs Discoloured Internally', p. 33.

VI—Twisted

The foliage of sweet corn which has been attacked by the Frit Fly (*Oscinella frit* L.), (May-June), becomes twisted and stunted with a tendency to roll at the tip.

Control. See 'Shoots Tunnelled', p. 88.

The terminal leaves of the young shoots of black currant become twisted and curled when infested by the Black Currant Leaf Midge (*Dasyneura tetensi* Rübs.), (May–Aug.), (Fig. 73).

Control. See 'Foliage Curled', p. 118.

Various races of the Stem and Bulb Eelworm (*Ditylenchus dipsaci* (Kühn) Filipj.), (Jan.–Dec.), may cause severe twisting, stunting and discoloration of the leaves of bulbous plants, including narcissi, snowdrops, hyacinths, bluebells and tulips (Fig. 84).

FIG. 84. Distortion of Hyacinth foliage by Stem and Bulb Eelworm (*Ditylenchus dipsaci* (Kühn) Filipj.).

Control. See 'Bulbs Discoloured Internally' p. 33 (narcissus, hyacinth, etc.) and 'Bulbs Discoloured Externally', p. 31 (tulip).

FOLIAGE DROPPING

Premature leaf-fall is associated with several factors other than pest attack, and may follow the application of insecticides and fungicides (e.g. lime-sulphur on sulphur-shy varieties of apple and gooseberry, and the incompatible mixture of lime-sulphur and lead

FIG. 85. Defoliation of Spruce due to infestation of Spruce Aphid (*Elatobium abietinum* (Wlk.).

arsenate when applied to apples during the immediate post-blossom period). Drought conditions and waterlogged soil due to defective drainage affect the healthy action of roots with the result that premature leaf-drop occurs. Again, infections of bacterial and fungal organisms produce similar symptoms on fruit trees.

Among the more common pests responsible for this type of injury are: (*a*) the Leaf and Bud Eelworm (*Aphelenchoides ritzema-bosi* (Schwartz) Stein.), which is responsible for the naked appearance of the stems of chrysanthemums, which are denuded of their leaves later in the season (see 'Foliage with Black or Brown Areas', p. 102). (*b*) The Glasshouse Red Spider Mite (*Tetranychus telarius* L.) may cause extensive leaf-fall on heavily-infested peaches and vines (see 'Foliage Mottled', p. 105). (*c*) The Fruit Tree Red Spider Mite (*Panonychus ulmi* Koch) causes premature leaf-fall on infested fruit trees (see 'Foliage Bronzed', p. 104). (*d*) The Spruce Mite (*Paratetranychus ununguis* Jac.) causes severe defoliation of spruce and other conifers (see 'Foliage Mottled', p. 106). (*e*) Aphids by reason of the amount of sap they extract from leaves are one of the chief agents responsible for premature defoliation. This symptom is specially marked when the Spruce Aphid (*Elatobium abietinum* Wlk.), (Mar.–July), attacks Sitka spruce (*Picea sitchensis*), upon which almost complete defoliation may develop. Leaf-drop is only partial with other species of spruce, namely, *P. abies* and *P. pungens glauca* (Fig. 85), while certain other species appear to be extremely tolerant of an attack (see 'Foliage Aphid-infested', p. 100). (*f*) Defoliation and subsequent death of the branches of yew may be caused by severe infestations of the Yew Scale (*Eulecanium pomeranicum* Kaw.) (see 'Stems Scaly', p. 79).

Control. The control measures against these pests are given in the relevant sections, mentioned above.

FOLIAGE EATEN

The injuries described below are all of the type directly caused by the feeding of biting insects and other pests, and should be distinguished from the type of damage which results from the feeding of Capsid Bugs (see 'Foliage Ragged', p. 153), where tearing and puckering takes place due to the cessation of growth around the feeding punctures made by these insects.

Within this section it is possible to distinguish four main patterns of damage.

I—Clean-cut Holes

The majority of biting insects cause this type of injury, which may occur on all garden plants with few exceptions. In many cases the leaves show a 'shot-hole' effect in the early stages of attack and gradually large irregular holes are eaten out. If the infestation is severe and unchecked the plant may be completely defoliated or the leaves reduced to a skeleton, only the midribs and main veins being left.

Pests which eat out small holes which are not enlarged or which cut small pieces from the edge of the leaves only are considered separately (see 'Foliage Perforated', p. 140, and 'Foliage Notched', p. 141).

The Garden Slug (*Arion hortensis* Fér.) is particularly destructive to seedlings and the Grey Field Slug (*Agriolimax reticulatus* Müll.) is a leaf-feeder and a widely-distributed pest in gardens. Other species of Slugs, including those that are normally soil-inhabitants, feed on the aerial portions of plants after dark and eat out holes in the leaves (Fig. 86).

FIG. 86. Iris foliage damaged by Slugs.

Snails are likewise responsible for a great amount of injury to the foliage of horticultural plants. The Large Garden Snail (*Helix aspersa* Müll.) and the Strawberry Snail (*Hygromia striolata* Pfeiff.) are particularly destructive in herbaceous borders and on rock gardens, feeding on the leaves of campanulas, *Chrysanthemum maximum*, iris, rudbeckias, *Sedum spectabile*, violets and numerous other plants.

Control. (1) Small infestations can be checked by hand-picking at night. (2) Spray attacked plants during dry weather with a metaldehyde suspension. (3) Lay down poison baits of bran and metaldehyde or Paris Green (see Appendix V, p. 216). (4) Ensure that the ground is well drained. (5) Where the ground has a high humus content refrain from using heavy dressings of organic manures for a year or so, substituting inorganic fertilizer.

Many species of Woodlice are destructive to garden plants, both in the open and under glass. The more common species are *Armadillidium vulgare* Latr., *A. nasatum* B.-L. and *Oniscus asellus* L. Some species are omnivorous, feeding on animal and vegetable matter; some are saprophagous and feed on dead and decaying organic matter; while others are chiefly herbivorous and attack the foliage of cucumber, French beans, various orchids, tomatoes and numerous other crops, and roots.

Control. See 'Roots Eaten', p. 48.

The European Earwig (*Forficula auricularia* L.), (June–Aug.), will eat out clean-cut holes in leaves, and causes a peculiar type of skeletonizing of the leaves of such plants as carrot, beetroot, parsnip and occasionally dahlia. The leaves have a lacy appearance due to inter-veinal injury.

Control. See 'Flowers Eaten', p. 166.

It is among the *Lepidoptera* (Butterflies and Moths) that is found the greatest number of species whose larvae eat out clean-cut holes in leaves, and space will allow only the briefest reference to this group of phytophagous insects. The 'looper' larvae of the Winter (*Operophtera brumata* L.), Mottled Umber (*Erannis defoliaria* Clerck), and March Moths (*Alsophila aescularia* Schiff.) are well-known pests of fruits, and of forest and ornamental trees and shrubs (Fig. 87). The Angleshades Moth (*Phlogophora meticulosa* L.) is a polyphagous species feeding on a wide range of plants both under glass and in the open. The Large and Small Cabbage White Butterflies (*Pieris brassicae* L. and *P. rapae* L.) and the Cabbage Moth (*Mamestra brassicae* L.) feed on the leaves of numerous plants, chiefly cruciferous, eating out holes and frequently completely skeletonizing the foliage. The Lackey (*Malocosoma neustria* L.) and the Vapourer Moths (*Orgyia antiqua* L.) are destructive pests on fruit trees and on ornamental trees and shrubs, including hawthorn. The Brown China Marks Moth (*Nymphula nymphaeata* L.) is responsible for the removal of oval portions from the leaves of water-lilies and other aquatic plants.

The larvae of many Tortricid Moths are leaf-rollers, though some, e.g. *Archips podana* Scop., *A. leacheana* L., and *A. xylosteana* L., are responsible for clean-cut holes, unaccompanied by leaf-rolling, in the leaves of rhododendrons.

Control. (1) Spray the infested plants with DDT. On fruit trees this is best applied about the green cluster stage. (2) Do not apply DDT to edible crops within 2 weeks of harvesting. If treatment is necessary use derris instead. (3) Where fish are present in ponds along with infested aquatic plants, the plants should be submerged to enable the fish to feed on the caterpillars. DDT and derris will poison fish. (4) To prevent egg-laying on fruit and ornamental trees by the wingless females of the Winter Moth group, a band of vegetable grease should be applied to the trunks before the end of October.

The number of Coleopterous insects (Beetles and Weevils) whose feeding habits comprise the eating-out of clean-cut holes in the foliage is considerable. This habit is particularly pronounced in the Families (I) *Chrysomelidae*, (II) *Curculionidae* and, to a lesser extent, in the Subfamily (III) *Melolonthinae*.

FIG. 87. Damage to Apple foliage by caterpillars of Winter Moth (*Operophtera brumata* L.). (*Shell Photograph.*)

FIG. 88. Leaves of Water-lily damaged by Water-lily Beetle (*Galerucella nymphaeae* L.). (*Photograph by R. P. Scase.*)

(I) Chrysomelid Beetles, e.g. (*a*) the Mustard Beetles (*Phaedon cochleariae* F. and *P. armoraciae* L.), (May–Aug.), which injure the foliage of various cruciferous crops, including mustard, water cress, cabbage and turnip. (*b*) Flea Beetles (*Phyllotreta* species), (May–July), which are among the most destructive pests of crucifers, especially to seedlings and young plants of radish, turnip and other brassicas (see 'Foliage Perforated', p. 141). (*c*) The Water-lily Beetle (*Galerucella nymphaeae* L.). (June–Aug.), which is a destructive pest of water-lilies in ornamental ponds and lakes (Fig. 88).

(II) Weevils, including (*a*) the Clay-coloured (*Otiorrhynchus singularis* L.) and (*b*) the Vine Weevils (*O. sulcatus* Fab.), are destructive in their adult stages to plants in glasshouses and in the open. They bite out holes in the foliage of such plants as cyclamen, ferns (especially *Phyllitis*), peach, raspberry, rhododendron and vine. (*c*) The several species of *Phyllobius* are true leaf-feeders, being found in vast numbers on the foliage of fruit and ornamental trees. (*d*) Pea and Bean Weevils (*Sitona* species) notch the leaf margins of leguminous crops, especially broad beans and peas (see 'Foliage Notched', p. 143).

(III) Chafer Beetles, more especially (*a*) the Cockchafer or May Bug (*Melolontha melolontha* L.) and (*b*) the Garden Chafer (*Phyllopertha horticola* L.), (May–June), attack the foliage of certain fruit and forest trees and eat out irregular-shaped portions.

Control. (1) Clean cultivation, including the disposal of crop refuse. (2) Spray or dust infested plants with DDT, but if they are edible, plants should not be treated for 2 weeks before harvesting. (3) Aquatic plants should be submerged for several days to allow fish to feed on the pests.

The Hymenopterous insects responsible for this type of damage are Sawflies. The damage consists of small, clean-cut holes in the foliage,

FIG. 89. *Left:* Foliage of *Aruncus sylvester* skeletonized by Spiraea Sawfly (*Pteronidea spiraeae* Zadd.).

FIG. 90. *Right:* Gooseberry foliage damaged by Gooseberry Sawfly (*Pteronidea ribesii* Scop.). (*Shell Photograph.*)

and these, with certain species, develop into a partial or complete skeletonizing of the leaf. Among the more common species attacking horticultural plants are: (*a*) the Iris Sawfly (*Rhadinoceraea micans* Klug.), (June–July), which feeds along the leaf margins of *Iris*

FIG. 91. Damage to Rose leaves by Leaf-cutter Bee (*Megachile* species).

pseudacorus in ponds; (*b*) the Solomon's Seal Sawfly (*Phymatocera aterrima* Klug.), (May–June), which often causes considerable damage to *Polygonatum*, especially in London gardens; (*c*) the Spiraea Sawfly (*Pteronidea spiraeae* Zadd.), (June–July), which may completely skeletonize the foliage of *Aruncus sylvester* in southern gardens (Fig. 89) and (*d*) the Geum Sawfly (*Blennocampa geniculata* Hart.), (June–July), which is often found attacking the foliage of geum in herbaceous borders. (*e*) The Large Rose Sawfly (*Arge ochropus* Gmel.), (Jul.–Oct.), (see 'Stems with Lesions', p. 77) and (*f*) the Banded Rose Sawfly (*Emphytus cinctus* L.), (Jul.–Oct.), are fairly common pests, feeding on the leaves of wild and cultivated roses.

Among the better-known species that attack the foliage of hardy fruits are: (*g*) the Gooseberry Sawfly (*Pteronidea ribesii* Scop.), (Apr.–Aug.), which is a destructive pest on gooseberry, and occasionally on red currant (Fig. 90). The larvae feed at first in the centre of the bush and later disperse to the outer foliage. (*h*) The Black Currant Sawfly (*Nematus olfaciens* Ben.), (Apr.–July), is a pest of increasing importance on black currants. Since it was first recorded in Britain in 1953 it has become distributed generally throughout the country. (*i*) The Hazel Sawfly (*Croesus septrentrionalis* L.), (June–Sept.), which is a polyphagous species feeding on the foliage of a number of trees and, on occasion, a pest on nut hedges. (*j*) The Antler Sawfly (*Cladius pectinicornis* Geoff.), (June–Aug.), which is an occasional pest in strawberry plantations, especially during the period when the fruit is colouring.

Control. (1) Spray ornamental plants with DDT or BHC. (2) Spray fruit bushes with DDT or derris when the damage is first seen, i.e. from the end of April onwards. Early applications should be directed to the centre of the bush.

The other group of Hymenopterous insects concerned consists of the Leaf-Cutter Bees (*Megachile* species), which cut out regular oval or circular portions from the foliage of many plants for the purpose of lining their nests to form larval cells. *M. centuncularis* L., (June–Aug.), is the chief culprit concerned with rose-leaf disfiguration (Fig. 91), while other species are concerned with similar injury to foliage of laburnum, lilac, privet, rhododendron and other ornamentals.

Control. Little can be done to prevent this unsightly damage other than destroying the nests and capturing the bees while they are engaged in collecting the leaf portions.

II—Epidermis Eaten

Some leaf-eating larvae restrict their feeding to one surface of the leaf and the underlying parenchyma. The other epidermis of the leaf, together with the veins, is left intact and later turns brown and shrivelled in patches where feeding has taken place. Usually it is the upper epidermis which is destroyed, but in some cases, e.g. the Willow Leaf Beetles, the lower epidermis is eaten. Some pests such as the Rose Slugworm are less particular and feed on either or both surfaces.

Many Lepidopterous larvae feed in this manner. The Apple Leaf Skeletonizer (*Anthophila pariana* Clerck), (June–Aug.), is a pest more commonly found in the southern counties than elsewhere. The larvae are found on the leaves of apple, pear, ornamental *Pyrus* species, and hawthorn, where they remove patches of the upper epidermis. In severe infestations the whole upper surface may be removed, leaving the skeleton and the thin tissue of the lower surface (Fig. 92). The larvae also roll the margins of the leaves which are secured by silk threads. Damaged foliage turns a rusty brown colour giving the appearance of having been scorched by fire. There are two broods each year. The larvae of the second generation also attack the skins of the fruit and cause russeting.

Control (1) Hand-pick and burn the attacked leaves where practicable. (2) Spray with BHC or DDT after petal-fall but if spraying on fruit trees is necessary later in the season an acaricide or summer ovicide should be added to prevent a build-up of Fruit Tree Red Spider Mite.

FIG. 92. Damage to foliage of Apple by caterpillars of the Apple Leaf Skeletonizer (*Anthophila pariana* Clerck). (*Photograph from A. M. Massee, 'Pests of Fruits and Hops'*.)

The Yellow Tail Moth (*Euproctis similis* Fuess.), (Sept.–Oct.), is a minor pest of fruit trees, especially apple, cherry, pear, plum and rose, the leaves of which are devoured by the larvae. The young larvae before hibernation feed on the upper epidermis of apple foliage producing characteristic skeletonized patches. This damage may continue until the leaves fall, at which time the larvae spin small, silken cocoons in the shelter of the rough bark and in the axils of branches.

Control. (1) Spray the trees when dormant with a tar oil wash, which will kill all larvae with which it comes into contact; and (2) the normal routine spraying of the foliage with DDT in spring will provide an effective control.

The Buff-Tip Moth (*Phalera bucephala* L.), (July–Sept.), is a pest of many trees, especially elm, lime and oak. The young caterpillars feed in colonies and are found to skeletonize the foliage of oaks during July and August.

Control. It may be found necessary to spray the foliage of specimen trees in early August with DDT, but there are few records of severe damage being done by this species.

The Diamond Back Moth (*Plutella maculipennis* Curtis), (July–Oct.), is a particularly destructive pest during certain years and in some districts. The larvae feed on the foliage of brassicas, more especially cabbage, cauliflower, kale, swede and turnip, and on cruciferous weeds, e.g. charlock and hedge mustard. The damage consists at first of the eating out of small holes in the leaf tissue and, later, the small caterpillars confine their attention mainly to the lower surface, so that only the shrivelled and split upper epidermis remains. In severe infestations, however, the entire leaf tissue between the mid-rib and the larger veins is devoured, so that the leaf appears in skeleton form.

Control. (1) Clean cultivation, including the destruction of wild cruciferous hosts in the immediate vicinity of kitchen and market gardens. (2) Spray or dust the lower surface of the foliage with DDT or, if within 2 weeks of harvesting, with derris.

The Fruit Tree Tortrix Moth (*Ditula angustiorana* Haw.), (June–July), is occasionally troublesome on rhododendrons, especially on *R. ponticum* and its varieties, *R. galactinum* and certain others. The larval habits of this species resemble those of some other species of Tortricids, for the type of injury consists of the fastening together of two overlapping leaves by means of silken threads, and the destruction of the lower epidermis of the leaf uppermost and the upper epidermis of the leaf so joined. This species may also girdle the petioles of the leaves causing them to break off easily.

Control. (1) Where practicable, hand-pick or crush the larvae within the fastened leaves. (2) Spray the foliage before leaf-tying commences, i.e. in May and June, with DDT.

Among the *Coleoptera* are found only a comparatively small number of species that, in their larval and/or adult stages, skeletonize the foliage of horticultural plants.

The Brassy Willow Beetle (*Phyllodecta vitellinae* L.), the Blue Willow Beetle (*P. vulgatissima* L.) and occasionally the Brown Willow Beetle (*Galerucella lineola* F.), (all June–Sept.), are in their larval and adult stages destructive to the foliage of specimen trees of *Salix* species, e.g. *S. alba* var. *vitellina*, *S. purpurea*, *S. triandra* and

S. viminalis. The larvae feed on the lower surface of the leaves so that only the upper parchment-like cuticle remains, while the beetles attack the upper surface and may cause complete defoliation. There are two broods in the year, but as the generations overlap to some extent both adults and their larvae may be found together during the summer months.

Control. (1) Clean cultivation, that is the elimination of the over-wintering quarters of the beetles, including rubbish heaps and old tree-stumps in the vicinity of specimen trees. (2) Spray both surfaces of the leaves with DDT.

FIG. 93. Rose leaves damaged by Rose Slugworm (*Endelomyia aethiops* F.).

The Nut Leaf Weevil (*Strophosomus melanogrammus* Fors.), (May–June), is an occasional pest of rhododendrons, more especially when they are grown in birch and oak woods and in the vicinity of nut plantations and hedges. The adult weevil partly skeletonizes the leaves by feeding on the upper epidermis, and may on occasion eat out large pieces and cause severe defoliation.

Control. Spray or dust the foliage of attacked plants with DDT.

The only Hymenopterous pests concerned with leaf skeletonization are certain Sawflies, including:

The Pear and Cherry Slugworm (*Caliroa cerasi* L.), (June–Sept.), so-called by reason of the larvae resembling black, slimy slugs, which attack pear and cherry by feeding on the upper leaf epidermis and leaving the lower surface and the veins intact.

Control. Spray the attacked foliage with nicotine, derris, DDT or BHC. If either DDT or BHC is used it is advisable to add an acaricide to check any build-up of the Fruit Tree Red Spider Mite.

The Rose Slugworm (*Endelomyia aethiops* F.), (June–Sept.), not only renders unsightly the foliage of garden roses, but materially checks the growth of the plants. The larvae feed chiefly on the lower epidermis, but in shade or during the night will also feed on the upper epidermis (Fig. 93). The result of the feeding is that the leaves become blotched, and later turn brown and shrivel up. There are two broods in the year—the first being found on rose foliage in June, the second and more serious attack occurring during August and September.

Control. Spray the undersides of the leaves with BHC, DDT, nicotine or derris.

III—Perforated

This category includes damage which consists of small holes eaten in the leaf and which are not liable to be enlarged to any great extent.

FIG. 94. Turnip seedlings attacked by Flea Beetles (*Phyllotreta* species).

The term 'shot-hole effect' aptly describes the appearance of such leaves.

Flea Beetles are responsible for extensive perforation and pitting of the foliage of cruciferous crops especially cabbage, mustard, radish, swede and turnip, and of various wild plants, e.g. shepherd's purse. Severe damage may be done to the developing seedlings before they appear above ground as well as to the cotyledons as they break through the soil. The critical period of attack is in spring, especially during a dry period in May. Injury is done, later, to the plants during their 'rough-leaf' stage, but the worst effect follows the attacks upon the seedlings in their cotyledon stage (Fig. 94). There are many species implicated, including *Phyllotreta cruciferae* Goeze, *P. nemorum* L., *P. atra* F., and *P. undulata* Kuts.

Similar damage may be done to potato foliage by the Potato Flea Beetle (*Psylliodes affinis* Payk), (May–June), and to certain ornamental plants, e.g. godetia, anemone, iris, stocks, wallflowers, by other species of Flea Beetles.

Control. (1) Clean cultivation, including the clearing and destruction during winter of all rubbish in the vicinity of the plots to reduce over-wintering populations, and the cutting of long vegetation which provides shelter near the crops during the growing season. (2) Dress the seed with lindane seed dressing or (3) spray or dust with DDT 7–10 days after sowing, repeating the treatment if necessary at fortnightly intervals until the rough-leaf stage is reached.

A 'shot-hole effect' on the leaves of leeks is produced by the caterpillars of the Leek Moth (*Acrolepia assectella* Zell.), (July–Sept.), which bore in all directions through the folded leaves in the centre of the plant. Rotting may often follow the attacks, and may cause the death of the plant. Onions, shallots, perennial onions and garlic are also attacked. The moth, which was first reported in Britain in 1943, is usually confined to coastal districts of south-east England.

Control. Spray or dust with DDT from early July onwards, as soon as damage is seen. Applications should be repeated at intervals of 2 weeks until the end of August.

IV—Notched

Damage of this type, where the margins of the leaves are eaten, is produced almost exclusively by Coleopterous insects. It is disfiguring in ornamental plants and may cause a decided check in growth of vegetable crops, e.g. broad beans, peas and celery. The chief pests concerned are:

(*a*) *Phaedon tumidulus* Germ., (May–July), a Chrysomelid beetle which normally feeds on the foliage of wild umbellifers (e.g. *Heracleum*), but is an occasional pest of celery upon which the beetles eat out notches from the leaf margins.

Control. (1) Clean cultivation, including the control of wild host plants in the neighbourhood of the vegetable garden; and (2) spray the foliage in June with DDT.

FIG. 95. Rhododendron leaves notched by Vine Weevil (*Otiorrhynchus sulcatus* F.).

(*b*) The Vine Weevil (*Otiorrhynchus sulcatus* F.), (Apr.-July), is a destructive pest of many plants in glasshouses and in the open. The injury it causes to the leaves of peach, vine, rhododendron (Fig. 95) and to *Phyllitis* ferns is characteristic, owing to the removal of notches from the leaf margins.

Control. (1) Spray infested foliage with DDT in April and May. (2) Trap the weevils in loosely rolled sacking or corrugated paper placed beneath attacked bushes to provide shelter during the day for this nocturnally active species. (3) For control of larvae see 'Bulbs Tunnelled', p. 39.

(*c*) The Bean and Pea Weevil (*Sitona lineata* L.), (Apr.–June), is a well-known pest of pulse, principally broad beans and peas. Other species attack leguminous crops, including clover and lucerne, but the one mentioned is responsible for the most serious damage to garden and field pulse crops. The injury comprises the eating out of the leaf margins by the adult weevils, so that the foliage appears to be notched (Fig. 96). The larvae feed upon the roots of the plants, though little damage is done by them except in severe infestations.

FIG. 96. Bean foliage notched by Pea and Bean Weevil (*Sitona lineata* L.). (*Shell Photograph.*)

Control. (1) Clean cultivation—including the eradication of their over-wintering quarters in heaps of rubbish, tufts of grass on headlands and ditch-sides, and accumulations of dried leaves beneath hedges, alongside fences and at the base of haystacks. (2) Spray the plants with DDT or dieldrin or dust with DDT when the damage is first seen. (3) Provide a good tilth for susceptible crops to allow the plants to grow away from an attack.

FOLIAGE EXCESSIVELY HAIRY

This condition is known as 'Erinose', a term applied to the hairy outgrowths of the epidermis arising from irritation set up by certain

Mites, e.g. The Glasshouse Red Spider Mite (*Tetranychus telarius* L.) and by microscopic Gall Mites (*Eriophyidae*). The Glasshouse Red Spider Mite spins a fine silken web over the leaves—usually on the underside—of a great variety of plants, but the presence of this webbing should not be confused with erinose. The general effect of this Mite is a mottling of the foliage (see 'Foliage Mottled', p. 105), but erinose is occasionally a symptom of severe Red Spider attacks on such plants as cineraria and vine.

There are many species of Gall Mites which produce erinose on the leaves of various plants. They set up irritation in the leaf tissue with the result that the entire leaf, the lower surfaces generally, or a portion of the leaf between the veins, becomes covered with fine hairs. This condition arises commonly on walnut leaves as a result of infestation by the Walnut Leaf Gall Mite (*Aceria erineus* Nal.), (May–Oct.).

Control. For Glasshouse Red Spider Mite, see 'Foliage Mottled', p. 105. Gall Mite infestations, when occurring on trees (e.g. lime, maple, poplar and walnut), are of little economic significance, although a recurrence may generally be avoided by spraying the affected trees, if small, with 3 per cent. lime-sulphur just when the leaf buds are bursting in the spring.

FOLIAGE WITH FROTHY MASSES

The presence of frothy masses on leaves is well known—the popular term being 'Cuckoo-spit'. This spittle-like excretion is produced by the larvae of Froghoppers (*Cercopidae*). The more common species are: (*a*) *Aphrophora spumaria* L. on alder (June); (*b*) *A. salicis* Deg., (June), on various willows; (*c*) *Philaenus leucophthalmus* L.), (June–July), which is sometimes a serious pest on apple, geum, lavender, rose, solidago and many other garden plants (Fig. 33), as well as upon weeds, especially sorrel. The larvae suck the sap and cause the leaves to wilt and become deformed. Serious distortion of young shoots and of the stems of lavender may follow an attack.

Control. Spray infested plants with parathion, malathion or BHC. This must be applied forcibly to remove the froth which protects the insects. Alternatively, the froth may be removed before spraying by syringing forcibly with water.

FOLIAGE GALLED

Galls result from a hypertrophy of living tissues that have been disturbed owing to the action of some irritant derived primarily from the organism concerned (see 'Stems Galled', p. 68). This local disarrangement of cellular tissue results in gall-formation—the galls varying considerably in shape, size, colour and consistency. Such terms as bean, blister, button, cherry, currant, kidney, marble, nail, red pea and spangle as applied to leaf-galls will enable one to visualize the range in form of the more common types. Leaf-galls are found on many annuals, biennials and perennials—weeds as well as cultivated plants—and on fruit and forest trees, and arise from the invasion of the cellular tissue by *Nematoda* (Eelworms), *Eriophyidae*. (Gall Mites), *Cecidomyidae* (Gall Midges) and *Cynipidae* (Gall Wasps). Other groups of insects are concerned with gall-formation, but are not considered here. According to some authorities the rolling and curling of leaves are considered to be symptomatic of gall-formation, but these particular injuries are considered elsewhere (see 'Foliage Curled', p. 117; 'Foliage Rolled', p. 122; and 'Foliage Puckered', p. 120).

Gall Mites whose galls are commonly found include the following: (*a*) *Auculus aucuparia* Liro, (June–Oct.), which produces reddish-brown blisters on both leaf surfaces of mountain ash. (*b*) *Aceria macrorhynchus* Nal., (June–Oct.), raises reddish pimples on the upper surface of the leaves of maple. (*c*) *Eriophyes tiliae* Nal., (June–Oct.), causes the growth of greenish-yellow or reddish-brown elongate 'nail-galls' on the upper surface of the leaves of the lime tree. These galls have little effect on the growth of the host plant but may be considered disfiguring. (*d*) The Pear Leaf Blister Mite (*Eriophyes piri* Nal.), (Apr.–Aug.), raises pustules, varying from yellowish green to brownish black in colour, on the upper surfaces of pear leaves (Col. Fig. I).

Control. (1) Where practicable, hand-pick and burn the affected leaves. (2) For Pear Leaf Blister Mite spray with 5 per cent. lime-sulphur at the end of March. For other species spray at the end of February.

A number of species in the *Aphididae* cause the formation of galls on the leaves of various plants but these are of little horticultural importance. In the *Phylloxeridae* the Vine Louse (*Phylloxera vastatrix* Planch.) may produce fleshy greenish-yellow or reddish-brown galls which are scattered over the surface and on the margins of the leaves of certain races of vines. It is a serious pest in Europe and America and may occasionally be introduced to Britain. Suspected outbreaks should be reported to the Ministry of Agriculture who will take the appropriate measures.

There are numerous species of Gall Midges that produce leaf-galls, the most important pest of horticultural plants being the Chrysanthemum Gall Midge (*Diarthronomyia chrysanthemi* Ahlb.), (July–Dec.). The larvae are found within thorn-like galls mainly on the upper surfaces of the leaves of chrysanthemum. In severe attacks the stems and bracts are also galled, the flower stems are distorted and the blooms malformed (Fig. 36). Galled cuttings do not root well and produce poor plants.

Control. (1) Remove and burn all heavily-infested leaves and stems. (2) Spray with BHC or parathion 3–4 times at weekly intervals, or with DDT emulsion 2 or 3 times at intervals of 10–14 days. (3) Dip stools and rooted cuttings in BHC or parathion. (4) Burn infested remnants if not needed for propagation. (5) Infested stools required for propagation should be stripped of all leaves and as much of the stems as possible.

FIG. 97. Spangle galls on Oak leaf due to Cynipid Gall Wasp.

The family *Cynipidae* includes not only gall-formers, but also inquilines ('guests' in galls), and a few parasitic species. Many Gall Wasps undergo a complicated life-cycle whereby the sexual generation gives rise to a totally different kind of gall to that produced by the asexual generation. It is estimated that over 80 per cent. of the known species of Gall Wasps produce galls on the roots, stems branches and leaves of the oak. Button and Spangle galls (Fig. 97) are commonly found on the leaves during autumn. Certain species of *Rhodites* produce galls on the foliage of wild roses, but injury to cultivated plants is uncommon (see 'Stems Galled', p. 70).

Control. Leaf-galls arising from Cynipids and from Sawflies, e.g. *Pontania* spp. on *Salix*, have little deleterious effect upon the host plant, and their presence on the leaves does not warrant any expenditure in labour and spray material.

FOLIAGE MINED

Leaf-mining insects are, with certain notable exceptions, of little economic significance to horticultural crops. The damage consists of the destruction of the palisade tissue and/or the spongy parenchyma, so that the affected leaf is not only rendered unsightly but its normal functions are partially or completely prevented. There are several different types of mines, e.g. linear, serpentine, trumpet, blotch, tentiform and community. Some mines commence as one type (i.e. linear) and develop into another (i.e. blotch). The leaf-mining habit among insects is confined to the larval stages, and is found chiefly in the following Orders, namely, (A) *Lepidoptera* (Families *Coleophoridae*, *Stigmellidae*, *Lyonetiidae* and *Gracillariidae*); (B) *Coleoptera* (*Chrysomelidae*, e.g. some Flea Beetles, and *Curculionidae*, e.g. *Orchestes*); (C) *Diptera* (*Cecidomyidae*, *Trypetidae* *Agromyzidae* and *Anthomyidae*); and (D) *Hymenoptera* (*Tenthredinidae*).

The more common leaf-mining pests of horticultural plants are considered under the headings (I) Linear Mines, including serpentine and trumpet; and (II) Blotch Mines, including tentiform and community.

(I) LINEAR MINES—Order *Lepidoptera*: (*a*) The Apple Leaf Miner (*Lyonetia clerckella* L.), (July–Oct.), is a common though not important pest of apple, cherry, hawthorn and birch. (*b*) The Rose Leaf Miner (*Stigmella anomalella* Goeze), (June–Oct.), frequently renders unsightly the foliage of bush and climbing roses, and is common on wild species. (*c*) The Apple Pygmy Moth (*S. malella* Staint.), (July–Oct.), mines the leaves of apple and wild crab apples.

Control. Control measures are usually only necessary on ornamental plants where the mines are unsightly. Hand-pick and burn mined leaves where possible. Otherwise spray in early May with DDT or BHC and repeat the application a fortnight later.

Order *Coleoptera*: (*d*) The Large Striped Flea Beetle (*Phyllotreta nemorum* L.), (June–July), the larvae of which mine the leaves of cabbage, radish, turnip and other cruciferous crops. The mines are linear at first but later become extended to the blotch type.

Control. Control measures should be directed against the adults (see 'Foliage Perforated', p. 141).

Order *Diptera*: (*e*) The Iris Leaf Miner (*Dizygomyza iraeos* R.-D.), (June–Aug.), the larvae of which occur in the leaves of wild and cultivated irises. (*f*) The Columbine Leaf Miner (*Phytomyza aquilegiae* Hard.), (June–Aug.), renders unsightly the leaves of aquilegias.

Control. Neither of these are serious pests and may be ignored unless the plants are being seriously disfigured. Hand-pick and burn the mined leaves, or spray with BHC or parathion at 14-day intervals from mid-May until the end of June.

(*g*) The Chrysanthemum Leaf Miner (*P. atricornis* Meig.), (July–Dec.), is a most destructive pest on chrysanthemums, cinerarias, and other composites. The larvae make whitish serpentine mines which meander through the leaf tissue (Fig. 98). The leaves may

Fig. 98. Severe damage on Chrysanthemum leaf by Chrysanthemum Leaf Miner (*Phytomyza atricornis* Meig.). (*Shell Photograph.*)

Fig. 99. Lilac foliage mined by Lilac Leaf Miner (*Caloptilia syringella* F.). (*Shell Photograph.*)

shrivel and die if heavily infested with the result that the plants are weakened and the blossoms affected. Spotting of the leaves may also occur, due to punctures made by the female fly when feeding on the sap (Col. Fig. XII). This and other related species may also attack the leaves of culinary and sweet peas.

Control. Chrysanthemum, etc. (1) Remove and burn the mined leaves. (2) Spray with lindane, malathion or parathion, giving 3 applications at 14-day intervals. To be effective, treatment must be started in the early stages of growth. (3) As an alternative to sprays, lindane or parathion smokes may be used 3 times at intervals of 7–10 days.

Peas. (1) Spray with DDT emulsion 10 days after flowering and again 4 weeks later. (2) Where the infestation is already severe spray with parathion or lindane.

The Tomato Leaf Miner (*Liriomyza solani* Macq.), (Jan.–Sept.), if present in large numbers, can cause reductions in crops of glasshouse tomatoes and attacked seedlings may be crippled or killed.

Control. Spray 3 times at 14-day intervals with lindane or parathion. Treatment should be started at the seedling stage if a heavy attack is expected. Alternatively lindane or parathion smokes may be used, giving 3 treatments at 7-day intervals.

(II) Blotch Mines—Order *Lepidoptera*: (*a*) The Laburnum Leaf Miner (*Leucoptera laburnella* Staint.), (June–Sept.), produces spiral blotches on laburnum leaves. (*b*) The Lilac Leaf Miner (*Caloptilia syringella* F.), (June-Sept.), mines the leaves of lilac and privet (Fig. 99), later emerging from the mines and feeding on the surface of the leaf, which rolls laterally or conically. (*c*) The Azalea Leaf Miner (*C. azaleella* Brants.), (Sept.–Dec.), is a serious pest of indoor azaleas, *Rhododendron simsii* and other deciduous rhododendrons. The larvae mine the leaves during the younger stages but later emerge from the mine and curl up the tips of the leaves which are secured with silk webbing. They may cause severe defoliation and stunting.

Control. (1) Pick off and burn the infested leaves where this is practicable. (2) Spray the foliage with BHC or parathion in May when the eggs are being laid on laburnum, lilac and privet. On azaleas treatment should be given about September or when they are brought into the glasshouse for the winter. In all cases several applications should be given at 14-day intervals.

(*d*) The Pear Leaf Blister Moth (*Leucoptera scitella* Zell.), (May–Sept.), attacks apple, pear and *Sorbus aucuparia*. (*e*) The Nut Leaf Blister Moth (*Lithocolletis coryli* Nic.), (May–Sept.), produces brown blisters on the leaves of hazel in hedgerows and in plantations. (*f*) *L. messaniella* Zell., (Apr.–Oct.), renders unsightly the leaves of the evergreen oak (*Quercus ilex*).

Control. Where mining is liable to be severe on ornamental or nursery trees, they should be sprayed with DDT in late April or early May. Mined leaves should be picked off and burned.

The *Coleophoridae* or Casebearers are only partial leaf miners but they are included here since the damage they do is very similar to the blotch type of mine (Fig. 100). The minute caterpillar constructs around its body a case made of leaf tissue and silk. It bores a hole in the surface of the leaf and, thrusting its head into the aperture, devours as much of the internal tissue as it can reach, producing a pale blotch which has a round hole in the centre.

FIG. 100. Elm foliage damaged by Casebearer Moth Caterpillars (*Coleophora* species).

The two chief fruit-infesting species are:

(*a*) The Apple and Plum Casebearer (*Coleophora nigricella* Steph.), (Apr.–May), which feeds on apple foliage, plum and cherry, and occasionally on bullace and sloe. The young larvae may be found during July and August feeding on the leaves, but the damage during this period is not serious. Hibernation takes place within the larval case, and feeding recommences in spring when the characteristic spotting of the foliage is observed.

(*b*) The Pistol Casebearer (*C. anatipennella* Hübn.) is often abundant on apple and cherry and undergoes a life-cycle similar to that of *C. nigricella*.

Control. (1) Spray in early spring with DDT or lead arsenate. (2) If damage has already started spray with parathion.

Order *Coleoptera*: The larvae of many species of *Orchestes* produce blotch mines in the leaves of deciduous trees, especially oak, beech and birch. These are unlikely to affect the growth of the trees and no control measures are necessary.

Order *Diptera*: (*a*) The Celery Fly (*Philophylla heraclei* L.), (May–Oct.), is a common and destructive pest of celery and parsnip. The attacked leaves shrivel and the growth of the plant suffers accordingly (Fig. 101). Seedlings are particularly vulnerable. (*b*) The Mangold Fly

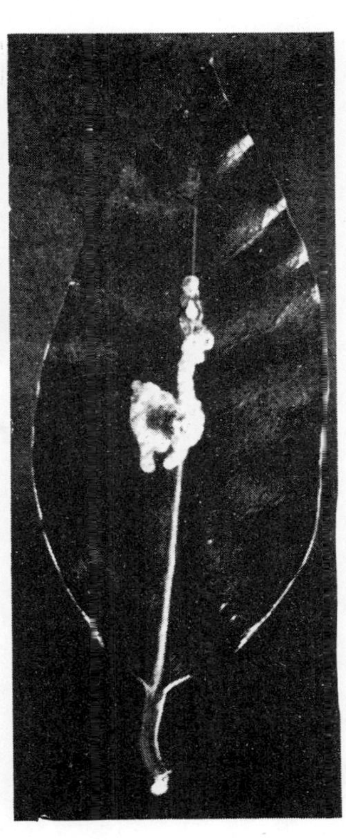

Fig. 101. *Above:* Damage to Celery foliage by Celery Fly (*Philophylla heraclei* L.). (*Crown Copyright Photograph.*)

Fig. 102. *Right:* Holly leaf mined by the Holly Leaf Miner (*Phytomyza ilicis* Curt.). (*Shell Photograph.*)

(*Pegomyia betae* Curt.), (June–Aug.), retards the growth of beetroot, mangold and spinach, and is particularly harmful during the early stages of growth.

Control. (1) Where practicable, remove and burn the mined leaves. (2) Where attacks are a regular occurrence, an application of DDT or lindane should be made at the egg-laying periods, i.e. late April (Celery Fly) or mid-May (Mangold Fly) and a close watch kept for subsequent damage. Otherwise (3) spray with lindane, malathion or parathion as soon as the damage is seen and repeat at fortnightly intervals as necessary.

(*c*) The Holly Leaf Miner (*Phytomyza ilicis* Curt.), (May–Dec.), is widely distributed on the foliage of wild and cultivated hollies which may be rendered unsightly by the brownish mines (Fig. 102).

Control. This is only practicable on small trees where hand-picking will check the pest. Spraying the undersides of the leaves with BHC will also reduce the damage.

Order *Hymenoptera.* The larvae of different species of *Heterarthrus* are leaf-miners on alder, birch, poplar and willows. They cause little harm and control measures are unnecessary.

FOLIAGE NARROWED

The leaves of phlox which are infested by the Stem and Bulb Eelworm (*Ditylenchus dipsaci* (Kühn) Filipj.), (Mar.–June), become narrow and strap-like, spongy in texture and distorted (Fig. 103). The stem may split in places and is often twisted and stunted.

FIG. 103. Damage to Phlox foliage caused by infestation of Stem and Bulb Eelworm (*Ditylenchus dipsaci* (Kühn) Filipj.). (*Shell Photograph.*)

Control. (1) Burn all heavily-infested plants. (2) Less severely attacked plants may be subjected to hot-water treatment, immersing them for 1 hour in water at a constant temperature of 110° F. (see

Appendix I, p. 208). (3) Clean stocks may also be raised from true root cuttings or seed taken from infested plants. (4) Infested ground should not be replanted with any likely host plant (see Appendix II, p. 210) for at least 3 years.

FOLIAGE RAGGED

The Common Green Capsid Bug (*Lygus pabulinus* L.), (Apr.–Aug.), has within recent years become a serious pest of many plants. The sucking of the young nymphs causes the leaves to become spotted but, as growth proceeds, the spots enlarge and holes with brownish edges appear, giving the foliage a scarred and tattered appearance. This type of injury is not apparent on all the host plants of this Capsid, but it is found in an acute form on currants (Fig. 104), gooseberry, blackberry, raspberry, wild and cultivated roses, potatoes, beans, dahlias and salvias, and on such weeds as bindweed. The fruits of pear, gooseberry and plum may also be damaged (see 'Fruits Scarred', p. 183). This Capsid migrates from its woody primary hosts (apple, currants and gooseberry) to many annual and herbaceous secondary summer hosts, both cultivated and wild.

Control. (1) Clean cultivation, i.e. the destruction of weed hosts in the vicinity of gardens, and the forking in of all weeds in fruit

FIG. 104. Black Currant foliage damaged by Common Green Capsid (*Lygus pabulinus* L.). (*Shell Photograph.*)

FIG. 105. Geranium foliage damaged by Capsids. (*Shell Photograph.*)

plantations and in flower borders before the end of July. (2) On soft fruits spray with DNC-petroleum in mid-March or DDT about the end of April either before or after, but not during the flowering period. (3) On other plants treat as for the Tarnished Plant Bug (see 'Flowers Distorted', p. 164).

The Tarnished Plant Bug (*Lygus rugulipennis* Popp.), (June–Sept.) is destructive to many herbaceous plants, especially chrysanthemum, dahlia, and zinnia. The buds and foliage are pierced by the feeding stylets which results in the malformation of the bloom. The leaves are misshapen, scarred and perforated with irregular holes (Figs. 78 and 105). This Capsid over-winters in the adult stage, and is a more difficult pest to control than the Common Green Capsid by reason of its active habits during its larval and adult stages, its manner of migrating from weed hosts to cultivated plants during the spring and summer months, and the difficulty of destroying it during the dormant season on woody plants.

Control. See 'Flowers Distorted', p. 164.

FOLIAGE SCALY

The leaves of a great variety of plants, particularly those grown in temperate and tropical houses, are rendered unsightly and frequently wither and die as a result of a thick encrustation of Scale insects or Coccids. Many such infestations are accompanied by a growth of Sooty Moulds on the honeydew-drenched leaves. The immature 'scale' stages of Aleyrodids (Whiteflies) and the coccid-like bodies of certain Fungi (e.g. *Pilobolus*, *Pilaira* and *Sphaerobolus*) may be confused with true Scale insects. Many Coccids that attack glasshouse plants, more especially orchids and palms, are exotic species, and have been introduced on imported plants.

Many of the species which infest the stems of plants are also found on the leaves (see 'Stems Scaly', p. 77). Among those which more commonly attack the leaves only are: (*a*) the Oleander Scale (*Aspidiotus hederae* Vall.) on glasshouse plants, including cyclamen, oleander and palms (Fig. 106), and, in southern England, on outdoor plants such as Japanese laurel and acacia. (*b*) The Bay Scale (*A. brittanicus* Newst.) on bay. (*c*) The Cymbidium Scale (*Lepidosaphes pinnaeformis* Bouché) on orchids (Fig. 107). (*d*) The Soft Scale (*Coccus hesperidum* L.), common on tender plants in glasshouses, e.g. citrus, figs, vines, etc., and occasionally on holly and ivy growing in sheltered spots in the open garden (Fig. 108).

Control. See 'Stems Scaly', p. 77.

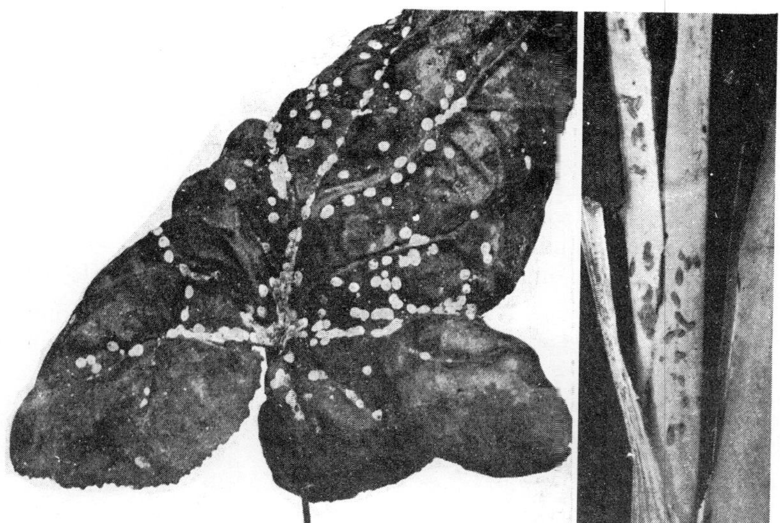

FIG. 106. *Left:* Oleander Scale (*Aspidiotus hederae* Vall.) on Cyclamen leaf.
FIG. 107. *Right:* Cymbidium Scale (*Lepidosaphes pinnaeformis* Bouché) on Cymbidium. (*Shell Photograph.*)

FIG. 108. Soft Scale (*Coccus hesperidum* L.) on underside of citrus leaf. (*Shell Photograph.*)

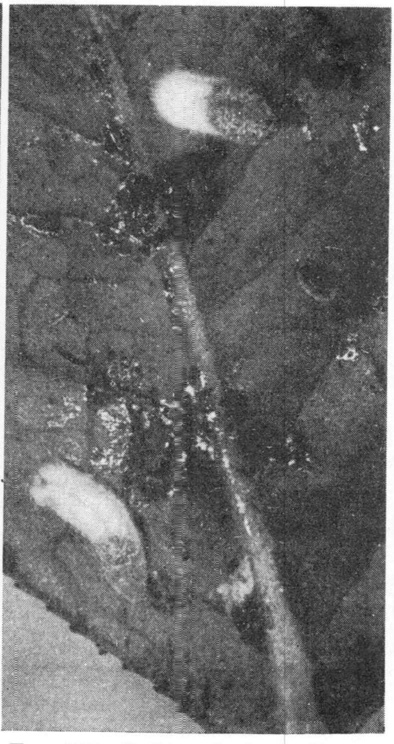

FIG. 109. Cushion Scale (*Pulvinaria floccifera* Westw.) on underside of Magnolia leaf. (*Shell Photograph.*)

FOLIAGE SCARRED

The young leaves of strawberry and chrysanthemum which are attacked by the Leaf and Bud Eelworms (*Aphelenchoides* spp.) may sometimes show rough greyish or brownish scars on the upper surfaces near the petioles (Fig. 110). These are caused by the eelworms feeding externally on the young leaves while they are still in the bud.

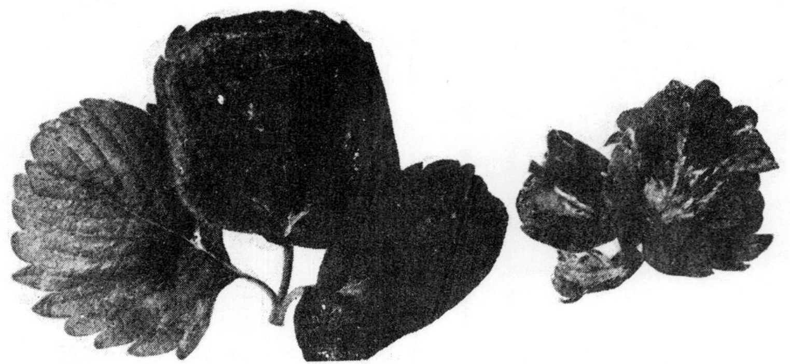

FIG. 110. Strawberry leaves with scars caused by external feeding of Leaf and Bud Eelworms. (*Photograph by East Malling Research Station.*) .

Control. Chrysanthemums: see 'Foliage with Black or Brown Areas', p. 103; strawberries: see 'Foliage Puckered', p. 120.

The Garden Slug (*Arion hortensis* Fér.) and the Grey Field Slug (*Agriolimax reticulatus* Müll.) in particular injure the leaves of iris, more especially *I. japonica*, *I. sibirica* and *I. unguicularis*, and aspidistra in a characteristic manner—the nature of the damage resembling somewhat the clawing of the foliage by a cat (Fig. 86). Young slugs are chiefly responsible but, owing to their nocturnal habits and to the absence of any appreciable quantity of slime on the leaves, the culprits are often unsuspected.

Control. See 'Foliage with Clean-cut Holes', p. 131.

The Common Green Capsid Bug (*Lygus pabulinus* L.), (Apr.–June), produces a scratched appearance on the foliage of certain of its host plants, more especially currants (see 'Foliage Ragged', p. 153).

FOLIAGE SEVERED

The damage here described is the partial or complete severance of the petiole or leaf-stalk, and is distinct from the injury caused by

Twig-Cutting Weevils, *Rhynchites* and *Caenorhinus* species (see 'Shoots Severed', p. 81).

The larva of the Fruit Tree Tortrix Moth (*Ditula angustiorana* Haw.), (May–June), has been found to girdle the petioles of rhododendron so that the leaves wilt and snap off during high winds. This species is concerned with somewhat similar injury to the shoots of yew so that they turn brown as if frosted.

The Clay-coloured Weevil (*Otiorrhynchus singularis* L.), (Apr.–May), feeds in a similar manner on the leaf-stalks of currants, raspberry and ornamental shrubs, causing them to wilt and hang down.

Control. Spray attacked plants with DDT as soon as the first damage is seen and repeat as necessary. The weevils may also be trapped in loose sacking or rolled corrugated paper, which should be placed under the infested plants at night and examined during the day.

FOLIAGE SPUN TOGETHER

The larvae of numerous species of Tortricid Moths are not only leaf-rollers (see 'Foliage Rolled', p. 123) but also leaf-tyers, for they fasten together the young leaves and shoots with strands of silk thereby providing a shelter in which they live and feed. This leaf-tying habit is characteristic of many Tortrix Moths, and is frequently observed on fruit and ornamental trees and bushes, on herbaceous plants, and on roses. Among the chief species concerned are the larvae of the following:

(*a*) The Fruit Tree Tortrix Moth (*Archips podana* Scop.), (May–June), which is a common pest of apple, apricot, pear, plum and indoor vines, and not only rolls the leaves but has the habit of fastening two leaves together by silken webs, or attaches a leaf to the side of an apple fruit and feeds on the skin.

(*b*) The Carnation Tortrix Moth (*Cacoecia pronubuna* Hübn.), (Jan.–Dec.), injures the young growths of carnations, chorizema, grevillea and many other glasshouse subjects by fastening the leaves together at the tips of the shoots.

(*c*) The Flax Tortrix Moth (*Cnephasia virgaureana* Treits.), (May–June), is concerned with the spinning-together of the young leaves and growths of heleniums, phloxes, rudbeckias and solidagos (Fig. 80).

(*d*) *Acroclita naevana* Hübn., (May–July), is the chief culprit in disfiguring the young growths on clipped holly hedges by tying together the tender new leaves.

(*e*) The Bramble Shoot Moth (*Notocelia uddmanniana* L.), (May–June), draws together the terminal leaves of wild and cultivated blackberries and of loganberry, producing a bunched-up appearance of the growth tips.

(*f*) The Bud Moth (*Spilonota ocellana* Schiff.), (Apr.–May), not only feeds on the buds of apple, pear, plum, cherry and other fruits, but draws together several leaves and lives within its little tunnel of silk.

The larvae of several Tineid Moths belonging to the genus *Depressaria* live in rolled and spun leaves, especially on umbelliferous and composite plants. This type of injury is apparent on such ornamentals as *Cytisus*, *Genista*, *Hypericum*, and on *Salix* species grown as specimen trees, while carrots and parsnips are frequently attacked by *D. heracliana* Deg. and *D. nervosa* Haw. respectively (June–July).

Control. See 'Buds Tunnelled', p. 98; 'Flowers Eaten', p. 168; and 'Foliage Rolled', p. 123.

FOLIAGE WILTING

The fact that a plant wilts is in most instances symptomatic of water shortage—the amount of moisture absorbed by the roots or checked in its upward movement in the plant being insufficient to meet the demand made by the aerial portions, especially the leaves. This effect is readily detected during periods of drought. Wilting of the foliage may be due, however, to waterlogged conditions arising from defective drainage and to cultural defects (e.g. over-watering of glasshouse borders and pot-plants), this meaning that the roots have been killed through lack of aeration, or, being diseased, are unable to function. This symptom is also produced by root- and stem-rots caused by bacterial and fungal infections.

Among the pests which cause wilting are the root feeders mentioned under 'Roots Eaten', p. 46, and also Root Aphids (p. 44), Root Mealy Bugs (p. 61), Potato Root Eelworm (p. 59), Cabbage Root Eelworm (p. 57), Pea Root Eelworm (p. 115) and Root Knot Eelworms (p. 54). Also responsible for this damage are Leaf and Bud Eelworm on chrysanthemums (p. 102), stem-boring insects (see 'Stems Tunnelled' p. 82), and sucking pests such as Capsid Bugs (p. 114), Aphids (p. 100), Scale Insects (p. 77), Mealy Bugs (p. 91) and Red Spiders (p. 114).

Again, wilting is observed in plants, more especially in flower borders and rock gardens, which have been upheaved as a result of Ants making their nests beneath them. The delicate root hairs wither as a result of exposure or by being loosened from the soil particles, causing the plants to wilt and die.

Control. (1) Destroy the nests by watering copiously with aldrin or dieldrin or pouring it into the entrance hole which should be sealed with earth or a turf. (2) Alternatively dust the entrance hole and the runs with lindane or aldrin dust.

FOLIAGE WITH WOOLLY MASSES

The presence of white, woolly patches on the needles of various coniferous trees indicates the presence of some member of the Family *Adelgidae*. The life-cycles of these insects are extremely complex, and

FIG. 111. Douglas Fir infested with *Adelges cooleyi* Gill.

space will not allow detailed reference to them. Many species of *Adelges* require two hosts—primary and secondary—in order to complete their cycle, and this fact has produced in the past some confusion for the systematist. The type of injury produced by these pests varies according to the host, the symptoms—other than the presence of woolly tufts on the foliage, shoots and stem—being: distortion of shoots, formation of galls, wilting and distortion of the foliage and premature leaf-fall, with the result that the sap flow is reduced and the vigour of the plants is lowered.

Among the more common species infesting coniferous trees in gardens are: (*a*) the Douglas Fir Adelges (*Adelges cooleyi* Gill.), which forms white woolly tufts on the lower leaf surface of Douglas Fir (Fig. 111). The gall-forming generation on Sitka Spruce is now known to occur in Britain.

(*b*) The Silver Fir Adelges (*A. nordmannianae* Eck.) forms tufts on the needles, branches and stem of *Abies nordmanniana* and *A. pectinata*.

(*c*) The Pine and the Weymouth Pine Adelges (*Pineus pini* Macq. and *P. strobi* Htg.) lives beneath woolly patches on the Scots pine and the Weymouth pine respectively.

(*d*) The Spruce Pineapple Gall Adelges (*A. abietis* L.) forms woolly patches on the needles of spruce and larch.

Control. See 'Stems with Woolly Masses', p. 89.

Certain other pests produce woolly patches on the foliage; for instance: (*a*) the Woolly Aphid or American Blight (*Eriosoma lanigerum* Hausm.) on apple, hawthorn, *Pyracantha* species and on *Cotoneaster horizontalis* (Fig. 56); (*b*) the Beech Aphid (*Phyllaphis fagi* L.), (May–July), which is a frequent and destructive pest of beech hedges and of specimen trees of the green and copper beeches. It occurs in dense woolly masses on the lower surfaces of the leaves, and also excretes quantities of honeydew, fouling plants growing beneath their shade; and (*c*) Mealy Bugs (*Pseudococcus* spp.), mainly on greenhouse plants, which also become disfigured by honeydew and Sooty Moulds (Fig. 57).

Control. For Woolly Aphid and Mealy Bugs see 'Stems with Woolly Masses', p. 89.

Spray the lower surfaces of infested leaves with BHC to which a succinate spreader has been added, or malathion, or parathion.

CHAPTER SEVEN

Flowers

Flowers Discoloured. Flowers Distorted. Flowers Eaten. Flowers Withered.

THE flower is a modified shoot bearing lateral appendages in the form of specially modified leaves, the whole forming an organ specially adapted for the production of seeds, so that pests that attack the floral organs are indirectly concerned with a partial or complete failure of the seed and/or fruit crop.

Insects that attack the non-essential parts of a flower—the perianth, comprising the calyx and corolla—are less injurious than those that attack the essential portions—the stamens, stigma, style and ovary—for these last-mentioned organs are directly concerned in fertilization and seed formation.

The supply of food—pollen and nectar—in flowers gives insects an inducement to visit them, while the coloured floral envelope acts as an attractant and guide to the visitor. Insect-pollinated flowers attract a vast number of insect visitors, some of which are useful and invaluable pollinating agents, while others are destructive by feeding on the petals and on the essential organs of the flower.

Both the flower and seed trades suffer heavy losses through the depredations of flower pests. The injuries consist of: (i) the destruction, distortion and discoloration of the petals, and (ii) the destruction of the essential floral organs, which may result in a partial or complete failure of the seed crop. Every gardener has witnessed at some time the spoliation of his floral display by flower-infesting species. The fact should not be overlooked that insects that attack fruit blossom are either directly responsible for (e.g the Apple Blossom Weevil and Pear Midge) or indirectly concerned with (e.g. the larvae of Green Pug, Winter and other Moths) crop reduction. The destruction of the floral envelope by mandibulate insects lessens the attractiveness of the flowers to pollinating insects.

There are certain species of insects and mites that attack the male flowers of amentaceous (catkin-bearing) trees, but these rather highly specialized species are not considered here.

The numerous species of Solitary (*Andrena* and *Halictus*), Humble (*Bombus*) and Hive (*Apis*) Bees are anthophilous, i.e. flower-loving, for they depend entirely upon flowers for food—pollen and nectar—for themselves and their offspring.

Humble bees are known to rob flowers of their nectar by piercing the corolla and/or calyx, and this type of injury may frequently be observed in spurred and tubular flowers, more especially on antirrhinum, aquilegia and certain leguminous plants (e.g. climbing beans 'scarlet runners' and sweet peas). Hive bees may also occasionally cause this type of damage. Again, ants will rob flowers of their nectar, and their presence in orchard houses is frequently attended by severe injury to the unopened blossoms of pear and cherry.

Woodlice are occasional pests of flowers, more especially in glasshouses. Details concerning their habits and control are given elsewhere (p. 48).

Attention is drawn to the danger of applying poisonous washes and dusts to plants which are in flower, owing to the danger of poisoning pollinating insects, especially Hive Bees.

FLOWERS DISCOLOURED

The Glasshouse Red Spider Mite (*Tetranychus telarius* L.), (Mar.–Dec.), is a notorious glasshouse pest, and besides severely injuring the foliage causes disfiguration and discoloration of the flowers of carnation, chrysanthemum, hydrangea and violet. In severe infestations the whole flower may be enmeshed with their webbing. During August, there is often a definite migration period when the mites tend to leave their host plants and seek over-wintering quarters in and around the house, although feeding may continue throughout the winter provided the temperature is above 65° F.

Control. See 'Foliage Mottled', p. 105.

Thrips, of which there are numerous flower-infesting species, invade and disfigure the blooms of many plants, and may so affect them that further development ceases. The chief flower-infesting species are:

(*a*) The Onion Thrips (*Thrips tabaci* Lind.), (Jan.–Dec.), which attacks the unopened and open blooms of carnation, cyclamen and other ornamentals, and gives rise to white flecks on coloured flowers.

(*b*) The Rose Thrips (*Thrips fuscipennis* Hal.), is occasionally a pest of cucumber flowers and of chrysanthemum and rose blooms.

(*c*) *Taeniothrips inconsequens* Uzel., (Mar.–Apr.), is commonly found in the blossoms of apple and plum, and later gives rise to a russeting of the fruits (see 'Fruits Scarred', p. 182).

(*d*) The Gladiolus Thrips (*Taeniothrips simplex* Mor.), (June–Sept.), feeds on the flowers of gladiolus, marking the petals with white flecks (Fig. 112), (see 'Foliage Mottled', p. 106).

(*e*) *Kakothrips robustus* Uzel., the well-known Pea Thrips, attacks the flowers of culinary peas and broad beans (see 'Fruits Discoloured', p. 173).

FIG. 112. Gladiolus blooms discoloured by Gladiolus Thrips (*Taeniothrips simplex* Mor.). (*Photograph by R. P. Scase.*)

FIG. 113. Mottled Arum Aphid (*Aulacorthum circumflexum* Buckt.) on Arum bloom.

Control. (1) Syringe the flowers of infested glasshouse plants with clean water during dull weather or when the sun is off the house. (2) Heavily infested blooms should be sprayed at dusk or in dull weather with an insecticide of short persistence such as nicotine or TEPP. (3) Other control measures under 'Foliage Mottled', p. 106, should be taken before or after flowering.

Conditions in glasshouses are particularly favourable to the rapid breeding of pests, e.g. Spider Mites, Thrips and Aphids. Aphids are responsible for a considerable amount of damage to flowers and render the blooms of many glasshouse plants unmarketable. Among the more important flower-invading species are:

(*a*) *Macrosiphum luteum* Buckt., which is a yellow species found infesting dendrobium flowers.

(*b*) The Mottled Arum Aphid (*Aulacorthum circumflexum* Buckt.) is essentially a glasshouse aphid, and injures the flowers of arum (Fig. 113), hippeastrum (amaryllis), chrysanthemum, cyclamen, cypripedium, lily and tulip.

(*c*) The Leaf-curling Plum Aphid (*Aulacorthum helichrysi* Kalt.), which infests the flowers of cineraria.

(*d*) The Peach-Potato Aphid (*Myzus persicae* Sulz.) occurs in the blooms of canna, chrysanthemum and tulip.

(*e*) The Water-Lily Aphid (*Rhopalosiphum nymphaeae* L.), in water-lily flowers.

(*f*) The Apple-Grass Aphid (*R. insertum* Wlk.), in apple and pear blossom.

Control. (1) Spray infested flower buds with TEPP or a nicotine-soap wash—spraying should not be carried out in bright sunlight or severe scorching of the blossoms may result. (2) Fumigate glasshouse plants with nicotine 'shreds'.

The tulip strain of the Stem and Bulb Eelworm (*Ditylenchus dipsaci* (Kühn) Filipj.), (Apr.–May), causes severe distortion of the blooms of tulips, parts of which may fail to colour.

Control. See 'Bulbs Discoloured Externally', p. 31.

FLOWERS DISTORTED

The Tarnished Plant or 'Bishop' Bug (*Lygus rugulipennis* Popp.), (Aug.–Oct.), is a serious pest of many garden plants, including herbaceous plants and annuals. The flowers of chrysanthemum (Fig. 114), dahlias and venidiums are distorted and malformed as a result of feeding on the flower buds. The extraction of sap from the buds results in the production of one-sided and disfigured blooms. Other species of Capsid Bugs are known to injure the blooms of chrysanthemum, namely, the Potato Capsid (*Calocoris norvegicus* Gmel.) and the Common Green Capsid (*Lygus pabulinus* L.), both of which are concerned with petal distortion.

Control. (1) Ensure clean cultivation and the control of weeds near borders to reduce the available hibernation quarters for the adult Capsids. (2) In the early stages of growth, while the flower buds are forming, spray with DDT, lindane or parathion, or dust with DDT, repeating the application 14 days later. (3) Treat the ground under the plants to kill any Capsids which drop off during spraying. (4) In glasshouses DDT or lindane smokes may be used.

FIG. 114. Damage to Chrysanthemum blooms caused by Tarnished Plant Bug (*Lygus rugulipennis* Popp.). (*Shell Photograph.*)

The Pea Midge (*Contarinia pisi* Winn.) will attack the pods, shoots and flowers of culinary peas. The presence of the legless, jumping, white larvae in the flowers may be recognized by the wrinkled appearance of the petals and the swollen sepals. The damage may somewhat resemble damage by Thrips, from which it may be distinguished by the presence of the maggots in the blooms. The flowers usually die without forming pods, or dwarfed and malformed pods may be produced. The larvae also attack the terminal shoots which results in clustering of the flowering stems, leaves and pods. In the pods they feed on the internal surface and occasionally on the peas themselves.

Control. Chemical control is not satisfactory On a garden scale the attacked parts of the plant should be picked off and burned and infested plants should be burned immediately the crop has been harvested. Infested land should be deeply trenched and dressed with aldrin dust. Where the pest is prevalent it is advisable to sow only early varieties of peas which are not so seriously damaged as later varieties.

Malformation of the flowers of chrysanthemum may result from an infestation by the Leaf and Bud Eelworm (*Aphelenchoides ritzema-bosi* (Schwartz) Stein.), (see 'Foliage with Blackened or Brown Areas', p. 102), and on tulips, hyacinth, etc., infested by the Stem and Bulb Eelworm (*Ditylenchus dipsaci* (Kühn) Filipj.), (see

'Bulbs Discoloured Externally', p. 31, and 'Bulbs Discoloured Internally', p. 33).

FLOWERS EATEN

The Garden Slug (*Arion hortensis* Fér.) and the Grey Field Slug (*Agriolimax reticulatus* Müll.) are omnivorous, prolific and hardy species, although injury to flowers is confined chiefly to the late spring, summer and autumn months. Gooseberry blossom and the petals of dahlias (chiefly Mignon), *Iris unguicularis*, narcissi and violas are frequently devoured. Not only are these species concerned in flower injury, but others, together with snails, will feed on the floral envelope of garden flowers. Considerable havoc often occurs in herbaceous borders where the flowers of *Chrysanthemum maximum*, coreopsis, heleniums and rudbeckias are ruined by these pests (Fig. 116).

Control. See 'Foliage with Clean-cut Holes', p. 131.

The Common Earwig (*Forficula auricularia* L.), (May–Oct.), is known to attack apple and plum blossom, and the flowers of several ornamentals, including chrysanthemum, clematis (Fig. 115) and dahlia, both in the open and in glasshouses.

FIG. 115. Clematis flower damaged by Earwigs (*Forficula auricularia* L.).

Control. (1) Shake the blooms to dislodge any sheltering Earwigs. (2) Spray or dust the lower foliage or, in the case of fruit trees the trunk and lower branches, with DDT, lindane or dieldrin, avoiding the flowers as much as possible. (3) Apply DDT to the ground under the attacked plant. (4) Remove rubbish, dead leaves and other shelter from the vicinity of the plant. (5) Trap with loosely-rolled sacking or corrugated paper.

FIG. 116. *Above:* Petunia flower eaten by Garden Slug (*Arion hortensis* Fér.). (*Shell Photograph.*)

FIG. 117. *Right*: Quince flowers eaten by caterpillars of the Green Pug Moth (*Chloroclystis rectangulata* L.).

Cockroaches, principally the American species, *Periplaneta americana* L., and Crickets (*Gryllulus domesticus* L.), are frequently destructive in glasshouses and conservatories. Seeds, seedlings, the foliage and stems of many plants, and the aerial roots of orchids are eaten with avidity, while the blooms of chrysanthemum, cineraria and orchids are damaged by these omnivorous and persistent pests.

Control. (1) Do not allow débris to collect under the staging. (2) Apply DDT or BHC dust to infested plants, to the soil underneath them and near hot pipes. (Do not allow DDT dust to come in contact with hot rusty pipes.) (3) Lay down poison baits (see Appendix V, p. 216).

The larvae of many Lepidopterous insects are concerned with floral injuries. Among the more important species are: (*a*) the Angle-shades Moth (*Phlogophora meticulosa* L.), (Sept.–Feb.), which is a polyphagous species and may continue to breed throughout the year under glasshouse conditions; the larvae feed on the blooms and flower buds of chrysanthemum (Fig. 118), especially of white-flowered varieties. (*b*) The Green Pug Moth (*Chloroclystis rectangulata* L.), (May–June), whose larvae feed on the floral organs of apple, pear, medlar and quince (Fig. 117). (*c*) The Winter Moth (*Operophtera brumata* L.), (Apr.–May), whose larvae, though normally foliage feeders, are destructive to the blossoms of fruit trees, especially apple, pear and quince, and to those of ornamental *Pyrus* species. (*d*) The Cherry Fruit Moth (*Argyresthia curvella* L.), (Mar.–Apr.), feeds on the buds and flowers of cherry in the early spring, later tunnelling into the fruitlets which are hollowed out (see 'Fruits Tunnelled', p. 188). (*e*) Tortricid Moths of which there are numerous species, some being destructive to fruit blossom, others to decorative plants, e.g. roses—the so-called 'Rose Maggots'—and many glasshouse plants. The larvae of the Carnation Tortrix (*Cacoecia pronubana* Hb.), (Jan.–Dec.), may be found throughout the year feeding on the flower buds and open blooms of acacia, carnation, cytisus and other plants.

FIG. 118. Chrysanthemum blooms injured by caterpillars of the Angleshades Moth (*Phlogophora meticulosa* L.).

Control. DDT applied as a spray or a dust will kill caterpillars, but this should not be applied to open blossoms because of the risk of poisoning bees and other pollinating insects. On fruit trees and ornamental *Pyrus*, *Malus*, etc., damage can be prevented by treatment about the green cluster stage; on other plants before the blooms open. After the flowers have opened spraying and dusting should be confined to the lower leaves and stems or should be done after picking all open blooms. Small infestations may be checked by collecting the caterpillars by hand.

Clean cultivation in and around glasshouses and flower beds will eradicate weeds which attract egg-laying female moths.

Of *Coleoptera*, the number of species found attacking flowers is proportionately high. With few exceptions, most species of Beetles and Weevils that visit blossoms are injurious, and are of little significance as pollinating agents. Large numbers of beetles are found in open flowers, e.g. those of the *Umbelliferae*, where the nectar and pollen are easily accessible.

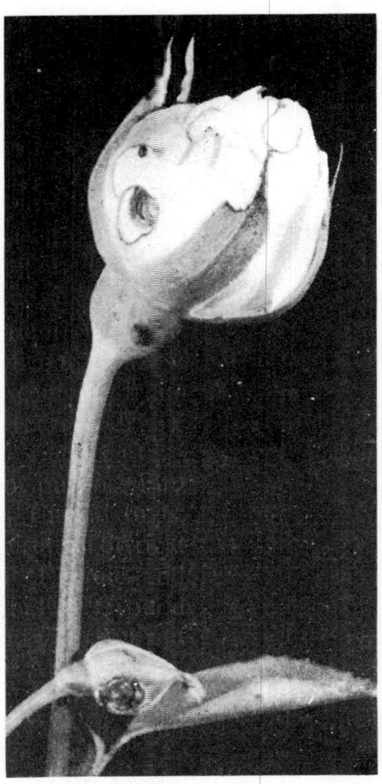

FIG. 119. Damaged Rose bloom and bud by Garden Chafer (*Phyllopertha horticola* L.). (*Shell Photograph.*)

The more important beetle and weevil pests of flowers are: (*a*) the Apple Blossom Weevil (*Anthonomus pomorum* L.), (see 'Flowers Withered', p. 171). (*b*) Chafer Beetles, including the Rose Chafer (*Cetonia aurata* L.), (May-Jul.), which attack the petals and anthers of bush and climbing roses, narcissi and other blooms, including white lilac; the Cockchafer (*Melolontha melolontha* L.), (May–June.), which devours with avidity the floral organs of rhododendron, roses and other decorative plants; and the Garden Chafer (*Phyllopertha horticola* L.), (May-June), which is a highly destructive species in orchards and roseries (Fig. 119).

Control. (1) Hand-pick, sweep and jar the Chafers from infested blooms during the evening or on dull days when the insects are sluggish. (2) Control the larvae, which feed on the roots of various plants, by either hand-picking, dressing the ground with aldrin or DDT (see 'Roots Eaten', p. 49). (3) Clean cultivation, including the correct disposal of rubbish and weed destruction. (4) Dust or spray infested plants with DDT.

(*c*) Blossom Beetles, especially *Meligethes aeneus* F., and *M. viridescens* F., (May–Aug.), are chiefly important as pests of cruciferous crops (e.g. mustard, swede and turnip) grown for seed, but when they occur in large numbers injure the flowers of irises and sweet peas.

Control. Spray with DDT when the flower buds are still green and repeat, if necessary, before the plants are in full flower. If Cabbage Seed Weevil is also present use dieldrin instead of DDT to control both pests.

The Raspberry Beetle (*Byturus tomentosus* F.), (June–July), is particularly destructive to the blossoms of cultivated blackberries, loganberry and raspberry, in the receptacles of which the larvae live. The blossoms of apple and rose are also frequently invaded by the small brown beetles, which feed on the anthers and petals.

Control. See 'Fruits Tunnelled', p. 189.

The Water-lily Beetle (*Galerucella nymphaeae* L.), (June–Aug.), is the most destructive pest of water-lilies in this country. The flowers of some varieties are ignored, but the white blossoms of *Nymphaea marliacea* var. *albida* are a constant source of attraction to the beetles and their larvae, while the foliage is often reduced to ribbons by their feeding.

Control. (1) Syringe the foliage and flower buds forcefully with water to dislodge the larvae and adults so that fish are enabled to feed on them, or (2) submerge the leaves for a few days by means of iron hoops placed over the plants. This will enable fish to clear the infested foliage of all stages of the pest. (3) Where fish are not present the foliage and buds may be sprayed or dusted with DDT or derris.

Many species of Weevils are responsible for extensive injury to the flowers of garden plants, including malvas, rose, rhododendron and others. The chief offenders belong to the genera *Apion* and *Phyllobius* (May–July).

Control. Dust or spray the foliage and flower buds with DDT.

FLOWERS WITHERED

The Apple Sucker (*Psylla mali* Schmid.), (Apr.–May), can cause serious damage on apples, particularly where routine spraying is not carried out. The Pear Sucker (*P. pyricola* Foers.), (Mar.–May), has become more prevalent on pears in recent years In both species the young suckers, which are flat and crab-like, make their way into the developing buds and suck the sap causing the leaves to pucker and the blossom trusses to wither and die. The insects excrete large quantities of honeydew which later in the season gives the foliage an unsightly appearance and encourages the growth of sooty moulds on the leaves and fruit.

Control. (1) A tar oil wash, applied during the dormant period in December or early January, will give a good control of Apple Sucker. (2) Apple Sucker can also be controlled by spraying with BHC at the green cluster stage. (3) For Pear Sucker spray with nicotine or malathion at the white bud stage and repeat at petal fall.

Gladiolus Thrips (*Taeniothrips simplex* Mor.) (June–Sept.), when present in large numbers, may cause the flowers of gladiolus to turn brown and die without fully opening.

Control. See 'Foliage Mottled', p. 107.

Damage to blackberries and loganberries may occasionally be caused by the Onion Thrips (*Thrips tabaci* Lind.) and the Honeysuckle Thrips (*T. flavus* Schrank), (July–Aug.). These insects feed on the blossoms and on the fruitlets, causing them to shrivel and turn brown.

Control. Spray with DDT or BHC just before the blossoms open. Apply the spray also to the ground under the plants.

The Apple Blossom Weevil (*Anthonomus pomorum* L.), (Apr.–May), was at one time a serious apple pest but is now of minor importance where routine spraying is carried out. The eggs are laid on the blossom buds of apple and occasionally pears, and the larvae feed and pupate inside the buds. These fail to open and the petals turn brown producing a 'capped' blossom (Col. Fig. XIII).

Control. Apply a DDT spray at the breaking stage. One application will give adequate control for several years.

CHAPTER EIGHT

Fruits

Fruits Blistered. Fruits Discoloured. Fruits Distorted. Fruits Dropping. Fruits Eaten Away. Fruits Punctured. Fruits Scaly. Fruits Scarred. Fruits Spotted. Fruits Tunnelled. Fruits Warted.

THE fruit consists of that part of a flower that persists and grows as a result of a physiological process known as fertilization. True fruits are those that are the product of the ovary only, while false fruits are those that are the product of the ovary together with any other organ that develops, e.g. the calyx and receptacle. Certain so-called fruits are not true fruits, e.g. the strawberry, which is a fleshy receptacle bearing achenes, and the rose hip, which is a fleshy receptacle enclosing achenes. The blackberry, raspberry and loganberry are, on the other hand, true or aggregate fruits.

The term 'fruit' is applied frequently to a number of different parts of the plant that may be in no way connected with the true meaning of the term. The edible portion of rhubarb—the leaf-stalk or petiole—is classified as a 'fruit' by most people, while, on the other hand, the tomato and cucumber, which are fruits, are classified as 'vegetables'.

While such conflicting terms are misleading, our attention is confined to a review of the pests of fruits, which are classified as follows: (I) dehiscent dry fruits (legume, capsule); (II) indehiscent dry fruits (achene, nut); and (III) fleshy or succulent fruit (berry, drupe, pome).

The pests of fruits may be grouped for our present purpose into two classes, namely, (A) Surface-feeders, e.g. Thrips, Capsid Bugs, Aphids, Scale insects, Mealy Bugs, the caterpillars of certain Tortricid Moths, and the Garden Chafer; and (B) Flesh- and/or Ovule- and immature Seed-feeders, e.g. (*a*) adults—Slugs, Carabid or Ground Beetles, and Wasps; (*b*) larvae—Tomato, Codling and Cherry Fruit Moths, Raspberry Beetle, Pear Midge, Fruit Flies, and Apple Sawfly.

Such pests as those mentioned as being surface-feeders are responsible for extensive injury that increases in effect as the fruit develops.

The effect of fruit pests is that there is (*a*) a partial or complete loss of crop; (*b*) a reduction in value due to infested fruits being deformed, spotted and small; (*c*) a considerable loss in time and labour in 'culling out' damaged fruits during grading operations; (*d*) a lessening of garden decorative value of infested fruits of ornamental trees, shrubs and climbers; and (*e*) a partial or complete loss of seeds due to the destruction of the ovules and maturing seeds.

FRUITS BLISTERED

The Pear Leaf Blister Mite (*Eriophyes piri* Nal.), (Apr.–July), is primarily a foliage pest but, in heavily-infested pear trees, the developing fruitlets and their stalks become covered with reddish pustules. The attacked fruits are malformed and fall prematurely.

Control. See 'Foliage Blistered', p. 101.

The Apple Capsid (*Plesiocoris rugicollis* Fall.), (Apr.–July), attacks apples causing, on the skin of some varieties, the formation of raised areas and scattered pimples with rough corky surfaces (Fig. 129). In severe attacks the fruit may be badly deformed.

Control. See 'Foliage Puckered', p. 122.

FRUITS DISCOLOURED

The Blackberry Mite (*Aceria essigi* Hass.), (Aug.–Sept.), is responsible for the condition known as 'Redberry Disease' of wild and cultivated blackberries, and also the Himalayan berry. During the spring and summer the mites feed in colonies on the leaves and petioles. At blossom time they migrate to the flowers but cause no apparent injury. Later the mites feed near the base of the fruits causing uneven development, some of the drupelets ripening prematurely while others take on an abnormal red colour. It is also thought that the mites are responsible for malformation of the fruit.

Control. (1) Cut out and burn all old canes immediately after fruiting. (2) Spray infested plants in spring, when the young growths are 3–5 inches long, with 3 per cent. lime-sulphur.

The skin of the pods of peas and broad beans becomes mottled and assumes a silvery appearance when attacked by the Pea and Bean Thrips (*Kakothrips robustus* Uzel), (June–Aug.), which also damages the flowers and haulms. In severe cases the pods fail to develop or are badly deformed and the whole plant may be crippled or stunted (Fig. 120).

Control. (1) In practice the measures used against the Pea Moth are also effective against Thrips, i.e. spraying with DDT 7–10 days after the beginning of flowering. Alternatively, (2) spray with DDT, malathion or TEPP as soon as the damage is first seen.

The Pear Thrips (*Taeniothrips inconsequens* Uzel), (Apr.–June), commonly causes russeting on apples, pears, plums and damsons and, in severe infestations, small lumps appear on the surface of the stone fruits. The blossoms are also damaged by this pest. The Cabbage Thrips (*Thrips angusticeps* Uzel), (Apr.–June), causes similar damage to fruit in the eastern counties of England.

FIG. 120. Pea pods scarred by Pea Thrips (*Kakothrips robustus* Uzel).

Control. (1) Spray the ground under the trees with DDT at the green cluster stage to kill insects emerging from hibernation, or (2) spray infested trees with DDT, nicotine or TEPP at the white bud or pink bud stage.

Apples which have been attacked by the Apple Fruit Miner (*Argyresthia conjugella* Zell.), (June–Sept.), develop sunken patches which become discoloured, giving the fruit a bruised appearance (see 'Fruits Tunnelled', p. 188).

FRUITS DISTORTED

As well as being caused by pests, distortion of fruits may occur as a result of defective pollination, especially in apple, pear, loganberry, raspberry and strawberry.

Distortion may be caused by almost any pest which feeds on the fruit, particularly when it is young and still growing. Among the most important of these pests are the Pear Leaf Blister Mite (p. 101), Pear Thrips (p. 174), Pea and Bean Thrips (p. 173), Rosy Apple Aphid (Fig. 121), (p. 117), Capsid Bugs (Fig. 122), (p. 153), Apple

FIG. 121. Apples distorted by Rosy Apple Aphid (*Dysaphis plantaginea* Pass.). (*Shell Photograph.*)

FIG. 122. Distortion and scarring of Pears following attack by Common Green Capsid (*Lygus pabulinus* L.). (*Shell Photograph.*)

Fruit Miner (p. 188), Codling Moth (p. 186), Winter Moth (p. 132), Apple Fruit Rhynchites (p. 180), Raspberry Beetle (p. 189), Apple Sawfly (p. 191) and Pear Midge (p. 191).

FRUITS DROPPING

The premature fall of fruits in orchards is not necessarily due to the presence of fruit-infesting insects, but may be caused by one or other of the following factors: drought, excessive soil moisture due to waterlogging, malnutrition, low temperatures (especially late frosts), high winds, defective pollination, and spray injury (e.g. the application of lime-sulphur to 'sulphur-shy' varieties of apple and gooseberry, and to the immediate post-blossom application of lime-sulphur and lead arsenate to apple trees (see 'Foliage Dropping', p. 129). The natural shedding of some fruitlets occurs with the 'June drop'.

A large proportion of the fruit falls prematurely as a result of attacks by Capsid Bugs (see 'Foliage Puckered', p. 122). Aphids (see 'Foliage Aphid-infested', p. 100), Codling Moth, Pear Midge,

Apple and Plum Sawflies (see 'Fruits Tunnelled', p. 186) and Apple Fruit Rhynchites (see 'Fruits Punctured', p. 180).

FRUITS EATEN AWAY

Under this heading are included miscellaneous pests which eat away considerable portions of fruits or excavate large open cavities in the flesh. Pests which eat out shallow holes on the surface, gnaw the skin or make tunnels in the fruit are dealt with elsewhere (see 'Fruits Punctured', p.180; 'Fruits Scarred', p.182; 'Fruits Tunnelled', p. 186).

Slugs, including the Grey Field (*Agriolimax reticulatus* Müll.), the Garden (*Arion hortensis* Fér.) and the Black Slugs (*A. ater* L.), and also Snails, more especially the Strawberry Snail (*Hygromia striolata* Pfeiff.), are destructive to strawberry fruits and to ripening gooseberries, especially in walled gardens and in neglected plantations. These several Molluscs eat out uneven holes in the fruit (Fig. 123) so that it speedily decays.

Control. See 'Foliage with Clean-cut Holes', p. 131.

FIG. 123. Strawberries attacked by Slugs.

Millipedes are often responsible for a considerable amount of damage to ripening strawberry fruits, more especially when the beds are scantily supplied with straw mulch, so that the fruits are in direct contact with the soil. These pests may also extend the injury produced by other fruit-attacking creatures, e.g. Birds, Mice and Carabid Beetles. The species chiefly concerned is the Spotted Millipede (*Blaniulus guttulatus* Bosc.), and many immature Millipedes may be found in the centre of a single strawberry fruit.

Control. See 'Bulbs Tunnelled', p. 36.

The European Earwig (*Forficula auricularia* L.) is an omnivorous feeder, and is occasionally destructive to ripe fruits, being specially partial to peaches, nectarines, apples, pears and plums. Their attacks often follow those of Codling Moth and Apple Sawfly, of Wasps and of Birds. They extend the initial injury by crawling into the wounds made in the fruits by other creatures and feeding on the flesh.

Control. (1) Trap the earwigs by placing bands of loose sacking or corrugated paper around the trunks of the trees. The bands should be soaked in BHC or dieldrin. Alternatively (2), place loose sacking soaked in BHC or dieldrin under the trees as traps, or (3) dust the base of the trunk and the ground under the tree with BHC.

Among the *Coleoptera* are found a number of important fruit-infesting species, the chief of which are given below.

Carabid or Ground Beetles, of which there are numerous species, are chiefly carnivorous in their habits and therefore beneficial. Many species occur in gardens and are, with certain exceptions, welcome inhabitants on account of the predacious habits of both the larvae and the adults. The chief culprits responsible for extensive damage in strawberry plantations are *Abax parallelopipedus* B. & M., *Nebria brevicollis* F., *Feronia madida* F. and *F. melanaria* Illig. (June). The beetles attack the berries and eat holes in the flesh, the damage resembling somewhat that produced by Slugs and Birds. The Strawberry Seed Beetle (*Harpalus rufipes* Deg.) confines its attack to the seeds, which are removed, thereby spoiling the fruits and causing them to shrivel (Fig. 124).

Control. (1) Clean cultivation, including the removal of natural shelter (e.g. heaps of pulled weeds, leaf-mould, sods, old compost, etc.) in the vicinity of the strawberry plantation; and the maintenance of a fine tilth in the bed so that the upper layer of soil is too dry for the larvae to exist. (2) Delay strawing as long as possible. (3) Apply aldrin dust to the soil surface and to headlands just before strawing. (4) Avoid growing strawberries near long herbage, hedges and woodland.

Wasps are omnivorous, and fruits provide one of their chief articles of diet in late summer and early autumn. The chief fruit-damaging species are *Vespula vulgaris* L. and *V. germanica* F. (July–Sept.). These much maligned insects do a vast amount of useful work during the summer by feeding upon a number of harmful insects, but as the season advances and ripening fruits become available, they become unwanted visitors in orchards, fruit houses and vineries. They feed on the fruits of apple, pear, plum, seldom on peaches, but often on nectarines, and on grapes (Fig. 125). Wasps show decided preferences for certain varieties, the sugar content being probably the decisive factor.

Control. (1) Find the nests and destroy them. A number of materials may be used but DDT, BHC and derris powders are the most convenient and safe. A tablespoonful of the dust should be placed at the

FIG. 124. Strawberries damaged by (*bottom left*) Strawberry Beetle (*Feronia melanaria* Illig.) and (*right and top left*) by Strawberry Seed Beetle (*Harpalus rufipes* Deg.). (*Photograph by East Malling Research Station.*)

entrance hole on a dry day and left for at least 24 hours. The entrances of hanging nests should be dusted with the powder. Alternatively, a small DDT or BHC smoke bomb may be attached to a cane, lighted and the smoke directed into the entrance hole. If derris is used the nest should be dug up and destroyed to kill wasps which are due to emerge from the pupal cells. All operations should be carried out in the evening when activity had ceased. (2) The doors and ventilators of glasshouses should be screened with fine netting or muslin. (3) Bunches of grapes and choice specimens of other fruit may be enclosed in muslin bags.

FIG. 125. Grapes eaten out by Wasps (*Vespula* sp.).

The Hive Bee, *Apis mellifera* L., is frequently accused of feeding on ripe fruits. It is found, however, that bees do not attack sound fruits, though they will feed on fruits that have been injured by Birds, Wasps and other fruit-infesting insects.

Ants are occasionally destructive in fruit houses where they attack ripe fruits, more especially peaches and nectarines.

Control. See 'Foliage Wilting', p. 158.

Severe damage to maturing pears and apples is often caused by magpies, blackbirds and jays, which peck out large holes in the flesh.

Smaller fruits such as raspberries, currants, strawberries and cherries are pecked or carried away whole by blackbirds and thrushes, and pigeons will carry away the young fruitlets of cherries and plums. Jays are commonly guilty of ripping open the pods of peas and broad beans to steal the maturing seed.

Control. See Appendix III, p. 213.

FRUITS PUNCTURED

The Apple Fruit Rhynchites (*Caenorhinus aequatus* L.), (May–July), is a pest of apples, and sometimes plums, in both the adult and larval stages. The weevils feed on and lay their eggs in the flesh of the fruit. The skin is pierced with the rostrum and the resulting hole resembles that which would be made by pushing the point of a lead pencil into the skin (Fig. 126). The hole may partly close up but

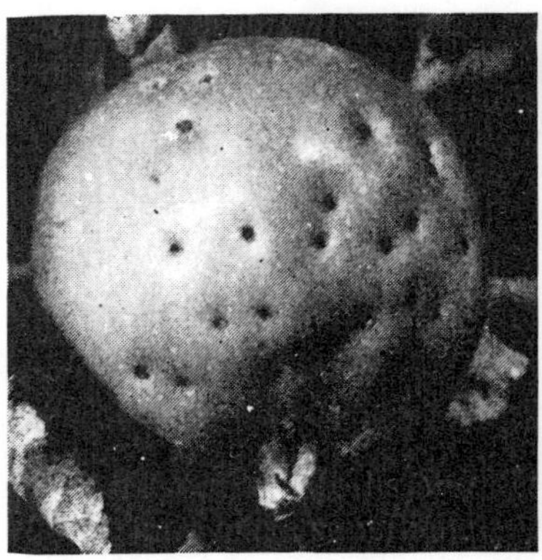

FIG. 126. Apple damaged by Apple Fruit Rhynchites (*Caenorhinus aequatus* L.). (*Shell Photograph.*)

FIG. 127. Apple pecked by Birds. (*Shell Photograph.*)

the fruit remains blemished and misshapen. The fruit, containing the feeding larvae, drops prematurely.

Control. (1) Collect and destroy all fallen fruits during June. (2) Apply a DDT or BHC spray at the pink bud stage.

The family *Trypetidae* includes the Fruit Flies which are serious pests in Mediterranean and tropical regions. The female fly pierces the fruits with her ovipositor and lays her eggs under the skin. Among the fruit-infesting species in this country are: (*a*) the Barberry Fly (*Anomoea permunda* Harr.), (Aug.–Oct.), the larvae of which render unsightly the fruits of many ornamental species of berberis and cotoneaster. The larvae feed on the fleshy pericarp and occasionally on the maturing seeds, the result being that the berries shrivel prematurely. (*b*) The Rose-Hip Fly (*Rhagoletis alternata* Fall.), (Aug.–Oct.), the larvae of which infest the fruits of many species of *Rosa*, e.g. *R. calocarpa*, *R. moyesii*, *R. villosa*, *R. rugosa* and certain others. The puncturing of the fruits allows the ready detection of this pest.

Control. (1) Spray the berries of ornamental shrubs subject to infestation—berberis and cotoneaster in particular—with DDT during the period of the fly's activity. (2) Prune off and burn shoots bearing shrivelled berries, by the end of September, to destroy the larvae before they leave the fruits for their pupation quarters in the soil. (3) Examine carefully all samples of seeds received from outside sources for the presence of puparia, which, if present, may be floated off from the seeds in water.

The larvae of the Winter Moth (*Operophtera brumata* L.) and the Clouded Drab Moth (*Orthosia incerta* Hufn.), (May–June), nibble small holes in the surface of apple fruitlets. The Winter Moth also attacks the fruitlets of plum and cherry. As the fruit grows sunken pits develop in the damaged area. Later in the season the larvae of the Fruit Tree Tortrix Moths (*Archips podana* Scop. and *Ditula angustiorana* Haw.), (July–Sept.), bite small holes in the surface of apples, usually under the protection of a leaf attached to the fruit with webbing.

Control. See 'Fruits Scarred', p. 184.

Some tunnelling pests such as the larvae of Codling Moths and Dock Sawfly, in their search for suitable sites, may make superficial punctures in the skin of apples without tunnelling further into the flesh (see 'Fruits Tunnelled', p. 186).

The fruits of apple and pear are frequently pecked by birds (Fig. 127), pears being usually attacked near the stalk. Tits and blackbirds are the main culprits and, although the damage is often slight, a large number of fruits may be attacked and rendered unfit for sale or storage. Also, the initial damage may often be extended by wasps, earwigs and other insects.

Control. See Appendix III, p. 213.

FRUITS SCALY

Many edible fruits are rendered unsightly and unsaleable by the presence of scale insects adhering to the skin. It is not uncommon to find lemons and oranges infested with various Coccids, the predominant species being *Lepidosaphes beckii* Newm. and *L. gloveri* Pack., while imported apples may be found at times to be infested with the San José Scale (*Quadraspidiotus perniciosus* Comst.).

FIG. 128. Pear infested with Oystershell Scale (*Quadraspidiotus ostreaeformis* Curt.). (*Photograph by East Malling Research Station.*)

The following species of Coccids are known to infest fruits in this country, viz.:

(*a*) the Oystershell Scale (*Quadraspidiotus ostreaeformis* Curt.) on apricot, pear, peach and nectarine (Fig. 128);

(*b*) the Mussel Scale (*Lepidosaphes ulmi* L.) in severe attacks invades the fruits of apple and pear;

(*c*) the Fig Mussel Scale (*L. ficus* Sign.) on indoor figs;

(*d*) the Soft Scale (*Coccus hesperidum* L.) on fig and citrus fruits in hothouses; and

(*e*) *Diaspis bromeliae* Kern. on frame-grown pineapples.

Control. The presence of numerous Coccids on the fruits indicates gross neglect on the part of the cultivator, for it is only under conditions of poor cultivation and general mismanagement that fruits become infested. For chemical controls see 'Stems Scaly,' p. 77.

FRUITS SCARRED

Thrips are responsible for the production of brown, scarred and roughened areas on many fruits, including imported citrus, and on apples, damsons and plums following an attack of the Pear Thrips (*Taeniothrips inconsequens* Uzel) (see 'Fruit Discoloured', p. 174).

The Apple Capsid (*Plesiocoris rugicollis* Fell.), (Apr.–Aug.), is a particularly serious pest of apples, and the injury it produces on the fruit is more obvious than that produced on the foliage. The skin shows russeted areas (Fig. 129), usually accompanied by a number of sunken pits or raised pimples rendering the fruits both unsightly and unsaleable,

Control. See 'Foliage Puckered', p. 122.

FIG. 129. Scars on Apple due to Apple Capsid (*Plesiocoris rugicollis* Fell.). (*Shell Photograph.*)

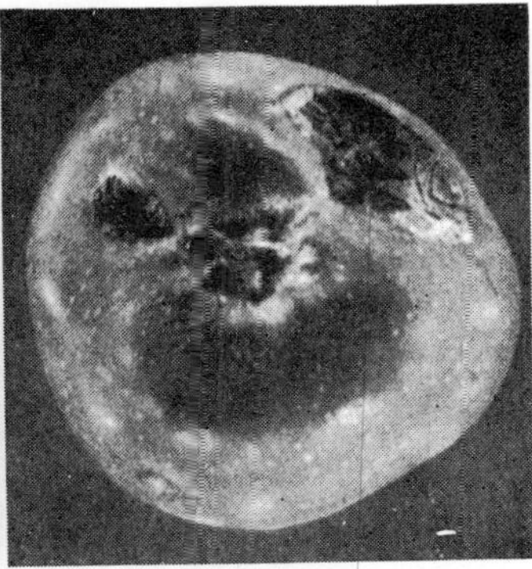

FIG. 130. Apple damaged by caterpillars of the Clouded Drab Moth (*Orthosia incerta* Hufn.). (*Photograph from A. M. Massee, 'Pests of Fruits and Hops'.*)

The Common Green Capsid (*Lygus pabulinus* L.), (Apr.–Aug.), feeds on the fruits of gooseberry, pear and plum. This causes the formation of rough brown patches on the skin which may be raised like warts (plums), or accompanied by splitting (gooseberries) or distortion (pears) (Fig. 122).

Control. See 'Foliage Ragged', p. 153.

The Cockchafer (*Melolontha melolontha* L.) and the Garden Chafer (*Phyllopertha horticola* L.), (May–June), are destructive to the young fruits of apple and pear. The beetles injure the blossoms and gnaw away patches of the skin of the fruit, leaving scarred areas (Fig. 131).

Control. As soon as the damage is seen spray with lead arsenate or DDT. If the latter is used precautions should be taken later to prevent an increase in the population of Fruit Tree Red Spider Mite (see 'Foliage Bronzed', p. 104).

The larvae of many *Lepidoptera* feed to some extent on the surface of fruits. Among the more destructive species are: (*a*) The Clouded

Drab Moth (*Orthosia incerta* Hufn.), (May–June), on apples and (*b*) the Winter Moth (*Operophtera brumata* L.), (May–June), on apples, plums and cherries. The larvae eat small holes in the fruitlets causing the formation of sunken scars as the fruit develops (Fig. 130).

FIG. 131. Pear fruitlets scarred by Garden Chafer (*Phyllopertha horticola* L.).

(*c*) The Fruit Tree Tortrix Moths (*Archips podana* Scop. and *Ditula angustiorana* Haw.), (July–Sept.), are found on a wide variety of fruit but the worst damage is caused on apple. The larvae gnaw small pits in the surface, often under the protection of a leaf which is attached by silk to the fruit (Fig. 132).

(*d*) The Summer Fruit Tortrix Moth (*Adoxophyes orana* Fisch. v. Rösl.), (Aug.–Oct.), is a new pest which is so far confined to Kent apple orchards. The larvae, as a rule, also feed under a leaf attached to the fruit, or where two fruits are touching. The damage is deeper and much more extensive than that caused by other Tortricids, large irregular areas being eaten out of the skin (Fig. 133).

Control. (1) Spray with DDT at the burst and green cluster stages. (2) Where only Winter Moth is present apply the spray at the green cluster stage and, if severe, at the pink bud stage also. (3) During the summer DDT should be applied only if absolutely necessary, in which case an acaricide should be added to keep Fruit Tree Red Spider Mite in check.

The Apple Sawfly (*Hoplocampa testudinea* Klug.), (May–June), is a serious pest of apple, but its presence is frequently over-looked on account of the larval injury resembling somewhat that produced by the Codling Moth. The young larvae often make ribbon-like scars on the fruits which become more pronounced as the fruit develops (Fig. 134).

Control. See 'Fruits Tunnelled', p. 191.

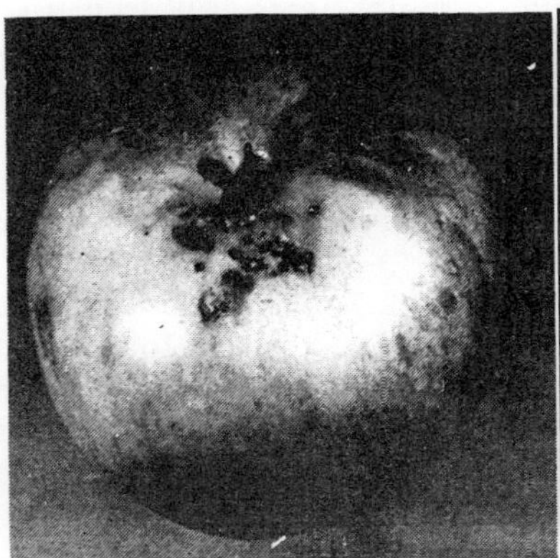

Fig. 132. Damage to Apple caused by caterpillar of Fruit Tree Tortrix Moth. (*Shell Photograph.*)

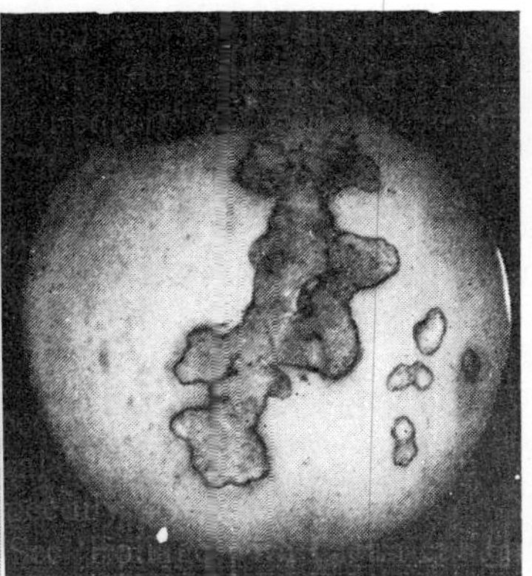

Fig. 133. Damage to Apple caused by caterpillar of Summer Fruit Tortrix Moth (*Adoxophyes orana* Fisch. v. Rösl.). (*Photograph by East Malling Research Station.*)

Fig. 134. Ribbon scars on Apple fruitlets produced by larvae of Apple Sawfly (*Hoplocampa testudinea* Klug.).

FRUITS SPOTTED

Among the more common pests responsible for fruit-spotting are the Pear Leaf Blister Mite (see 'Foliage Blistered', p. 101), Thrips (see 'Fruits Discoloured', p. 174), Apple Capsid (see 'Foliage

Puckered', p. 122), Rosy Apple Aphid (see 'Foliage Aphid-infested', p. 100) and Scale insects (see 'Shoots Scaly', p. 77).

FRUITS TUNNELLED

Many insects in their larval stages, and, to a far less extent, in the adult stage, tunnel and bore into fruits. Certain insects, e.g. the Pea Moth and the Bruchid Seed Beetles, are not necessarily fruit pests even though their eggs are laid in or on fruits. The larvae of such insects feed almost entirely upon seeds, so that they will be considered under the heading of 'Seed Pests', p. 193.

Among the *Lepidoptera* are found a great number of fruit-tunnelling species, and space will allow only the briefest reference to the more important fruit pests.

The Tomato Moth (*Diataraxia oleracea* L.) often causes extensive damage in tomato houses, where the larvae feed on the foliage and stems and eat into the green and ripe fruits (Fig. 136). The losses due to this pest can be severe and carnations, chrysanthemums and cucumbers may also be damaged. Under glasshouse conditions there are two generations each year.

Control. (1) Clean cultivation, including the sterilization or rejection of compost infested with pupae, the control of weed hosts such as dock, nettle and knot-grass in and around the glasshouse and the thorough cleansing of the staging and walls. (2) Collect and destroy fallen and damaged fruits. (3) Treat infested plants with DDT applied as a dust, spray or smoke, several applications being given throughout the season.

The Codling Moth (*Cydia pomonella* L.), (June–Aug.), is the most widespread of all apple pests, being found in nearly all countries in which this fruit is grown. The larvae are known to attack other fruits, e.g. pear, and some ornamental species of *Sorbus* and *Pyrus*. Confusion still exists as to the characters that distinguish the larva of this pest from that of the Apple Sawfly, for both are responsible for the condition known as 'maggoty' apples. The larva of the Codling Moth has eight pairs of legs while that of the Apple Sawfly has ten pairs. Sawfly attacks are generally seen earlier in the season, about May and June, when the young fruitlets show a conspicuous hole exuding a wet, brown mass which has an objectionable smell. Codling damage, on the other hand, becomes noticeable from July onwards. There is no objectionable smell or brown exudation, and the damage is mainly restricted to the region of the core. On apples the entry hole is usually surrounded by a reddish ring, particularly when it occurs on the side of the apple. The larvae may also enter through the 'eye' of apples and pears (Fig. 135).

Control. (1) Clean cultivation, including the destruction of dead branches and rubbish, and the removal of rough bark, moss, lichens, etc., in which the larvae may hibernate. (2) Collect and destroy all fallen fruits or feed them to pigs and poultry. (3) Spray with lead arsenate or DDT in mid-June to early July according to the season and repeat 3–4 weeks later. If DDT is used an acaricide should be added to it to prevent a build-up of Fruit Tree Red Spider Mite.

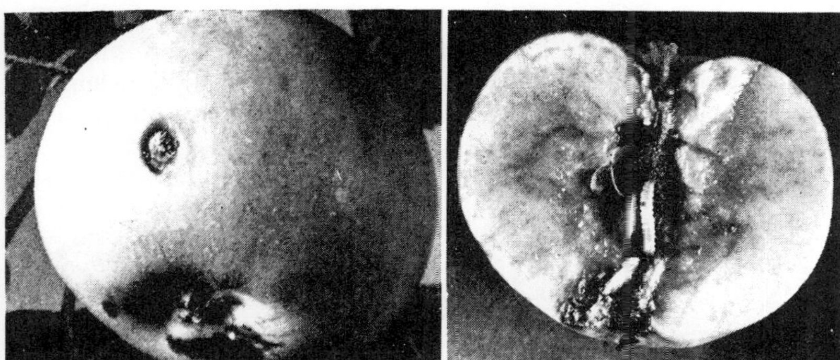

FIG. 135. Apple tunnelled by caterpillar of Codling Moth (*Cydia pomonella* L.). *Left:* entrance hole. *Right:* internal damage. (*Shell Photographs.*)

(4) In June place loose bands of sacking or corrugated paper round the trunks to catch hibernating caterpillars. Destroy the bands during the winter. (5) In mid-May sheds and boxes which have been used for storing apples should be sprayed with DDT to kill moths emerging from pupation.

The Red Plum Maggot (*Laspeyresia funebrana* Treits.), (June–Aug.), is destructive to the fruits of plum, damson, peach and sloe, but is frequently overlooked since affected fruits may appear sound and the presence of the larvae may not be detected until after the fruit is cooked. The larva burrows into the fruit near the stalk and feeds in the vicinity of the stone. The entrance hole is conspicuous, and from it exudes a brown liquid surrounded by frass. Later, the caterpillar leaves the fruit at the side as it prepares to seek its hibernation quarters either among crevices in the bark, in rubbish or in the soil.

Control. (1) Apply the hygienic measures and banding as for Codling Moth. (2) A 5 per cent. tar oil wash applied in December will reduce future infestations. (3) Spray in mid-June with DDT to which has been added an acaricide to prevent a build-up of Fruit Tree Red Spider Mite.

The Apple Fruit Miner (*Argyresthia conjugella* Zell.), (June–Sept.), is a fairly common pest of apples in certain districts of England and Scotland. The small larvae tunnel into the flesh of apples, crab apples and mountain ash berries. The damaged fruits are distorted, showing discoloured sunken patches which give them a bruised appearance. On cutting through the flesh the typical winding larval tunnels may be seen (Fig. 137). The larvae burrow into the centre of the fruit and into the seeds, finally emerging and pupating in silken cocoons among dead leaves or rubbish.

FIG. 136. Tomato tunnelled by caterpillar of Tomato Moth (*Diataraxia oleracea* L.). (*Photograph by R. P. Scase.*)

FIG. 137. Tunnelling by caterpillars of the Apple Fruit Miner (*Argyresthia conjugella* Zell.). (*Photograph from A.M. Massee 'Pests of Fruits and Hops'.*)

Control. (1) Collect and destroy fruits which fall prematurely, and also any rubbish accumulating in the orchard. (2) Spray the trees with lead arsenate, DDT or derris in mid-June, ensuring that the fruitlets are thoroughly wetted. If DDT is used a summer ovicide or acaricide should be added to prevent a build-up of Fruit Tree Red Spider Mite.

The Cherry Fruit Moth (*Argyresthia curvella* L.), (Apr.–May), is frequently a destructive pest in cherry orchards and on wall trees. The larvae enter the trusses of blossom buds and feed on the peta' and stamens. Later, they burrow into and hollow out the developing ovary and young fruits.

Control. (1) Apply a 7 per cent. tar oil wash in December, using high pressure to drive the spray into the crevices in the bark and to reach all parts of the tree. (2) In addition spray with DDT at the bud burst stage and, where the infestation is serious, at the white bud stage also.

Among the *Coleoptera* there are several fruit-tunnelling species, of which the following are the most important.

The Raspberry and Loganberry Beetle (*Byturus tomentosus* Deg.), (June–Aug.), is by far the most serious pest of raspberries, loganberries and cultivated blackberries. The damage consists not only of the destruction of the floral organs by the adult (see 'Flowers Eaten', p. 170), but in the production of small, distorted and 'maggoty' fruits. The female beetle lays her eggs in the flowers and on the young fruits, and the larvae, after first feeding on the surface of the berries (Fig. 138), tunnel in at the base of the berries and feed on the flesh.

Control. Spray or dust thoroughly with derris. Two applications should be given, the first 10 days after flowering begins and the second 10 days later.

FIG. 138. External damage on Raspberry by larva of Raspberry Beetle (*Byturus tomentosus* Deg.). (*Shell Photograph.*)

FIG. 139. Exit holes of Nut Weevil (*Balaninus nucum* L.) in Cob nuts.

The Nut Weevil (*Balaninus nucum* L.), (June–Oct.), is a common pest of cob, filbert and wild hazel nuts. The adult, long-snouted weevils appear in May and June, at which time the female bores a hole in the nutlet with her rostrum, and deposits an egg in the hole. The larva feeds on the kernel until it is mature, when it bores a circular hole in the shell (Fig. 139) through which it escapes into the soil where it pupates in an earthen cell. The holes made in the young nuts by the adult weevils also allow the entry of the Brown Rot fungus.

Control. (1) Spray or dust the bushes with DDT in late May, and give a second application 3 weeks later. (2) The soil under the bushes should be cultivated to a depth of several inches during the winter to expose or kill hibernating larvae.

The only Dipterous pest of fruits deserving mention here is the Pear Midge (*Contarinia pyrivora* Ril.), (Apr.–June), which is particularly destructive in pear orchards and responsible for reducing the crop considerably. The female Gall Midge lays her eggs in the flower buds and open blossoms, and the young larvae make their way down into the ovary and feed on the developing fruits. This pest may be detected by the presence of swollen, distorted and discoloured fruitlets (Fig. 140). As the larvae develop, the interior of the fruit decays and the skin cracks thus allowing the maggots to escape and to fall to

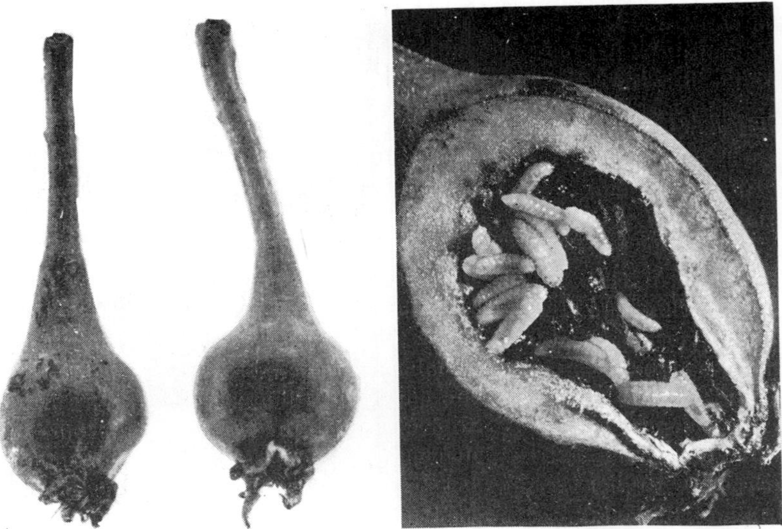

FIG. 140. External symptoms (*left*) and internal damage (*right*) on Pear fruitlets due to attack by Pear Midge (*Contarinia pyrivora* Ril.). (*Photographs by East Malling Research Station and Shell.*)

the ground, where they pupate. The blackening of the fruitlets is often considered to be due to frost injury.

Control. (1) Spray with DDT at the early white bud stage, ensuring that all parts of the tree are thoroughly drenched. (2) Where practicable, hand-pick all attacked fruitlets before they fall, and collect all fallen fruitlets during May and June. These should be buried, burned, or fed to pigs and poultry. (3) The soil under infested trees should be cultivated at weekly intervals during June and July to destroy pupating larvae.

The most important Hymenopterous pests are Sawflies, more especially the Apple Sawfly (*Hoplocampa testudinea* Klug), (May–June), which appears in spring and may be found about apple blossom on bright sunny days. The female lays her eggs beneath the calyx of the flower and frequently within the bases of the stamens. The young larva may tunnel for a short time just under the skin of the fruit which splits, giving rise to a ribbon-like scar (Fig. 134). It also tunnels into the flesh and feeds for several weeks eating out a large cavity in the centre. The exudation of moist, brown frass which is found on the fruit at the entrance to the tunnel provides a ready means of recognizing this pest. The larva may desert one fruit and enter another. When fully grown, it leaves the fruit and pupates in the soil.

Control. (1) Spray with BHC about 7 days after 80 per cent. petal fall ensuring that the trusses are thoroughly wetted. (2) Collect and destroy all infected fruits.

The Dock Sawfly (*Ametastegia glabrata* Fall.), (Sept.–Oct.), is a pest of apples which appears to have increased in recent years in many parts of England. There are 2 or 3 generations of larvae each year which, during the summer, feed on dock, sorrel, plantain, fat hen and other related plants. The last generation, when fully fed, search for hibernation quarters and may climb nearby apple trees and burrow into the mature fruit, often to a depth of 2 inches. However, since this is not a suitable site for hibernation it is soon abandoned by the larva, leaving the apple unfit for sale or storing.

Control. Since the apples are almost ready for picking at the time of attack spraying cannot be advised. Some protection may be obtained by the application of tree-banding grease in early September. Otherwise steps should be taken to eradicate the weed food plants in and around the orchard.

The Plum Sawfly (*Hoplocampa flava* L.), (June–July), is not so general a pest as the Apple Sawfly though it is often destructive in plum orchards. The female deposits a single egg in each fully open blossom, and the young larva bores into the fruitlet and eventually hollows it out. The larva may then migrate to other fruit. The attacked fruits can be recognized by the sticky black frass exuding from the entrance holes, and they drop to the ground prematurely.

Control. Spray with BHC or parathion at the cot split stage (i.e. about 8 days after petal fall).

FRUITS WARTED

The presence of warts and pimples on fruits is an indication that the skin has been punctured during the early stages of growth by the proboscis of some haustellate insect or the rostrum of some weevil. The size of the warts necessarily varies according to the organism and to the plant's reaction to the injury. Such factors as the depth to which the stylets of a sucking insect are thrust or the snout of a weevil is pushed during the process of feeding, the length of time spent in sucking the juice of the fruit, the extent to which rupturing of the cell walls has occurred, and the injection of a toxin during the process of feeding, will affect the size, shape, colour and persistency of the warts or pimples. The injury varies with the organism concerned in the damage, while there are definite varietal reactions to insect injury.

The insects chiefly concerned with this type of damage are: the Common Green Capsid, the Apple Capsid (Fig. 129), the Rosy Apple Aphid, various fruit-infesting Scale insects, and Fruit Flies, though with the last-mentioned the injury is due to oviposition punctures.

Control. See 'Foliage Puckered', p. 122 (Apple Capsid); 'Foliage Ragged', p. 153 (Green Capsid); 'Foliage Aphid-infested', p. 100; 'Shoots Scaly', p. 77; 'Fruits Punctured', p. 180 (Fruit Flies).

CHAPTER NINE

Seeds

Seeds Attacked on the Plant. Seeds Attacked after Sowing. Seeds Attacked in Store.

THE seed is the product of the ovule after fertilization and the term is misapplied when reference is made to 'seed' potatoes—such terminology being comparable to the classification of rhubarb as 'fruit'. The seeds of plants vary greatly in the number that are produced by a single flower, and in their size, shape, colour and composition. The testa or seed-coat may be smooth or rough, covered with tubercles, ribs, granules and so on, and may be winged or hooked to aid dispersal by wind and animals.

The store of reserve food in most seeds is sufficient to supply the nutriment essential for the early development of the seedling until such time as the plant is able to manufacture food for itself with the aid of its leaves. It is not surprising that this reserve of food is attractive to many insects, and such pests as Bruchid Seed Beetles feed on it to the detriment of the plant's future existence—the effect being that the developing plant may exhaust its food reserves before it is able to produce leaves, so that exhaustion and lack of vigour and even death may result.

In addition, there is the danger of parasitic organisms invading the ruptured testa so that the seed may decay soon after sowing. A further example of exhaustion is observed as a result of too deep sowing, in which event the reserve food is used up in the effort to produce a shoot sufficiently long to lift the cotyledons above ground into the air and light.

Injury to seeds by insects and other pests may be either (A) Direct, or (B) Indirect.

(A) Direct injury arises from pests attacking (*a*) the maturing or ripe seed on the plant (e.g. Pea Moth and Clover and Grass Seed Midges); (*b*) the sown seed before and after germination (e.g. Millipedes, Wireworms, Mice and Birds); and (*c*) the dried seeds in storage (e.g. Store Beetle, Bean Seed Beetle, and the Brown House, Mediterranean Flour and Indian Meal Moths).

(B) Indirect injury is caused when the ovules and/or seeds are partially or completely devoured by insects that are primarily fruit pests (e.g. the larvae of the Tomato, Codling and Cherry Fruit Moths and the Barberry and Rose-Hip Fruit Flies).

Some pests are entirely dependent upon seeds for their development and are dispersed in them (Bruchid Seed Beetles); some invade the seeds and are distributed with them (e.g. the Stem and Bulb Eelworm (*Ditylenchus dipsaci* (Kühn) Filipj.) on onion seed), while others are conveyed with seeds as puparia (Agromyzid Flies, e.g. the Aquilegia Leaf Miner; and Trypetid Flies, e.g. the Barberry and Rose-Hip Flies).

The seedsman is primarily concerned with seed-infesting insects and is aware of the desirability of taking every measure to ensure freedom from such pests, not only to avoid wide-spread infestations among stocks in the warehouse resulting in depreciation, but to reduce the chance of claims being made from the sale of inferior seed and the loss of prestige that would follow the distribution of pest-ridden samples.

The result of pest injury to seeds is that the seeds are partially or completely destroyed. Injuries will be considered under three headings, namely, (I) Seeds attacked on the plant; (II) Seeds attacked after sowing; and (III) Seeds attacked in store. It is found, however, that not all pests fall conveniently into one or other of these categories, for some, e.g. Ants, may attack not only the ovules and developing seeds, but also seeds after they have been sown and when stored. Others, e.g. Bruchid Beetles, possess different habits according to the species concerned—some being injurious only as field pests to the growing crop (the Pea and Bean Beetles, *Bruchus pisorum* L. and *B. rufimanus* Boh.), others attacking seeds both on the plant and continuing to breed among the dried seeds in storage (Dried Bean Beetle, *Acanthoscelides obsoletus* Say.).

SEEDS ATTACKED ON THE PLANT

It is among the Order *Coleoptera* that the most important pests of seeds are found.

The Strawberry Seed Beetle (*Harpalus rufipes* Deg.), (June), is one of the Carabid or Ground Beetles, and is responsible for serious injury to strawberry fruits owing to the removal of the seeds from the ripening and ripe berries. The effect is that the fruits become discoloured, misshapen and shrivelled.

Control. See 'Fruits Eaten Away', p. 177.

Over 800 species of Bruchid Beetles are known and are widely distributed throughout the temperate, sub-tropical and tropical regions. Their larvae mostly live in the seeds of the *Leguminosae*, while others are associated with the seeds of the *Palmae*. Members of the Family *Bruchidae* are beetles, though they are erroneously known as 'Weevils' in the United States and elsewhere. It is difficult to discover the country of origin of many species as they have been carried from one country to another in consignments of seeds, and have in many instances become adapted to their new conditions so that their present distribution is cosmopolitan.

Some of the troubles arising from the introduction of Bruchid-infested seeds are: (i) exotic species of beetles may be introduced into a country or district in cargoes of seeds; (ii) a reduction in the crop, quantitatively as well as qualitatively; (iii) a loss in the germinating power, both directly owing to any injury to the embryo and indirectly by hastening decay after sowing because of invasion through the ruptured testa by soil-inhabiting pests, e.g. Millipedes, and of bacterial and fungal organisms; and (iv) a considerable loss in food as heavily infested cargoes are unfit even as food for stock.

It is found, however, that infested seeds will usually germinate, but the resultant plants may be poor, less vigorous and give a lower yield than pest-free seeds. The larger the seed, the less the amount of direct injury committed by the beetles—the amount of reserve food in many leguminous seeds being sufficient to supply nutriment to the developing plant and to the beetles. While this may be applicable to such pests as the Bean Beetle (Fig. 141), of which usually one larva only

FIG. 141. *Left:* Broad Bean Seeds infested with Bean Beetle (*Bruchus rufimanus* Boh.). *Right:* French Beans attacked by Dried Bean Beetle (*Acanthoscelides obsoletus* Say.).

occurs in a single seed, the reverse is true of the Dried Bean Beetle, in which there appears to be no limit to the number of larvae that can be supported in a single seed other than the matter of space and the amount of food material available, for as many as 20–30 Bruchids have been bred from a single French bean seed (Fig. 141).

Among the more important Bruchid pests of leguminous seeds in this country are: (*a*) the Pea Beetle (*Bruchus pisorum* L.), in seeds of culinary peas; (*b*) the Bean Beetle (*B. rufimanus* Boh.), in seeds of broad beans (Fig. 141) and horse beans; (*c*) the Spanish Bean Beetle (*B. affinis* Fröl.), in seeds of broad beans, more especially the variety 'Seville Longpod' imported from the Mediterranean region; and (*d*) the Dried Bean Beetle (*Acanthoscelides obsoletus* Say.), in seeds of French, dwarf and kidney beans (Fig. 141), cow-peas and lentils—this species being more important as a pest of dried seeds in warehouses and stores than of the green seed so far as this country is concerned.

Control. (1) The application of a DDT spray or dust to the crop immediately after flowering will reduce the infestation. (2) Stored infested seed not required for human consumption should be thoroughly mixed with DDT dust to prevent any spread of the infestation. (3) Seed containing live insects should not be sown. (4) Fumigate infested seed with carbon tetrachloride or carbon disulphide. The seeds should be placed in an airtight container and covered with a piece of cloth which has been dampened slightly with the fumigant. The container should be left for 36–48 hours at a temperature above 50° F.

The Cabbage Seed Weevil (*Ceuthorrhynchus assimilis* Payk.), (May–July), lays its eggs in the seed vessels of cruciferous plants, both cultivated and wild (e.g. charlock). The larvae feed on the floral organs and, later, on the ovules and developing seeds.

Control. (1) Spray with dieldrin when the flower buds are still green. If necessary a second application can be made just prior to flowering. (2) Infested land should be ploughed deeply to bury the pupae. (3) Seed from infested fields should be fumigated to kill any pupae.

The most important Lepidopterous pest of seeds is the Pea Moth (*Laspeyresia nigricana* F.), (July–Sept.), which is more destructive to the late than to early and mid-season sowings. The caterpillars bore through the pods into the developing seeds which are devoured—the injury resulting in 'maggoty' peas (Fig. 142). The losses arising from the damage done both to the green peas and to the ripe seeds are considerable and, the consumer may have to discard many seeds, while the seedsman must of necessity sort out the healthy from the injured seeds before packeting.

Control. (1) Practise crop rotation. Peas should be grown as far away as possible from the previous year's crop. (2) Keep the plants free from weeds to reduce available shelter for the moths. (3) In badly-infested areas avoid growing varieties which come into flower between mid-June and mid-August, the peak egg-laying period.

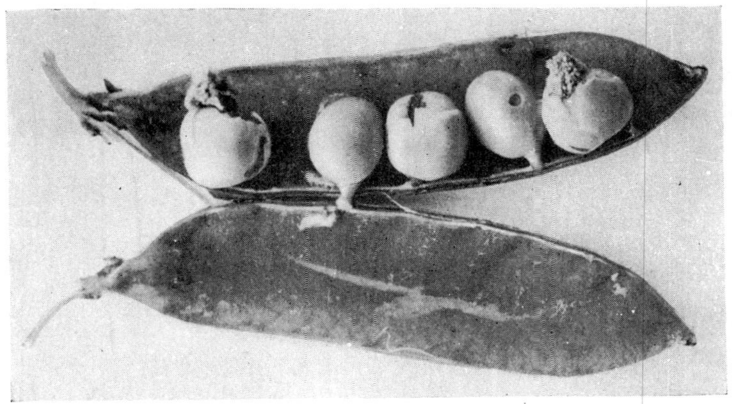

FIG. 142. Peas attacked by caterpillars of Pea Moth (*Laspeyresia nigricana* F.).

(4) Where crops are flowering during the peak egg-laying period spray with DDT 7–10 days after the beginning of flowering. Where crops are to be harvested dry a second spray should be applied 14 days later.

The Cherry Fruit Moth (*Argyresthia curvella* L.), (Apr.–May), is in its larval stage destructive to the floral organs of cherry and, later, by the injury done to the ovaries and ovules.

Control. See 'Fruits Tunnelled', p. 188.

The Order *Diptera* contains a number of seed pests among the *Cecidomyidae* or Gall Midges, including many important agricultural pests, such as the Clover Seed Midge and the numerous Grass Midges, which seriously affect seed production.

The species chiefly concerned with seed injury to horticultural plants are dealt with below:

The Brassica Pod Midge (*Dasyneura brassicae* Winn.), (May–Aug.), mainly attacks cruciferous crops which are infested by the

Cabbage Seed Weevil (see p. 196). The larvae feed inside the seed pods, causing them to become swollen and distorted, this condition being known as 'Bladder-pod'. Serious damage can be done to rape and also to mustard, radish, swede and turnip.

Control. It is found in practice that this pest is controlled by the treatment used against the Cabbage Seed Weevil (see p. 196).

The Pea Midge (*Contarinia pisi* Winn.), (July–Sept.), is mainly responsible for damage to the flowers, shoots and pods of pea plants. The larvae feed on the inner lining of the shuck, causing swelling and deformation. They may sometimes feed on the peas themselves though the damage done to them is negligible. However, the presence of large numbers of the larvae among peas served at the table and in shelled peas for market causes serious depreciation of the crop.

Control. See 'Flowers Distorted', p. 165.

The Barberry Fly (*Anomoea permunda* Harr.) and the Rose-Hip Fly (*Rhagoletis alternata* Fall.), (Aug.–Oct.), whose larvae not only render the fruits unsightly, but feed to some extent upon the unripe seeds. When infested berries of *Berberis* and *Cotoneaster* are harvested for seed and kept in store, the larvae leave the fruits and pupate among the decaying pulp, and may, during subsequent cleaning, be overlooked and conveyed as puparia with the seeds.

Control. See 'Fruits Punctured', p. 180.

Among Hymenopterous insects, the Chalcid Seed Flies (*Megastigmus*) attack the seeds of *Coniferae* and *Rosa*. The best known is the Douglas Fir Seed Fly (*M. spermotrophus* Wachtl.), which causes serious losses in home-grown seed of Douglas fir. The small female flies with their long ovipositors are frequently found among seeds of coniferous trees and of roses in storage, having emerged through a minute circular hole cut in the seed in which their larvae have lived.

Control. (1) Where practicable, spray the ground under the trees with DDT about the time when the adults are emerging from pupation, i.e. late May to early June. (2) Before sowing seed which is partly infested the larvae should be killed by fumigation with carbon disulphide or hydrocyanic acid gas, or by exposure to a temperature of 120° F. for 4 hours.

The seeds of sweet corn are often picked from the cob by crows which reach them by tearing through the husk. In the same way jays will rip open the pods of peas and broad beans to feed on the seeds inside.

Control. See Appendix III, p. 213.

SEEDS ATTACKED AFTER SOWING

Millipedes, of which the most destructive seed-infesting species is the Spotted Millipede (*Blaniulus guttulatus* Bosc.), (Mar.–July), feed on various seeds when they become swollen and soft before germination. Both young and adult Millipedes may be found feeding between and boring into the cotyledons of beans (Fig. 143), peas, beetroot, New Zealand spinach and other seeds.

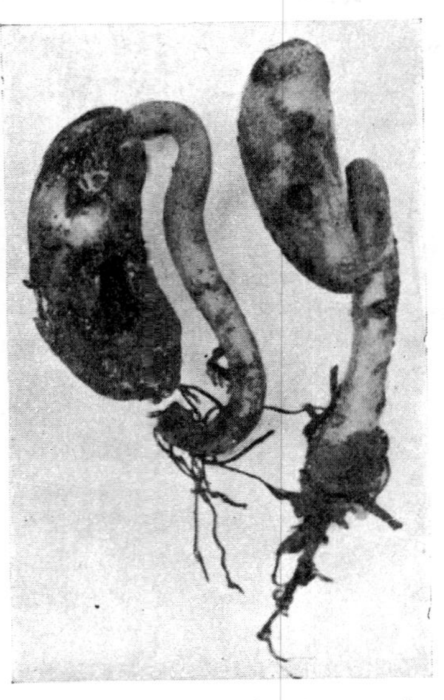

FIG. 143. Germinating Bean seeds attacked by Millipedes.

Control. See 'Bulbs Tunnelled', p. 36.

Cockroaches, especially the American species (*Periplaneta americana* L.), and Crickets (*Gryllulus domesticus* L.), (Jan.–Dec.), are frequently destructive in seed-houses owing to their depredations among sown seeds in pots and boxes. Both large and small seeds of a wide variety of plants are eaten with avidity.

Control. See 'Flowers Eaten', p. 167.

Of Coleopterous insects, the most destructive pest of sown seeds are Wireworms, which riddle the seeds of beans and peas so that they fail to germinate. So partial are they to germinating wheat that these seeds prove to be the most effective bait for Wireworms in glasshouse borders before planting such susceptible crops as tomato.

Control. See 'Bulbs Tunnelled', p. 38. The placing of manure some inches below the level of seed drills is stated to divert the attention of these pests from the germinating seeds, though it would be unwise to rely upon this measure to avert attack.

The Bean Seed Fly (*Delia cilicrura* Rond.), (May–June), causes heavy annual losses to germinating beans of all varieties in certain parts of the country. The larvae penetrate the cotyledons as soon as the testa splits and make winding tunnels in the interior. They also tunnel into the developing radicle and stem making the seedlings blind and checking root development. The injuries are usually followed by rotting and the collapse of the seedling. Peas are also liable to attack but this is less common.

Control. Dust the seed drills when sowing with aldrin dust and dress the seed with thiram fungicide to prevent rots. Alternatively, a combined seed dressing of lindane and thiram may be applied.

Ants are frequently destructive to seeds, which they collect and harbour in their nests. Seeds that contain oil are especially favoured, and will be collected both in the field, in gardens and in glasshouses —where they will raid seed-pots and boxes and remove the sown seeds bodily away.

There are a number of British species that, according to Donisthorpe ('British Ants', 1927), collect the seeds of such plants as cardamine, cerastium, centaurea, galium, ulex, viola, and certain grasses, which are transported to their nests for food for the larvae or to add as vegetable refuse on the nest.

The most destructive Ant is a cosmopolitan species, Pharaoh's Ant (*Monomorium pharaonis* L.), which is a serious pest in many glasshouses and propagating-pits where it collects the sown seeds of buddleias, meconopsis, rhododendron and violas and disturbs the soil in the seed-pots and boxes. It is difficult pest to exterminate since it makes its nests in walls, in the foundations of glasshouses and in other equally inaccessible situations.

Control. (1) For outdoor ants see 'Foliage Wilting', p. 158. (2) Pharaoh's Ants are more difficult to control and persistent treatment is necessary until they are completely eradicated. If possible the nests should be located and the entrance and surrounding structures sprayed or dusted with aldrin or dieldrin. The insecticide should also be applied to surfaces over which the ants are walking.

Mice may sometimes be responsible for digging up and eating the seeds of peas and beans after they have been sown.

Control. See Appendix IV, p. 215.

SEEDS ATTACKED IN STORE

The number of species of insects that are associated with seeds in storage is very considerable, and many that attack stored products (grain, dried fruit, nuts and other foodstuffs) are equally important as pests of dried seeds.

Only a comparatively small proportion of the *Lepidoptera* are injurious to seeds, the more important being: (*a*) the Brown House

Moth (*Hofmannophila pseudospretella* Staint.), whose larvae are recorded as feeding on a wide variety of products. It is often destructive to pulse, especially dried beans and peas, and more particularly occurs in neglected warehouses where the caterpillars feed on the dust and débris that collect on window-ledges and between floor boards. (*b*) *Ephestia* species, though primarily pests of dried fruits and similar commodities, attack the seeds of numerous plants in storage. (*c*) The Warehouse Moth (*Ephestia elutella* L.), which is a cosmopolitan species, is specially important as a pest of stored grain.

The order *Coleoptera* contains the greatest number of seed-infesting species, of which the most important from the horticultural standpoint are: (*a*) the Biscuit Beetle (*Stegobium paniceum* L.), which is closely related to the Furniture Beetle, was formerly abundant in ships' biscuits, which were said to be 'weevily'. The larvae feed on a wide variety of products, including cereals, spices, dried herbs, books, dried animal products, leather, wool, hair, horn, bread, flour, and may even exist on such drugs as aconite and opium. Damage is done to various seeds, including aubergine, caraway, carrot, coriander, lettuce and tropaeolum. (*b*) The Australian Spider Beetle (*Ptinus tectus* Boield.), which has become a pest of dried seeds within recent years, feeds on a number of plant products. Breeding is continuous in storage, and high populations are rapidly built up so that infested seeds become reduced to dust. Serious infestations have occurred in seeds of *Anemone rivularis*, *Platycodon*, beans, peas and wheat. (*c*) The Dried Bean Beetle (*Acanthoscelides obsoletus* Say.) is by far the most destructive of all Bruchids, and is the most pernicious pest of dried pulse by reason of its continuous breeding in stored seeds and for the number of larvae that reach maturity in a single seed (see 'Seeds Attacked on the Plant', p. 196). (*d*) The Grain Weevil (*Calandra granaria* L.) and the Rice Weevil (*C. oryzae* L.) are cosmopolitan in distribution and are among the most important pests of dried cereals, dried peas and beans, and of other products.

Control. See 'Seeds Attacked on the Plant', p. 196. (1) General cleanliness in the warehouse and store will tend to avoid serious outbreaks of these pests—infestations are rapidly built up where hygienic principles are ignored; the pests pass from one infested consignment to hitherto clean stocks, while a permanent population is maintained by allowing dust and débris to accumulate in the store, in sweepings and empty sacks, and among seed spilled during cleaning and trucking. (2) The application of a continuous strip of banding grease to the upper parts of walls prevents the moth larvae climbing up to the eaves and rafters to pupate. It may also be applied to the floor around infested material to prevent larvae spreading to clean commodities. (3) Fumigate infested seed in air-tight containers with ethylene dichloride or carbon tetrachloride, or (4) mix DDT or lindane dust with the seed.

Among the Order *Diptera* are found a number of important Gall Midge or Cecidomyid pests of seeds (see 'Seeds Attacked on the Plant', p. 197), some of them leaving the seed heads before the crop is harvested or the seed is threshed (e.g. the Red Clover Seed Midge), while others (e.g. certain of the Meadow Foxtail Midges) remain with the seed though no further harm is done after the seed is placed in the store.

It is not uncommon to find consignments of seed infested with the larvae of Gall Midges, and the outside of the sacks covered with the puparia of harmless species of *Clinodiplosis* and *Lestodiplosis*, which are either 'inquilines' or predacious forms respectively. The orange-coloured or blood-red larvae of these Midges occur in a variety of seed, including antirrhinum, China aster, cosmos, gentian, gladiolus, lettuce and lobelia, and no remedial measures against them require to be taken.

Mites belonging to the Family *Acaridae* are common pests of seeds in store, especially in ill-ventilated, damp, unclean warehouses. The Flour Mite (*Acarus siro* L.) is cosmopolitan and is found to attack an enormous range of stored products, including grain and seeds. Feeding is concentrated on the germ of the seed and the presence of the mites can be recognized by the sweetish odour which they produce.

Control. (1) Store seed off the floor in a dry cool place. (2) Infested seed should be mixed with lindane or malathion dust.

Rats and mice cause serious losses of stored seeds not only by eating them but by the spillage resulting from holes being gnawed in the bags,

Control. See Appendix IV, p. 215.

CHAPTER TEN

Lawns

Lawns with Earth Mounds. Lawns with Torn Turf. Lawns with Withered Patches.

THE ideal conception of a lawn as a smooth uniform expanse of grass is frequently spoiled by the presence of moss, weeds and fungal growths. The number of insects and other pests which spoil the turf is small but if they are present they can seriously damage and disfigure one of the most pleasant features of the garden. In conjunction with the control measures outlined below it should be remembered that cultural measures play a considerable part in pest control. A well-drained soil is less liable to be infested by Leatherjackets, and these pests and Chafer Grubs are kept in check by regular rolling. The application of fertilizers not only promotes good growth but also helps the grass to withstand the attacks of these pests.

LAWNS WITH EARTH MOUNDS

The burrowing of Earthworms in the soil helps to aerate it and keep it well drained. Some species, in particular *Allolobophora nocturna* Evans and *A. longa* Ude, deposit their excrement, consisting of earth and vegetable matter, on the surface in the form of worm casts. The casts are most abundant in the spring and autumn and, while they have a beneficial action on the turf they can also cause unevenness on lawns and are a great nuisance on golf and bowling greens and tennis courts. The casts also form bare patches on which weeds can become established.

Control. (1) Brush away the casts when dry. (2) Various materials can be used to kill the worms and are best applied in spring and autumn when the worms are most active, e.g. mowrah meal (6–8 oz. per sq. yd. followed by copious watering), potassium permanganate ($\frac{1}{2}$ oz. in 1 gal. water per sq. yd.), copper sulphate (1 lb. in 10 gal. water applied over 50 sq. yd.), derris (applied according to maker's instructions), colloidal lead arsenate (2 lb. or 1 pt. per gal. water applied over 25 sq. yd.). All except lead arsenate cause the worms to come to the surface where they should be swept up, particularly if copper sulphate is used, as the worms are then poisonous to poultry and other birds. Lead arsenate is longer lasting in its effect than the other materials and the worms die underground. Only potassium permanganate should be used in the vicinity of ponds containing fish where there is a danger of seepage into the water.

The Yellow Mound Ant (*Lasius flavus* F.) is common on grassland where the soil is sandy and raises mounds which resemble grass-covered mole-hills. These ant-hills are often troublesome on newly-made lawns.

Control. Make a hole in the centre of the nest and pour in enough aldrin solution to soak it thoroughly, afterwards closing the hole tightly with a turf. Alternatively, dust the entrances and runs with aldrin dust.

The Tawny Burrowing Bee (*Andrena fulva* Schr.) often makes its nest in lawns and garden paths in the early spring, digging down to a depth of 6–12 inches and throwing up a small pile of fine soil around the entrance hole. These insects tend to congregate in the same area every year, disfiguring the lawn and obstructing mowing.

Control. (1) Roll the lawn to flatten out the mounds. (2) Dress the infested area with BHC dust in April, renewing it 3 weeks later.

Moles can cause considerable damage on lawns by throwing up large mounds of earth on the surface. In addition, shallow workings cause unevenness of the surface through collapse of the burrows or by turf being pushed up into a ridge.

Control. (1) Lay down poison baits consisting of worms dusted with strychnine, brucine sulphate, red squill or a proprietary mole poison. The runs should be opened with a dibber, the bait inserted, and the opening closed with a turf to exclude the light. (2) Trapping may be employed but this usually requires some skill and practice to obtain successful results. (3) The runs may be fumigated with calcium cyanide preparations or with smoke generators sold to control moles.

LAWNS WITH TORN TURF

Some types of birds, in their search for insect larvae, tear up the turf of lawns with their beaks and claws. Rooks and blackbirds are most commonly responsible for this damage, and woodpeckers may also occasionally tear up the ground around ants' nests in search of food (Fig. 144). Occasional damage may also be done by badgers and hedgehogs.

Control. The only effective way of preventing damage by birds and mammals is to eradicate the insects to which they are attracted, i.e. Chafer Grubs and Leatherjackets mainly (see below).

FIG. 144. Turf damaged by birds in search of insects.
(*Photograph by Sports Turf Research Institute.*)

LAWNS WITH WITHERED PATCHES

The occurrence of withered patches on lawns may be due to fungal infection such as Brown Patch or Red Thread or to the presence of unbroken pieces of clay under the surface. The condition is also frequently caused by the activities of root-feeding insects.

The most widespread and destructive of these pests are the Leatherjackets, the commonest species being *Tipula paludosa* Meig. and *T. oleracea* L. The grubs cannot tolerate dry conditions and are most active in late summer, autumn and early spring. They will also feed throughout the winter if the weather is mild.

Control. (1) On small lawns Leatherjackets may be trapped under tarpaulins spread on the grass overnight after it has been thoroughly watered. (2) Water with DDT emulsion or apply a top dressing of

DDT or aldrin dust. These insecticides are best applied in mild humid weather in autumn or early spring, when the grubs are near the surface.

The larvae of Chafer Beetles, in particular the Garden Chafer (*Phyllopertha horticola* L.), can cause extensive damage on lawns in some districts where the soil is light and well-drained.

Control. Use insecticides as for Leatherjackets.

APPENDIX I

Hot-water Treatment of Plants

At present the only easy way to eradicate Eelworms in bulbs and plant material to be used for propagation is to immerse them in hot water. This treatment is also useful for eradicating other pests such as the Bulb Scale Mite and Strawberry Mite, and for some plant diseases. The period of immersion and the temperature of the water must be sufficient to kill the pests concerned and yet avoid permanent injury to the plant. It is important that the temperature does not fluctuate too widely during the time of immersion, otherwise complete control may not be achieved, or, conversely, the plant may be killed or damaged. Thermostatically controlled water baths are available but are usually too expensive for the small grower or private gardener. It is possible, however, for the handyman to build a simple apparatus at reasonable cost. Details of its construction and operation are available in Advisory Leaflet No. 379, issued by the Ministry of Agriculture (H.M.S.O. Price 2d.).

Details of the hot-water treatment of various plants are as follows:

Bulbs. These should be completely dormant at the time of treatment. Narcissus bulbs are usually treated 4–6 weeks after lifting, i.e. in August or early September. Where the bulbs are infested by the Stem and Bulb Eelworm hundreds of young eelworms, coiled together in a woolly-looking mass, may be found protruding from the bases of the bulbs. This 'wool' is very resistant to ordinary hot-water treatment and to kill these eelworms chlorphenol should be added to the water at the rate of 2 fl. oz. to 5 gal. To allow penetration of the 'wool' a wetter such as is used for insecticides should also be added.

Eelworm-infested bulbs should be immersed for 3 hours at a temperature of 110° F. Bulbs infested by Narcissus Bulb Flies or by the Bulb Scale Mite should be immersed for [illegible]½ hours at the same temperature. After treatment the bulbs should be allowed to cool slowly in trays and to dry off before planting out in clean soil.

Note: Tulip bulbs should not be given hot-water treatment.

Chrysanthemums. Treatment of stools infested with the Leaf and Bud Eelworm should be given as soon as the plants are dormant. The stems are cut down to 3–9 inches in length—if stem cuttings are to be taken the longer length should be left. Wash the roots thoroughly, pouring the washings into a drain to avoid soil contamination, and allow the surplus water to drain off the roots. Immerse the stools for 5 minutes in water at 115° F. and on removal from the bath plunge them in cold water. Allow the stools to drain, keeping them well away from untreated material and soil, and plant out or box them in soil free from eelworm.

Mint. The runners of mint infested with the Leaf and Bud Eelworm (*Aphelenchoides fragariae* (Ritz. Bos) Christie) should be lifted when dormant, washed thoroughly, drained and immersed for 10 minutes at 115° F. They should then be cooled rapidly in cold water and planted out in clean soil. This treatment will also control Mint Rust.

Phlox. The Stem and Bulb Eelworm is eradicated in dormant phlox stools by immersion for 1 hour in water at 110° F. The stools should be treated in the same way as those of chrysanthemum.

Strawberry. Runners should be treated in the autumn or spring. Wash the roots to remove the soil and immerse in water at a temperature of 115° F. Where only the Stem and Bulb Eelworm is present an immersion period of 7 minutes is sufficient, and this will also kill the Strawberry Mite and other pests present. If Leaf and Bud Eelworms are present an immersion period of 10 minutes is necessary. After treatment plunge the runners into cold water and plant out in clean soil, firming them thoroughly.

APPENDIX II

The Plant Hosts of Eelworm Pests

MOST species of Eelworms can live on a number of hosts which may be either cultivated plants or weeds. In most cases, particularly out of doors, the only practical method of eradicating eelworms from infested soil is to starve them out, and since the pests can often live in a dormant state without food for a long time, this may take a number of years. It is essential therefore that, during this time, none of the host plants of the species in question should be grown on or near the infested land. Great care should also be taken to prevent the growth of weed hosts.

The lists of host plants given below have been limited to those which are commonly grown in gardens and nurseries together with the weeds which may be found in these places. The list cannot be considered complete, however, since the host range of eelworms, particularly among horticultural plants, has by no means been fully investigated.

THE POTATO TUBER EELWORM

(*Ditylenchus destructor* Thorne)

Field Mint (*Mentha arvensis*)
Gladiolus
Iris (bulbous)
Lilac
Marsh Woundwort (*Stachys palustris*)
Perennial Creeping Sowthistle (*Sonchus arvensis*)
Potato
Tigridia
Tropaeolum polyphyllum

THE STEM AND BULB EELWORM

(*Ditylenchus dipsaci* (Kühn) Filipj.)

There are a number of 'strains' of this Eelworm each of which is restricted to a limited range of plant hosts. There is, however, considerable overlapping and some plants may be hosts of several different strains. Only the strains important in horticulture are dealt with.

Narcissus Strain

Begonia
Bluebell (*Endymion nonscriptus*)
Cat's Ear (*Hypochaeris radicata*)
Crow Garlic (*Allium vineale*)
Gladiolus
Goosegrass (*Galium aparine*)

Narcissus Strain—*cont.*

Narcissus
Nerine
Onion
Parsnip
Rayless Mayweed (*Matricaria matricarioides*)
Ribwort Plantain (*Plantago lanceolata*)
Scilla species
Sea Plantain (*Plantago maritima*)
Snowdrop
Sprekelia formosissima
Strawberry
Swine Cress (*Coronopus squamatus*)
Triquetrous Garlic (*Allium triquetrum*)

Tulip Strain

Bluebell (*Endymion nonscriptus*)
Hyacinth
Narcissus
Phlox
Scilla sibirica
Strawberry
Tulip

Hyacinth Strain

Hyacinth
Onion
Scilla species
Snowdrop

Phlox Strain

Aubrieta
Collomia biflora
Gilia species*
Gladiolus
Gypsophila
Hairy Bittercress (*Cardamine hirsuta*)
Mayweed (*Matricaria* sp.)
Oenothera species*
Pea
Phlox species*
Potato
Primula sinensis
Shepherd's Purse (*Capsella bursa-pastoris*)
Speedwell (*Veronica agrestis*)

Onion (Oat) Strain

Bean (Broad, French and Runner)
Black Bindweed (*Polygonum convolvulus*)
Chickweed (*Stellaria media*)
Chives
Curled Dock (*Rumex crispus*)
Garlic
Goosegrass (*Galium aparine*)
Leek
Mouse-ear Chickweed (*Cerastium vulgatum*)
Narcissus
Onion
Parsnip
Rhubarb
Sandwort (*Arenaria serpyllifolia*)
Strawberry

The Stem and Bulb Eelworm has also been found on carrot, pea, lettuce, spinach and kniphofia. The strains to which they belong have not yet been defined.

* For further information on susceptible species see G. Fox Wilson (1943), Annals of Applied Biology, Vol. 30, pp. 364–70.

BEET EELWORM
(*Heterodera schachtii* Schmidt)*

Many cruciferous plants including
Aubrieta
Alyssum species
Arabis species
Brassicas
Candytuft
Charlock (*Sinapis arvensis*)
Cress
Honesty
Mustard
Radish
Shepherd's Purse (*Capsella bursa-pastoris*)
Siberian Wallflower
Swede
Turnip
Virginian Stock
Wallflower

and also

Beetroot
Canary Creeper
Carnation
Chickweed (*Stellaria media*)
Docks (*Rumex* species)
Fat Hen, Goosefoot, etc. (*Chenopodium* species)
Gypsophila species
Hempnettles (*Galeopsis* species)
Love-lies-Bleeding
Maiden Pink
Persicaria (*Polygonum persicaria*)
Rhubarb
Silene species
Soapworts (*Saponaria* species)
Spinach

CABBAGE ROOT EELWORM
(*Heterodera cruciferae* Frankl.)*

Alyssum species
Arabis species
Brassicas
Candytuft
Charlock (*Sinapis arvensis*)
Cress
Deadnettles (*Lamium* species)
Honesty
Moricandia species
Mustard
Shepherd's Purse (*Capsella bursa-pastoris*)
Siberian Wallflower
Swede
Turnip
Wallflowers

PEA ROOT EELWORM
(*Heterodera göttingiana* Liebs.)*

Broad Bean
Pea
Vetches (*Vicia* species)
Vetchlings (*Lathyrus* species)

POTATO ROOT EELWORM
(*Heterodera rostochiensis* Woll.)*

Potato
Tomato
Woody Nightshade (*Solanum dulcamara*)

* A more detailed list of host plants is given by R. D. Winslow (1954), Annals of Applied Biology, Vol. 41, pp. 591–605.

LEAF AND BUD EELWORM
(*Aphelenchoides fragariae* (Ritz. Bos) Christie)

Adiantum species
Asplenium species
Begonia
Coleus
Ferns
Gloxinia
Lily
Saintpaulia
Strawberry
Violet

LEAF AND BUD EELWORM
(*Aphelenchoides ritzema-bosi* (Schwartz) Stein.)

The majority of composite plants including

Aster
China Aster
Chrysanthemum
Dahlia
Doronicum
Groundsel (*Senecio vulgaris*)
Pyrethrum
Sowthistle (*Sonchus oleraceus*)
Zinnia

and also

Blackcurrant
Calceolaria
Chickweed (*Stellaria media*)
Creeping Buttercup (*Ranunculus repens*)
Delphinium
Goosegrass (*Galium aparine*)
Lavender
Paeony
Phlox
Speedwell (*Veronica* species)
Strawberry
Verbena

ROOT KNOT EELWORMS
(*Meloidogyne* species)

These Eelworms have such a wide variety of plant hosts that it is quite impracticable to try to starve out the pests as recommended for other species. In greenhouses they can be controlled by sterilizing the soil with steam or with chemicals.

APPENDIX III

The Prevention of Bird Damage

THE severity and extent of damage by birds to growing garden plants, to ripening fruit and to dormant blossom buds of fruit and ornamental plants has reached such proportions in recent years that some species now rank as major pests in gardens, nurseries and orchards. The problem of preventing this damage has not yet been satisfactorily solved and it is to be hoped that the investigations at present being carried out by Ministry of Agriculture scientists will provide an answer in the not too distant future.

Many chemicals have been tested in the hope of finding one which will act as a repellent. So far none of these, including the much recommended method of spraying with alum, has proved satisfactory. Many scaring devices, both traditional and recently invented, suffer from the disadvantage that they are only temporarily effective and the birds quickly become accustomed to them. However, if a number of these are used in rotation, each one for a few days only, it is possible that some degree of control may be obtained.

Visual scarers such as strips of aluminium folded to cause them to glitter and make a clattering noise when hung in the wind, or strips coloured on one side and twisted to give the illusion of movement in the wind, should be hung a few feet away from the plants so that they are seen as the birds approach. Replicas of hawks may be hung over attacked plants or toy cats may be partly hidden in the foliage, but these and scarecrows are only effective for long if they can be kept constantly in motion. One commercially produced scarecrow is mounted on a pivot and swings constantly in the wind.

Clappers, rope-cartridges, acetylene bangers and other noise-making devices will also scare birds away for a time but, to be effective, the noise should be intermittent and irregular. Such methods, moreover, are not suitable in built-up areas. It should be noted that the efficiency of scarers in general is greatly reduced by the presence of nearby hedges, shrubs and woodland. These act as a refuge from which the birds will emerge as soon as the effects of the scare have worn off.

Physical methods of keeping birds off plants include the use of black thread strung on sticks over the plants. This is effective against some birds, e.g. sparrows, but does not deter bullfinches and other species. The only permanently effective method of keeping birds away is to use a fine-mesh net which should be suspended on poles over the plants. The netting has also the advantage of protecting fruit trees from frost. It may also be considered worth while to protect ripening fruit in muslin or cellophane bags. If this is done some of the fruit should be left uncovered to act as decoys and as indicators of ripeness.

APPENDIX IV

The Control of Rats and Mice

OCCASIONALLY rats and mice may cause considerable damage in the garden by gnawing the stems of plants, eating bulbs in store or in the ground, and feeding on fruit in store or on the trees. The most convenient and effective method of control is to lay down poison baits containing warfarin. This material, when taken regularly in small doses, causes fatal internal bleeding in rats and mice. Since it causes no immediate ill effects it does not give rise to 'bait shyness' before a lethal quantity has been taken and pre-baiting is therefore unnecessary.

Warfarin is available in ready-mixed baits, and small piles should be placed near damaged plants or produce. In the open the bait should be placed in drain-pipes or in jars and tins lying on their sides to protect it from the rain, but with rats these receptacles should be laid out some days before baiting to allow the animals to become used to their presence. Although warfarin must be taken in considerable quantities to harm domestic animals and birds every endeavour should be made to prevent them eating it.

The baits should be visited every two or three days and replenished where necessary. Untouched baits should be removed after 4 or 5 days. Continue to replenish the baits until all feeding has stopped and after a few more days, if no further feeding takes place, remove the remainder of the bait.

APPENDIX V

Useful Garden Formulae

Nicotine-soap wash

Dissolve 1 lb. of potash soft soap in about ½ gal. of warm water. Allow to cool, then add 1 fl. oz. of nicotine (95–98 per cent.). Make up to 10 gals. with water (preferably rain water).

This is chiefly useful as a control for Aphids, Thrips, Pear Sucker, Capsids and Sawflies. It is an insecticide of short persistence and produce for human consumption can be used 48 hours after treatment. Used during the summer on fruit trees it does not encourage the increase of Fruit Tree Red Spider Mite.

Nicotine-White Oil Emulsion

Nicotine (95–98 per cent.)	1 fl. oz.
Summer White Oil	1 pt.
Water	10 gal.

This formulation is now being superseded by organo-phosphorus chemicals as a control for Scale Insects and Mealy Bugs. It is useful, however, on delicate plants where the newer products cannot be used. The emulsion should not be used on cattleyas or on plants which are sensitive to petroleum oil.

Metaldehyde Bait

Metaldehyde Powder	1 oz.
Bran (or Bone Meal)	3 lb.

Used as a bait for Slugs and some Snails. For the underground Keeled Slugs bone meal should be used instead of bran. The mixture may be spread thinly on the ground or placed in small heaps which are protected from the rain by raised tiles, or in overturned flower pots.

Paris Green Bait

Paris Green	1 oz.
Bran	2 lb.

Thoroughly mix and add sufficient water to moisten but not enough to make it lumpy. This bait is effective against Slugs, Woodlice, Cockroaches and Crickets. The mixture can also be used dry for controlling Cutworms and Leatherjackets.

Host Plant Index

THE references listed are restricted to those plants mentioned by name in the main part of the book. Others may be mentioned by implication in the text and therefore, if a particular symptom does not appear in the index, it may be described in the appropriate section of the book although the host plant is not mentioned specifically.

The plant hosts of eelworm pests listed in Appendix II, pp. 209–212, are not listed in the index.

Where a symptom is described on a plant more than once on the same page the number of references is given in parentheses after the page number.

Abbreviations

B. Bulbs	Fr. Fruit
Bd. Buds	Rt. Roots
Cm. Corms	St. Stems or shoots
Fl. Flowers	Tb. Tuber
Fol. Foliage	Sd. Seeds

Pest Index

References are given, wherever possible, under the common names. Where more than one reference is given for a species the more important are shown in heavy type.

General Index